RANCHING AND THE AMERICAN WEST

THE **BROADVIEW**
SOURCES SERIES

Ranching and the American West

A HISTORY IN DOCUMENTS

edited by SUSAN NANCE

broadview press

BROADVIEW PRESS – www.broadviewpress.com
Peterborough, Ontario, Canada

Founded in 1985, Broadview Press remains a wholly independent publishing house. Broadview's focus is on academic publishing; our titles are accessible to university and college students as well as scholars and general readers. With 800 titles in print, Broadview has become a leading international publisher in the humanities, with world-wide distribution. Broadview is committed to environmentally responsible publishing and fair business practices.

Library and Archives Canada Cataloguing in Publication

Title: Ranching and the American West / edited by Susan Nance.
Names: Nance, Susan, editor.
Series: Broadview sources series.
Description: Series statement: The Broadview sources series | Includes bibliographical references.
Identifiers: Canadiana (print) 20210285478 | Canadiana (ebook) 20210285508 | ISBN 9781554814817 (softcover) | ISBN 9781770488168 (PDF) | ISBN 9781460407653 (EPUB)
Subjects: LCSH: Ranching—West (U.S.)—History—Sources. | LCSH: West (U.S.)—History—Sources.
Classification: LCC SF196.U5 R36 2021 | DDC 636/.010978—dc23

Broadview Press handles its own distribution in North America:
PO Box 1243, Peterborough, Ontario K9J 7H5, Canada
555 Riverwalk Parkway, Tonawanda, NY 14150, USA
Tel: (705) 743-8990; Fax: (705) 743-8353
email: customerservice@broadviewpress.com

For all territories outside of North America, distribution is handled by Eurospan Group.

Canadä Broadview Press acknowledges the financial support of the Government of Canada for our publishing activities.

Copy-edited by Juliet Sutcliffe
Book design by Em Dash Design

PRINTED IN CANADA

CONTENTS

PREFACE

Historians are known to be very good at a number of things: predicting the future, telling interesting stories, and vetting evidence. The evidence that historians work with comes in two forms. A primary source is any item created in a particular place and time that we use to understand that place and time. It can include paper documents found in an archive or someone's attic, old media like newspapers, books, and magazines, material objects of all kinds, buildings, archaeological finds, sound or video recordings, as well as archived electronic data like websites and social media posts. Secondary sources are the historical writing that explains the past using primary sources as evidence, and interpreting and contextualizing that evidence for a contemporary audience. Imagine telling the story of a particular interaction between historical actors using some photographs taken on the day, a news broadcast interview given by one participant, a magazine story about the event, plus, say, a book written a little later by different participant. Each primary source gives some information about what took place, but together they offer a much fuller picture. Thus, in this book, the historical item (text or image) presented to you is the primary source, my introduction to the book and the brief introductions to each primary source constitute secondary sources to contextualize the primary sources.

Although historical facts do not change, the kinds of secondary sources produced vary over time. That is, the meaning and conclusions we draw from historical evidence are shaped by the questions we ask when looking at primary sources, which are in turn determined by our current politics and interests. This is a good thing, to be sure. Each generation of historians builds on the work of previous historians, adding nuance, finding or looking at previously unknown primary sources, or filling in gaps that previous historians left in their work because they were focused on their own questions. For instance, in the late nineteenth century, historians such as Hubert Howe Bancroft wrote about the West but said little of women's lives or about people of color of the region. His readers seemed not to mind since, at the time, "history" was taken to be a record of the accomplishments of important white men. By the latter half of the twentieth century, historians were increasingly researching and writing about women and Indigenous peoples in the West on their own terms using primary sources that previous historians had ignored. Building on those new secondary sources—those histories of women and people of color—the authors of textbooks, popular histories of the West, and other academic studies have been able to write about a broader range of people. Increasingly, historians had come to see "history" as the record of all of the people in a given place. Others include also the history of the environment and of animals. Thirty years from now, historians and students will be asking still different questions about the transformation of the West that this book explores.

Primary sources are equally complicated. They do not represent "the truth" of the past necessarily, but a reflection of that past created by the people who lived at the time and had their own foibles, politics, rivalries, and fixations. So, they require some careful analysis and cannot always be taken at face value. When you consider these primary sources in this book, and the contextual statements about them, make sure to ask and find out: Who produced any given item, for what purpose, why, and to what effect? Knowing how primary sources came to be is crucial to understanding what they actually show us.

In putting together this collection here was the puzzle I thus confronted: How might anyone take this three-dimensional, impossibly complex history of people, animals, and environment in the West and put it in a straight line as a book? Some choices need to be made! This collection aims to give you some insight into the endlessly complex past of a large region and millions of people and animals with a selection of sources focused around a few themes: animals, people, land, environment, capitalism, and the development of consumer society.

Ranching and the American West offers you a way to see the transformation of the American West as a historical process for the environment, animals, the land, and people in ways that explain how the rural West became what it is today. Once you have worked through the primary sources here, it is fair to be critical about this particular collection: Do the sources enhance or complicate your understanding of the past? Do they convey the complexity of the past? What is missing from this collection, with respect to your own interests about the past? What other selections of historical evidence might one include in a book, say, twice the length?

INTRODUCTION

The transformation of the American West is one of the key topics in the study of United States history and global environmental history. It is also central to the growing field of animal history. It is a story driven by a combination of phenomena, which produced some intended consequences and many unintended ones. A list of those phenomena would include global human migrations, the introduction to North America of **settler colonialism**, capitalism, new technologies and organisms. To distill all that down into one more comprehensible theme, or big picture, we might focus on one broad change: the transformation of animals and the land from beings and entities with intrinsic value to entities taken to be property or commodities.

There are many approaches one could use to learn about this transformation and each one would expose different elements of the past. In this book, we will follow horses, cattle, and the men and women who worked with them, to understand the ways the West changed over the last three centuries, and why. Rural people and animals, and their lives and stories, shed light on many of the concepts and processes historians seek to understand: drivers of environmental change, the market and its development over time, the integration of rural regions into national economic markets, the nature of labor and gender, changing human–animal relationships, the development of consumerism, how Americans conceived of and managed food security, and the origins and circulation of popular national myths, as well as the interrelation of all these things. Or to put it another way: why does anyone live in the West and how did horses, cattle, and people persevere there in spite of all the obstacles the environment put in the way?

The American West is a symbol of American power and a site of contentious land, animal welfare, and environmental disputes. Indigenous nations are still there in spite of the fact that their political, economic, legal, social, and cultural networks have been overlaid with the United States government and many waves of in-migration by people from around the world. Westerners of many backgrounds, but especially rural people, pride themselves on their resilience and self-sufficiency. Some people say that much of the non-urban West has become, in effect, a federally subsidized and controlled feedlot, and a symbol of American hubris and stubbornness on the one hand, and rural decline on the other. Still others say that the West is the last place on earth where a person can be truly free. As you examine the primary sources here, you will work out your own interpretation of that debate, of this history, and the lessons it offers.

Taking nothing for granted, we should also start out by asking a perhaps provocative question: does the "American West" exist as a region? If so, what

settler colonialism:
Broadly defined, settler colonialism is a process in which people migrate to a new region and set about imposing their own political, economic, legal, social, and cultural systems there at the expense of—or even with the overt purpose of displacing or destroying—existing civilizations. Many historians explain the formation and expansion of the United States across the continent as a process of settler colonialism.

are its boundaries and characteristics? For our purposes, we can take the American West to be the area of the continental United States west of the 100th meridian. It is a diverse and globally unique geography that includes the high-elevation Great Plains, consisting before the twentieth century mostly of grasslands with few trees and winds that never seemed to stop blowing. To the northwest is the continental great divide and the Rocky Mountains and a region covered by relatively arid forests and, at the coastline, rainforests. Across the Rockies to the south is the Great Basin, an extremely dry semi-desert and desert region now spanning most of Utah, Nevada, and inland southern California. Along the south from Texas to California is another arid strip, referred to as the "sunbelt" by political scientists, who name that demographic region for its hot climate and scant rainfall. If for a moment we set aside the coastal areas of Oregon and Washington state, and large urban centers like Las Vegas, Denver, Houston, and Los Angeles (which grew dramatically after World War II), two things that we find in common over this large region are aridity and sparse human populations mixed with cattle, horses. Other species that once subsisted off the bison ecology remained, such as the prairie dogs who harassed cowboys and cow-girls with their chirping and their ground tunnels that tripped horses, and the coyotes who defied many wars of extermination against them by ranchers and bounty hunters, or native grasses that supported crucial prey animals like deer and elk. Others like bison, wolves, and the grizzly were hunted to near extinction or total extinction by market and sport hunters, removing ecologically important keystone species most settlers viewed as antithetical to extensive ranching, homesteading, and other ventures.

History is a representation of the past that speaks to contemporary questions about the world. *Ranching and the American West* offers you a way to be the historian and see the transformation of the American West as a historical process for the environment, animals, the land, and people. We should not take that transformation for granted or see it as inevitable. When you examine the historical sources here and the questions they raise, think about what particular things we learn from these artifacts of the past that are unique or important to your understanding of this history.

Below you will find short introductions to each of the six parts of the book. Read them all now and you will find it easier to put each primary source or group of sources in context as you proceed. Throughout the book, the original spelling and punctuation of the historical sources have been preserved except in cases when it was necessary to silently correct an error in the original for clarity of meaning.

I. ENTER HORSES AND CATTLE

The first sources we examine in this book are drawn from a period of history in which there was little published media in or about the West, so sources are far fewer than for the nineteenth and twentieth centuries. They consist of published textual and graphic travel accounts plus some early photographs of people and their horses in what is today Montana. The sources for this period in history are limited. Indigenous tribes and nations tended to rely upon oral histories and kept few written records we might refer to now. Explorers and travelers of European descent wrote about their travels there, some of which were published. At this time there were no electronic media so all sources were textual, either written documents or printed, or hand drawn and colored. Equally, photography only became available in the 1850s and for some decades the equipment was heavy and fragile, and not generally feasible for common use outdoors until the last decades of nineteenth century.

To begin, think back several centuries. People had been living in North America for thousands of years already and the total population was probably between 15 and 18 million.[1] It consisted of dozens of nations and language groups, each with their own goals, assets, and rivalries. Many Indigenous peoples, whether nomadic or settled, had found labor-efficient, sustainable means of subsisting or profiting from the land and its animals. Early non-Indigenous visitors to the area who chronicled what they saw commented on the variety and abundance of plant and animal species there, including frequent sightings of bears, wolves, elk, deer, countless varieties of birds, and herds of bison so large that one could look across them from a hillside or cliff top but not see where they ended.[2] The landscape was in places harsh and unforgiving, as in the deserts of the Great Basin or the frigid alpine regions of the Rocky Mountains, while others had seemingly limitless resources like the rainforests and salmon-bearing rivers of the Northwest, and the Great Plains grasslands so flat and vast that some compared them to an ocean. The region was proceeding on its own timeline and historical trajectory when people from other parts of the globe began arriving, exploring the coastlines by ship or traveling in overland from the south, looking for trade and resources to exploit. When Indigenous peoples first encountered evidence of those Europeans, it was often through trade rather than direct

---

1   Roxanne Dunbar-Ortiz, *An Indigenous People's History of the United States* (Boston: Beacon Press, 2014), 40–41. On the controversies over who has estimated pre-colonial population numbers and how, see Ted Steinberg, *Down to Earth: Nature's Role in American History*, 4th ed. (Oxford: Oxford UP, 2019), 6.

2   Dan Flores, *American Serengeti: The Last Big Animals of the Great Plains* (Lawrence: UP of Kansas, 2016), 1–4.

meetings. European goods circulated quickly on the continent and many people sought them as novelties, tools, or valuable items one might trade for something else in time.[3]

The first settled European presence in the West appeared in the seventeenth century, in what is today the American Southwest and northern Mexico, as a **mission** complex sponsored by the Spanish empire. Many Europeans in North America held a firm belief that, as Christians, their culture, civilization, and even race was superior, which gave them a God-given right to control people, land, and resources as they saw fit. They routinely referred to Indigenous peoples as "savages" in the seventeenth and eighteenth centuries as a way to express and justify their colonial intentions. It was an attitude that early Anglo-North Americans would share and adapt to the colonial project of expanding the early United States all the way to the Pacific. At its founding in 1776, the United States consisted of states situated on the eastern seaboard and, in time, a series of federally controlled non-state territories spreading west, decade by decade. Most Americans resented and sought to destroy Indigenous and Mexican (i.e., Spanish) political, economic, legal, social, and cultural systems in order to monopolize the West and provide a place for any white American to own land.

Visitors and migrants to the midwestern and western sections of the continent brought with them new technologies, devastating diseases, and livestock, including cattle and horses. Horses of a sort had been there before in the form of a direct ancestor of the modern horse, Eohippus, a hooved ungulate native to North America that went extinct approximately 10,000 or 12,000 years ago. Horses returned to the Americas as domesticated equines (*Equus ferus caballus*) with the Spanish who brought Iberian horse breeds (also known as the colonial Spanish horse) beginning in the sixteenth century. They were small, sturdy horses known to be extremely intelligent and, when at large on the land, exceedingly wary of humans and dangerously difficult to catch.

Horses were among the valuables from Europe that people traded in regions that had few if any visitors from the east. The appearance of horses was an unsettling process in the southwest and Great Plains as "the transformational power of horses was simply too vast," as one historian explains. Indigenous peoples did not keep domesticated animals except for the dogs that lived in and around their communities. Although Indigenous populations would later be devastated by the diseases and unintentional environmental changes caused by European exploration and settlement in North America, the horse was both an ecological actor and a living technology that radically

mission: Missions were Spanish outposts that generally consisted of a campus of buildings, including a church, built around a large courtyard. The goal of these institutions was to establish Spanish colonial civilization among local Indigenous peoples and convert as many as possible to Catholicism (they were only superficially successful in that respect).

---

3   Daniel K. Richter, *Facing East from Indian Country: A Native History of Early America* (Cambridge: Harvard UP, 2001), 41–68.

changed every aspect of life for many tribes. People adapted horses to what had been a "pedestrian" life with dogs, exacerbating disparities of power and wealth, or privileged access to environmental resources, among tribes and nations.[4] During the early seventeenth century Numunuu (Comanche) in the southwest, then Niitsitapi (Blackfeet) and Apsáalooke (Crow) to the north had acquired them in Santa Fe (today in New Mexico). That town had an important early market at which people purchased, then sold horses in a network moving north. People of all kinds used horses for transportation (riding and carrying belongings), for raiding and waging war on rival tribes and settlers, hunting bison and other wild animals in greater numbers, and as a form of currency or wealth that could be given away, sold, or stolen.

Horses who escaped from captivity or were turned loose by owners with no use for them became feral, or, many people surmised, had always been wild and simply reverted to inborn ways the moment they could. Young horses traveled with a dominant stallion and his harem of several to two dozen mares in a highly sociable band, with "tag-along geldings" keeping their distance in a loosely organized herd of their own. Older horses trained new foals to avoid humans, and were famously difficult to capture. People called them "wily," "trickish," and generally exasperating. Lead stallions or sometimes a dominant mare would spy humans on the horizon and charge off at a gallop with mares and their young following, stopping after some distance to watch if they were still being pursued. At times stallions would start mares and their young galloping away, then suddenly turn to run toward human stalkers, challenging them with kicks, stomps, and bites.[5] These horses learned how to forage on even the harshest western lands and had many foals, laying the foundations for the populations of wild horses, or mustangs, much romanticized by westerners and non-westerners alike.

By the eighteenth century, Indigenous, **Californio**, and Mexican horsemen drove a lively trade in horses captured with difficulty from wild herds, most of which fed demand for workhorses in growing east coast cities and burgeoning frontier areas just inland. While many Indigenous tribes held large herds of horses, many families on the eastern seaboard might only own one horse, a mule, or a pair of oxen. Indigenous peoples viewed European and later American travelers, traders, and settlers with caution. Many were interested in trading and purchasing European goods but had no intention of surrendering their political, economic, and cultural autonomy in the process. Indeed, traders and travelers visiting from further east noted

Californio: Spanish-speaking people of mixed Spanish and Indigenous descent who first appeared in the 1680s southwest (today California). They were absorbed into the Chicano/Mexican-American community in the state during the 19th century.

4   Pekka Hämäläinen, "The Rise and Fall of Plains Indians Horse Cultures," *Journal of American History* 90, no. 3 (December 2003): 833–62.

5   J. Frank Dobie, *The Mustangs* (New York: Little, Brown & Co, 1952), 132–34; Walker D. Wyman, *The Wild Horse of the West* (Lincoln: U of Nebraska P, 1963), 264–67.

that they were latecomers to Great Plains horse markets, dominated as they were by Hispanic and Indigenous buyers and sellers.[6]

Like horses, cattle were not native to North America. Cattle appeared with the Spanish, who routinely brought livestock on exploratory trips so that they could be disembarked and left to multiply. A handful of Northern European cattle had arrived in the 1620s with some of the first colonists from Europe who landed on the east coast. The cattle at the root of the cattle trade so central to the transformation of the West, however, were long-legged, long-horned Spanish breeds, or *criollo* cattle, like the famous Texas Longhorns. Spaniards in the Southwest kept herds or captured feral or **wild** cattle to produce meat and products like tallow and hides for the production of finished products. An initial group of 200 cattle in California was the foundation of the region's economy, which, by the 1830s, was dominated by a trade in hides, meat, and tallow. Mexican land grants to long-time residents as well as Americans and other immigrants from Europe willing to take up Mexican citizenship created a network of ranchos run day-to-day by Indigenous and **mestizo** Californio **vaqueros** who made California a critical trade centre, even before the discovery of gold in 1849.[7]

Spanish modes of ranching spread across the Southwest to Texas. When the US Civil War began in 1861, many Texan ranchers traveled east to fight, abandoning their herds. Returning after the war, ranchers found that in just four years those herds had multiplied, representing a once-in-a-lifetime financial opportunity. Yet, as with wild horses, capturing these autonomous cattle was not easy. They traveled in small matrilineal herds consisting of a number of cows, calves, and yearlings all led by a dominant cow. Adult bulls hovered around the fringes of the group, challenging one another occasionally by pawing the ground with a hoof or facing off with head butts to determine a hierarchy. The most dominant bulls would join the matrilineal herd temporarily whenever cows were in oestrus. Spanish cattle were self-sufficient, intelligent, curious, and fiercely protective of their young. In the absence of regular exposure to and handling by people, plus experience living at large on the land and traveling long distances for foraging and finding water, they developed and passed survival skills from generation to generation, including how to avoid predators such as humans. Texas Longhorns hid in dense thickets and brush, forging tunnel-like openings that a man on horseback could not navigate. People used a term of Spanish origin, *landinos*, meaning crafty or sagacious, to specify these "outlaw cattle of the brush country," and appreciated them for the ways they tested a cowboy's

wild: Feral animals were (and are) formerly domesticated animals who had been abandoned or had escaped human control to become autonomous again, often pointedly avoiding people once free. Wild cattle or horses, in this context, were the offspring of feral individuals who had no experience of captivity. However, the categories of feral and wild are just approximations of an animal's experience and lineage. In many cases, whether a herd of free-roaming cattle or horses was feral or wild could be a matter of debate or speculation. Free herds adopted or mated with newly escaped or abandoned individuals, living in hybrid herds that collectively avoided human contact so appeared "wild" (resistant to human contact) to many ranchers, cowboys, or cowgirls who attempted to break them for ranch work.

mestizo: Californio of combined Spanish and Indigenous ancestry.

vaqueros: Spanish, later Mexican, Hispanic cowboys who adapted ranching and horsemanship traditions from Spain to North America and devised the equipment and practices later adopted by American cowboys.

---

6   Flores, *American Serengeti*, 63–69.

7   Kevin Starr, *California: A History* (New York: Modern Library, 2015), 46–51.

skills.[8] When people still found ways to confront these feral cattle, they were quick to defend themselves. In fact, people frequently interpreted defensive cattle behavior, like charging or attempting to gore horses or people with a horn, as anger and aggressiveness when it was probably an expression of fear or frustration. Either way, it was a truism that one must remain on horseback to venture safely across the land in case of unexpectedly encountering some of these creatures.[9] People still slaughtered and ate these cattle, although Spanish cattle produced only limited amounts of stringy, dry meat in contrast to the relatively more docile and heavy beef breeds that proliferated later. (For the life cycle of modern beef cattle see Document 24.)

At this early stage, horses were the big story in the West. From Spanish trading centers in Texas and the Southwest, owned and free horses spread north from tribe to tribe for a century. By the beginning of the nineteenth century people reported seeing enormous numbers of wild horses throughout an arid band of territory from California to Texas and across the southern parts of the Great Plains in herds numbering up to 6,000 animals. By then, all the Indigenous nations used horses although the Nʉmʉnʉʉ (Comanche), Suhtai and Tsitsistas (Cheyenne), and Niimíipuu (Nez Perce) were especially known for the horses they bred systematically for both performance and appearance.[10]

2. BEEF BONANZA

The historical sources in this part of the book document the early boom in beef production as the cattle trade spread from Texas and the Southwest into the Great Plains. The sources include a book and map that investors consulted, plus memoirs by and images of cowboys who worked with cattle in remote, sparsely populated regions of the country on the one hand, and popular fictional accounts about those cowboys on the other. For the first half of the nineteenth century, Americans living east of the 100th Meridian knew relatively little about the West. Members of the Lewis and Clark expedition (1803–06), tasked by the US government with traveling through and documenting the north west territories from St. Louis to the Pacific coast (now Oregon), and other travelers sent back reports of enormous grass lands, vast deserts, and impossibly massive mountains, then, on the north Pacific Coast, rainforests that transformed into grasslands as one traveled south

---

8   Ramon F. Adams, *The Old-Time Cowhand* (New York: Macmillan Company, 1961), 155–56.

9   Larry D. Christiansen, "The Extinction of Wild Cattle in Southern Arizona," *Journal of Arizona History* 29, no. 1 (Spring 1988): 93–94.

10 Flores, *American Serengeti*, 70–73.

toward Mexico. Often those reports spoke of abundant animals to be hunted and fished, giving the impression that living was easy in the West. At the same time, the Great Plains was sometimes popularly known as the Great American Desert due to the region's aridity. Although Indigenous peoples had been living and flourishing there for thousands of years, migrants and explorers who arrived beginning in the 1840s on the overland trails from the east found it was hard work to make a living. Means of producing food or commodities that people practiced in the eastern half of the continent, like logging and farming, or commodity agriculture, were impossible in much of the Southwest, Great Basin, and Great Plains since there was no mechanized agriculture or interstate irrigation systems to support them yet. There were some extraordinary silver and gold strikes before the 1860s, and certainly a long history of ranching in the Southwest. Boosters seeking to promote settlement would publicize the West as an "Eden," a land of unlimited wealth that God providentially wished Anglo-Americans to exploit in various ways, not least by raising horses and cattle there.

From a pre-contact population of over 15 million, by the 1890s only about 250,000 Indigenous people remained. Many tribes had experienced catastrophic trauma as millions died due to the uncontrolled spread of diseases Europeans brought with them, in battle during the various "Indian Wars" that century in which the US military and armed settlers attacked Indigenous nations and their resources, or from starvation and other health problems created by economic and social dislocation in turn caused by settler colonialism. Those who remained migrated or were forcibly removed from their homes by the federal government. Many landed in what was known during the late nineteenth century as "Indian Territory," today the state of Oklahoma. On the Great Plains, people who had practiced settled agriculture and other means of living from the land resorted to subsisting off the bison herds to survive, hunting them for meat and hides to sell for cash. For instance, when the bison herds collapsed in Niitsitapi (Blackfoot) country, today Montana and Idaho, where the tribe was confined on limited, minimally productive land, a full quarter of the tribe died of starvation.[11] Historians believe that the bison ecology was seriously threatened as early as the 1840s due to competition with horse herds who monopolized forage and water in grasslands the bison had relied upon. Equally, migrants headed overland to California and Oregon brought along oxen and other cattle carrying brucellosis, a non-deadly bacterial infection in cattle that was fatal in bison. Then in the 1870s and 1880s, the expansion of the cattle trade north and west from Texas combined with years of drought to reduce bison

11   Sara Dant, *Losing Eden: An Environmental History of the American West* (Malden, MA: Wiley Blackwell, 2017), 86.

numbers further just when market hunting (clothing and conveyor belts were made from bison hides in these years) was at its peak. The herds were completely destroyed in about 15 final devastating years leaving behind the new "exotic" species: cattle and horses.[12]

Into these spaces market cattle flooded, creating an economic bubble many called the "Beef Bonanza." In Texas, the Southwest, and northern Mexico, criollo cattle were dominant. Their numbers rose and fell over the nineteenth century, largely depending on human consumption. After the US Civil War, men who had been at war returned home, hunted, and slaughtered feral Texas Longhorns, a practice that went on for only a decade or so before the famed cattle of Texas were dwindling.[13] Entrepreneurial men drove these hardy animals north on hoof into Kansas along the storied Chisholm Trail, a wide dirt highway beginning near Austin, Texas and ending at railheads in Kansas, for sale and loading onto railcars headed east and west. (More on the midwestern inter-state food system that took the place of the longhorn cattle drives appears in Part 3.)

The Texas Longhorn and Longhorn-shorthorn cattle crosses people created as the cattle business spread north and west toward Montana and Washington state were still just a minor part of North American life since, in white settler culture, people mostly ate pork if they ate meat. Nonetheless, for many absentee ranch owners and cattle investors on the east coast and, especially, in Britain who poured money into the trade between the end of the Civil War and the mid-1880s, there was a belief that the business was a foolproof way to make a fortune. Simply set feral cattle loose on land recently confiscated from Indigenous tribes—or still held by them—and come back some months later to capture the animals and reap the profits. Use of grass-lands in that period was entirely uncoordinated and unregulated. Ranchers with limited knowledge of or long-term concern for grassland ecologies collectively put too many animals out to graze, often with the idea that it was gamble but might pay off. They ignored a growing group of scientists, government officials, and long-term residents who explained the dangerous environmental changes underway as the number of acres required to support one head of cattle spiralled upward that decade. Horses and cattle ate native grasses with such ferocity that invasive foreign plants like cheatgrass (carried by travelers and cargo) began to take over; in 1890s California an estimated 50 to 90 per cent of native grasses had been lost.[14]

---

12 Andrew Isenberg, *The Destruction of the Bison* (New York: Cambridge UP, 2000), 142–43.

13 Terry G. Jordan, *North American Cattle-Ranching Frontiers: Origins, Diffusion, and Differentiation* (Albuquerque: U of New Mexico P, 1993), 275.

14 Dant, *Losing Eden*, 92.

remuda: The herd of horses available on a ranch, generally running loose on a small range, for use as saddle horses. The cowboys would choose a few to work each day.

mavericks: Cattle born on the range but missed during yearly round-ups during which animals were marked and counted as the property of a specific cattle operation. On these days, yearling cattle were marked by branding and also notches cut in the ear or neck skin, while bull calves were castrated to become steers that would be sold for fattening and slaughter around the age of two.

The culmination of over grazing with "exotic" species, namely cattle plus wild horse bands or a ranch's **remuda**, occurred over the winter of 1886 and 1887, less than a year after the cattle trade had finally made its way up to Wyoming and Montana. Piikáni (Piegan) cattle and horse raisers called that season "Many Cattle Died Winter," while the settler community called it, not a big round-up, but the "Big Die-Up." Lack of central oversight or government management of land use allowed each ranching operation to seek its own self-interest, which produced a tragedy of the commons event as many parties exploited public land without coordination. Stressed and drought-stricken grasslands bearing more cattle each year began to collapse, unable to supply sufficient grasses and water to grow healthy animals. In turn, overstocking forced weakened cattle to travel longer distances for what food and water there was. Finally, over the winter of 1886–87, millions of already-run down cattle froze to death in extended and cruelly frigid blizzards. Countless were found in the spring caught on the new barbed-wire fencing that had blocked their search for sustenance in the blinding winter storms. Many ranch operations lost most or all their cattle.

In the midst of all this disruption, many families and individuals had set up small homesteads with a few cattle, hoping to sustain themselves as independent ranchers on what seemed like the limitless expanse of the Great Plains. The vast majority of land in the West was the property of the federal government, much of it acquired by breaking treaties and other legal agreements with Indigenous nations and tribes that promised but failed to protect their autonomy and access to the land. Conflict ensued as big cattlemen used extra-legal means to harass or force out small operators, some of whom absconded with **mavericks** or cut illegal or disputed fences that the big operations installed on public land. Independent ranchers had as much right to the land as anyone, but the powerful cattlemen saw things differently. Wyoming in particular became known for "fence cutting wars," although they occurred all over the West wherever powerful people attempted to monopolize federally owned land.

In spite of these tragedies and conflicts, the 1870s and 1880s have been imagined as the golden age of the working cowboy. The young and middle-aged men who worked with cattle on remote ranges formed a diverse group that included Indigenous, Black, Mexican, Spanish-speaking Hispanic American, and settler laborers. Many young men headed into the West looking for work, or an escape from family obligations and the boredom of their hometowns. In an age when few people finished high school, they tended to have modest levels of education and to have worked for their families or themselves throughout their teen years. Contemporary observers noted their diversity, some "rude and unlettered," others "men of culture and ability."[15] Formerly enslaved Black men who had left the South to start their lives over on their own terms were common among them and numbered between five and ten thousand.[16] In the Southeast, Black people (free or enslaved) had long been known for their work with cattle in small subsistence operations in which a family might own just a few dairy cows or beef cattle. Likewise, Indigenous men familiar with cattle work cowboyed to earn cash, and in time Indigenous ranching operations sprung up on reservation land as various tribes sought food security.

The line dividing cowboys and small cattlemen or family ranching operations could be blurry, as many cowboys aspired to marry, then buy a homestead and a small herd and try to make a living as ranch owners themselves. Of course, the cowboys' techniques, equipment, and work clothes came from the *vaqueros*, or cowboys of Mexico and South America, and centuries before that, Spanish horsemen. Many Hispanic families living in Texas and the Southwest dated their ancestry there back a century or more before the US acquired those regions with the Treaty of Guadalupe Hidalgo (1848) and the Gadson Purchase (1854). Still today one can find many southwestern families who will tell you that their ancestors lived under Spanish imperial rule followed by Mexican government far longer than they have lived within the boundaries of the United States—hence the old saying: "We didn't cross the border, the border crossed us."

In the midst of all of this unsettling and sometimes violent change, many people took solace in stories about these cowboys. Although in reality their work was usually boring, often dangerous, and always underpaid, the cowboy as a mythical figure and stereotype was an appealing and resilient one. First in sensational newspaper stories and inexpensive dime novel tales of the 1860s and 1870s, cowboys were portrayed as wild men—bad boys who brought misrule and excitement into small western towns when they emerged from the range with their pay seeking whisky, women, and gambling, prone to swearing and settling disagreements with gun play. By the 1880s and 1890s, the traveling Wild West show, a Western-style traveling show that featured demonstrations of cowboy skills and dramatic vignettes of settler life or the Indian wars in the West, featured cowboys as expert horsemen and heroes who rescued people threatened by Indians. With the birth of the Western genre in cinema and literature just after the turn of the century, as well as the proliferation of community rodeos, the cowboy hero became a staple of American culture. Likewise, the growing network of community rodeos was a form of entertainment where working cowboys

---

15   Emerson Hough, *The Story of the Cowboy* (London: Hodder & Stoughton, 1896), 41.

16   Bruce A. Glasrud, "Introduction: Don't Leave Out the Cowboys!" in *Black Cowboys in the American West: On the Range, On the Stage, Behind the Badge*, ed. Bruce A. Glasrud and Michael N. Searles (Norman: U of Oklahoma P, 2016), 10.

and cowgirls competed in extraordinary or reckless roping and riding feats, which they did not normally perform with the boss's livestock, in order to win a little money and some notoriety.

The cowboy and cowgirl have often been a vehicle in fiction or colorful journalistic writing for a sense of belatedness, that is, the idea that in the West the best times are in the past and through living cowboys we can get a glimpse of that past. As early as the 1900s and 1910s, people imagined cowboys as symbolic of the "free grass" days before fencing and federal management of land, a period of great individual freedom. The cowboy laborer ironically evoked nostalgic ideas about the supposed unlimited bounty and economic opportunity of the Beef Bonanza days popularized by boosters seeking to sell land or books. Equally, many were nostalgic for the period before 1890, when the famous historian Frederick Jackson Turner declared that the frontier had "closed" since the military operations against Native Americans had ceased and there was no region of the West without settlers. Americans, he said, needed to find some new war to which to send its sons to prove themselves and for Americans to define themselves as superior people—the Spanish–American War and US annexation of Hawai'i both took place in 1893.[17]

The range of historical primary sources expands considerably here, since beginning in the later nineteenth century there were new media formats and more of them in circulation. They included illustrated newspapers, cowboy adventure story "dime novels," **stereo card photography**, photograph postcards, and published novels and memoirs about life in the West. Starting in the 1880s, public demand for information about life on the range was fed by cowboy memoirs, which are particularly important for this book. Today they are still a rich source of historical lore and factual information about the labor and lives of range cowboys. Often, the authors were talented writers who as young men spent some months or years working as cowboys. Hence the genre overrepresents white men and privileges a few more articulate or educated voices over the larger number of men who worked as cowboys but did not produce manuscripts or know how to get them published. Those

stereo card photography:
A stereo card was a cardboard plate that held the same image on the right and left halves. One viewed the two images through a viewer placed against the face such that when one looked through the eyeglasses there, one saw each image with a different eye, producing the appearance of a three-dimensional image. People owned stereo card viewers and bought cards displaying photographs of famous people and places, current events, novelties—just about anything.

17   Turner was a University of Wisconsin historian whose 1893 essay, "The Significance of the Frontier in American History," argued that American democracy and uniqueness were cultivated by the nation's expansion across the continent. Known as the "Turner Frontier Thesis," the argument has been refuted by several generations of professional historians. Most now describe American expansion as a product of imperialism, capitalism, and other factors that produced problematic environmental change and irrefutable inequalities among people in the West that defy Turner's vision of a democratic, equalitarian West for white men. Still, the idea that the Old West of Turner's era represents the most authentic period and culture in US history is central to popular ideas about cowboys, cattle ranching, and the West. Frederick Jackson Turner, "The Significance of the Frontier in American History," *Proceedings of the Forty–First Annual Meeting of the State Historical Society of Wisconsin* (Madison, WI: State Historical Society of Wisconsin, 1894), https://catalog.hathitrust.org/Record/008371809.

cowboys' stories can be found in oral tradition among families or sometimes the "old-timers" interviews in newspapers and Western-themed magazines. Similarly, in the Southwest, Mexico, central and south America, there is a parallel tradition in Spanish of cowboy nostalgia, poetry, and lore known as *gauchesco*. Since literacy rates among Spanish-speakers could be low, there was less of this type of literature than of the cowboy memoir feeding the large US book and magazine market.

3. FATTENING, SHIPPING, SLAUGHTERING, SELLING

In this section we examine sources that reveal the public debate over the expanding industrial beef trade in the United States that people found in promotional accounts from books, newspapers, and advertising as well as reports and depictions of the costs of the trade to cattle well-being that appeared in both private and public sources. People talked about the beef trade since the food system was changing quickly. Railroads and, in time, refrigerated railcars would make the modern industrial meat system possible. That system was emblematic of the industrial power of the United States, which by the turn of the century would be the most productive nation on the planet due to its abundance of natural resources, labor from heavy immigration, and robust business sector.[18] The roots of industrial beef lay in early cattle drives of longhorn cattle out of Texas and the Southwest beginning in the late 1860s. Drovers hired by cattle owners herded animals overland to new railheads in Kansas, where they waited at stockyards for sale and then shipping to slaughterhouses in Chicago and beyond.

The cattle investors who restocked and carried on after the Big Die-Up of 1886–87, put smaller herds on smaller ranges, fed them stored hay over the winter, then sold them via Kansas cattle markets to corn feedlots in Illinois. Suddenly, extensive ranching under this "midwestern system" required range workers—the famed, free-spirited cowboys of lore—to spend their time putting up hay.[19] The storied cattle drives of previous decades were stripped down in time to twice-yearly round-ups for branding, marking, and castrating, moving herds from one seasonal range to another, or cutting out steers from a herd for transfer to the railhead.

The meat-eating population on the east coast and overseas was growing and in the last two decades of the nineteenth century the number of beef cattle in the US doubled. Western beef appeared in American markets as

18 Dant, *Losing Eden*, 92.

19 Jordan, *North American Cattle-Ranching Frontiers*, 267–74; Richard White, "Animals of Enterprise," in *The Oxford History of the American West*, ed. Clyde A. Milner II, Carol A. O'Connor, and Martha A. Sandweiss (New York: Oxford UP, 1994), 261–62.

popular, inexpensive tinned products like corned beef hash (often made from rotten chopped meat treated heavily with preservatives—the predecessor to "mystery meat") or as dressed beef, that is cuts of meat from an animal that had been slaughtered in a different city and shipped to the consumer's local market. The public was at first skeptical and in time alarmed about all this. In much of the nineteenth century, people kept agricultural animals in urban spaces—the feral pigs of New York were famous for biting and knocking people over. Equally, dairy cattle, chickens, and other poultry were common in backyards and empty lots such that people often could see where their meat came from. Even at the butcher's shop, the staff would hang whole carcasses in the store for customers to inspect. One could see if the animal had been healthy when killed and point out to a butcher one knew and trusted the cut one wished to take home. Haggling over price was expected.[20] To find meat from an animal slaughtered far away (and how long ago?) precut or canned in packages and at prices set by an anonymous person was unsettling to many consumers, as were regular reports of people sickened by canned meat. The "Big 4" meat packers (Swift, Armour, Wilson, and Cudahy) poured money into attractive advertising campaigns that portrayed modern beef as wholesome, healthy, and convenient. In time, consumers came to accept pre-cut and processed, packaged meats, especially inexpensive ones, although they expected regulation (for instance the 1906 Meat Inspection Act) to limit toxic fillers and preservatives.[21]

Meanwhile, investment in beef cattle soon focused on more energy efficient, meat-productive cattle, who were more labor-intensive to manage but more profitable in the system. Although people had eaten criollo cattle like Texas Longhorns, these cattle had been valued primarily for their equally valuable hides and tallow. Texas Longhorns bulked up slowly; with their long legs and modest girth, their limited and tough flesh was increasingly unpalatable to eastern and foreign meat buyers. In an attempt to combine hardiness and speedy meat growth in one animal, ranchers began stocking with shorthorns of European descent and shorthorn-longhorn cross cattle. These heavier breeds were specifically bred for meat production. Artists often depicted these cattle in paintings and drawings as almost rectangular in shape—like a beef cube resting on short legs. Equally, by the 1880s fear of the tick-borne Texas fever, a cattle disease that criollos could tolerate, but to which shorthorn and dairy breeds were devastatingly vulnerable, drove many states to limit or stop cattle drives from Texas into their territories.[22]

---

20 Joshua Specht, *Red Meat Republic: A Hoof-to-Table History of How Beef Changed America* (Princeton: Princeton UP, 2019), 224.

21 Specht, *Red Meat Republic*, 227–31.

22 White, "Animals of Enterprise," 220–23.

In time, the railhead stockyards became just a transition point, not directly to a distant slaughterhouse (many cattle died in transit when shipped by rail for many days), but to feedlots in Illinois and other midwestern states. The new system was a precursor to the commercial feedlots beef producers use today, in which, for a month or two before slaughter, cattle are held in small paddocks and given calorie-rich feed for maximum weight gain. All of this was subsidized by a series of administrations in Washington that gave land grants and tax breaks to railway companies, in effect subsidizing beef production with crucial infrastructure as well as with the use of land confiscated from Indigenous peoples. Modern beef cattle funneled through the midwestern system seemed somehow less Western than the old-time Texas Longhorns, some cowboys said. Less able to defend themselves on the land from humans and wild predators, these purpose-bred meat cattle, sometimes dehorned, lived on fenced ranges where ranch hands (i.e., cowboys working at the main property of a ranching outfit) brought them hay to eat in winter. Many said that they submitted more easily to round-ups and the trip to the slaughterhouse because they lived in closer proximity to, and had more frequent contact with, humans. Some cowboys disliked the new cattle since the self-sufficiency and fierceness of the old, wild criollo cattle had made cowboy work more challenging and dangerous, enhancing the ruggedly manly status.

Still, beef cattle were dangerous and unwittingly contributed to the idea that western life was risky and rough. At work cowboys could be pulled off their horses and gored by a cow or fall under a stampede, or they might have digits or limbs twisted, broken, or severed by a taut rope pulled by a resistant steer. Word of mouth and the papers told of people killed or grievously injured by steers and other cattle. Especially in railhead towns where livestock routinely moved through business and residential districts, people had to trust transient drovers and vaqueros to control cattle who sometimes tried to escape or became frightened or frustrated when approached by unknown or threatening people. Cattle were also a legitimate public safety issue as they grazed on unfenced properties and were known to charge passing pedestrians and horses, tossing them in the air or impaling them on their long horns. Frightened or irritated horses also bit, kicked, threw, and otherwise injured people with regularity, not least the cowboys who periodically captured them from their semi-wild bands and forced a saddle on them.

For this section, the relevant sources are published accounts of the cattle trade in books, newspapers, and graphic illustration, as well as color **lithograph** images representative of the ubiquitous and often-beautiful advertising of the late nineteenth century. Literacy rates in the United States had always been some of the world's highest, especially in the northeastern areas where there had long been public schools and an expectation that

lithograph: Lithography is a means of mass-producing color illustrations with metal plates and colored inks that was in common use in the nineteenth century.

everyone would know how to read a newspaper and the Bible. In the South and West, literacy rates were lower, especially among migrants who had just arrived or people living in serious poverty who had worked as children and so had limited education.

4. TWENTIETH CENTURY RANCH LIFE, IMAGINED AND REAL

In this part of the book, the primary sources we examine include popular graphic items like postcards and advertisements that glamorized ranching and cattle people in the first half of the twentieth century, as well as memoirs and documentary accounts of the lives of ranch people and their neighbors. It is important that we look beyond romantic ideas that have circulated in order to instead see the history of cattle production as part of larger resource-extraction history in the West and the very difficult work that it was. Along with mining and, in time, oil and tourism development, the destruction of the bison ecology and the transplanting of cattle and horse agriculture was a transition away from human subsistence from the environment to a system of using the environment, land, and animals to generate profits and capital—with the expectation of perpetual growth.

Yet, in fact, for many cattle operations, ranching was not a money-making venture but a lifestyle to which people dedicated themselves, often struggling to make the business financially viable. Over the course of the twentieth century, many individuals and families exploited state and federal laws to raise cattle. Beginning with the Homestead Act of 1861, then the Enlarged Homestead Act of 1909, and finally the Stock-Raising Homestead Act of 1916, legislation helped settlers gain title to land in acreages too small to support a full herd of market cattle but substantial enough to serve as a base of operations. Equally crucial was the acquisition of water rights that guaranteed access to water in arid regions. Especially after the 1930s, water from the rural West was being funneled into huge aqueducts and dams to supply growing western cities and various irrigation schemes, known as land "reclamation," even though much of that land had been arid for centuries.[23] Once acquired, the water rights that made land viable for livestock raising were guarded carefully, with people handing them down to adult children along with their land titles.

The cow-calf operation was typical of family ranches. This type of business was often family owned and handed down to sons—pastoral societies

---

23   William Cronon, "Landscapes of Abundance and Scarcity," in *The Oxford History of the American West*, ed. Clyde A. Milner II, Carol A. O'Connor, and Martha A. Sandweiss (New York: Oxford UP, 1994), 617.

are usually patrilineal. The business was to breed cows, grow the resulting calves until one or two years old (depending upon what decade it was), then sell and ship them to a feedlot, where they would be fattened before slaughter. Twentieth-century ranches had long dispensed with criollo longhorn cattle and the northern European shorthorn cattle employed the previous century. Modern beef markets utilized new breeds like Herefords, colloquially known as "white faces," as well as Angus, Limousin, and Simmental cattle that produced the exact proportion of fat and lean consumers preferred. Usually based on a small ranch property where the family home, barns, and other main buildings were located, the business functioned by employing "hired men," or modern cowboys who managed stock, now using a pick-up truck or ATV as often as in the saddle. Much of the cattle grazing took place on leased public lands made possible by the Taylor Grazing Act of 1934. Like the water rights and land titles, grazing leases were crucial and families guarded them carefully from generation to generation. Twentieth-century ranchers who lived on site were generally more knowledgeable about the radically altered grass and plant ecologies they inhabited than those who had originally overseen the Beef Bonanza bubble. For instance, during the terrible Dust Bowl crisis of the 1930s, it was cattle ranchers who remembered the crises of the 1880s and 1890s, warned of cyclical droughts, and admonished settlers and government boosters for tearing up the plains grasses that remained in order to plant commodity crops like wheat.

Many family ranch businesses went out of business, or their proprietors gave up on them when their children decided they wanted to live a different way. It was common to find ranch families in which one or more members had a job in town in order to subsidize the meager or unpredictable earnings from cattle sales. That is, ranching was a lifestyle and a difficult one that people persevered with because they loved it. Ranching was a way to live on that vast Western landscape on one's own terms (in some ways, at least) as an independent business owner in charge of one's own destiny. They were rural people willing to do the work that others—especially supposedly delicate city people—were unwilling to do in order to put steak on the table since they had no long-term, multigenerational connection to the land in a particular place.[24]

Beef consumption nearly doubled between 1950 and 1972 as American consumers adopted beef steak as a middle-class status symbol. At the same time, the independent ranchers outsiders idealized as symbolic of a proudly independent western identity coped with volatile beef prices, which became

---

24 Paul F. Starrs, *Let the Cowboy Ride: Cattle Ranching in the American West* (Baltimore: Johns Hopkins UP, 1998), 71–73.

inflated in a speculative bubble, then crashed in 1952, taking a decade to recover.[25] Increased beef consumption did not translate to a better living in rural parts. Tourist and retiree in-migration also drove up the cost of living in rural areas, as did neighbors who sold out to developers of "ranchette" properties (large acreages that would be divided into smaller residential lots) that weakened the inter-reliance between small operations and made other ranches vulnerable to corporate beef operations that bought them up and put waged workers on site.[26]

Still, the family ranch and the lone male cowboy were archetypes the public found compelling and meaningful as a way to think about American exceptionalism. Meanwhile Hollywood movies and television Westerns idealized ranching and cattle raising as honorable and necessary, romanticizing a period in American history actually characterized by economic uncertainty and, in places, environmental degradation. Likewise, the popular culture depicting cowboys, cowgirls, and the West ignored the long-term environmental change caused by cattle, horses, and the many sheep operations[27] in order to "perpetuate the American ideal of ... the rugged individual—the tumbleweed cowboy—who can tame it but use it well."[28] In this imagining, cowboys, cowgirls, and ranchers were heroic stewards of a perpetually abundant western landscape characterized by powerful animals who likewise benefited the environment.

Historians of the twentieth century have an overwhelming abundance of primary sources to choose from, and this is equally true for the final three sections of this book. With respect to our history of Western lifestyles and ranching, real and imagined, the focus is on promotional images and documentary photography. Cameras were far less expensive, more durable and portable by the twentieth century than previously. Equally, the diversity of voices recorded telling their stories about life with cattle had increased

---

25   During the Great Depression, federal legislation protected ranch businesses with subsidies, loans, emergency feed distribution, and other supports. Then, the US government legislated and froze beef prices during World War II. Thereafter followed a period of high inflation and speculation in beef as a commodity. When the bubble burst and there was a "price break" (collapse), ranchers still coped with growing operating costs for feed, labor, land, new stock, and insurance so suffered financial losses. James R. Gray, *Ranch Economics* (Ames: Iowa State UP, 1968), 20–21; John T. Schlebecker, *Cattle Raising on the Plains, 1900–1961* (Lincoln: U of Nebraska P, 1963), 205–06.

26   Nathan Freeman Sayre, *Ranching, Endangered Species, and Urbanization in the Southwest: Species of Capital* (Tucson: U of Arizona P, 2002), 121.

27   Historically, sheep-herding outfits have been very common in the West, although less celebrated since work with such animals defies the stereotype of the cowboy and cowgirl as rugged individuals who seek to control powerful broncs and half-wild cattle. As with wild horses, many cattlemen resented sheep-herding businesses as voracious competitors for animal forage or government grazing leases. Such competition resulted in periodic violence. Andrew Gulliford, *The Woolly West: Colorado's Hidden History of Sheepscapes* (College Station: Texas A&M UP, 2018), 23–149.

28   Robin L. Murray and Joseph K. Newmann, *Gunfight at the Eco-Corral: Western Cinema and the Environment* (Norman: U of Oklahoma P, 2012), 53.

from the old cowboy memoir days, and now included women ranchers and Hispanic informants documented by academic researchers working on the oral history and ethnography of rural America.

5. THE CULTURES AND POLITICS OF HORSES

In this section, we examine a series of government and commercially produced accounts of life with wild horses in the West, plus one more cowboy memoir.

Between the 1910s and 1940s, with the mass production of the gasoline engine, people in the United States transitioned away from using horses as workers. Thereafter, horses were companions, farm pets, and tools for leisure riding. In the West, that transition was a little less clear cut than in other regions of the country since people still found horses indispensable for getting around on rough terrain where wheeled vehicles could not easily go. Horses remained indispensable for ranching and cowboying, of course, and also for the growing tourism industry. Dude ranches and pack-tour companies along with ski resorts and national and state parks settled into the western economy, competing for land with the old resource-extraction industries. Outside the West and among a minority of rural westerners, people thus began seeing horses, especially the much romanticized "Mustangs of the Old West," as beings of intrinsic value and symbolic of rugged western freedoms, just like cowboys and cowgirls.

When not hunted, countless horse bands seemed to accumulate on every ranch property of any size, as well as public lands, reservation lands, and private ranges. Cowboys and landowners would often attempt to manipulate the reproduction of these herds, shooting or gelding (capturing and castrating) most of the stallions, then adding intact draft stallions, heavy workhorses bred for hauling and pulling, in order to increase the size of offspring.[29] People who did that sort of wild horse ranching employed hands-off management techniques, letting such horses overwinter without aid, and rounding up surviving animals each spring. Many horses suffered severe weight loss after months pawing the ground to find frozen grass under the snow. Like cattle, when caught those semi-wild horses were branded while young, then rounded up at the age of three or four to be pressed into somebody's service. They might be various breeds or types, such as Quarter Horses (a versatile sporting breed), thoroughbred crosses (descended from

---

29 James A. Young and B. Abbott Sparks, *Cattle in the Cold Desert*. Expanded edition (Reno and Las Vegas: University of Nevada Press, 2002), 217.

Arabian stock, used for racing), or mustangs (the hardy Western horse descended from Spanish stock).

Horses left to themselves on a range or pasture and not ridden frequently were known to evade capture when a person with a halter approached since, as the wisdom went, the horse had decided he did not want to go to work. For horses in private-range bands, this was especially so because they were only seasonally exploited as temporary saddle horses, and thus had no chance to develop trusting or pain-free relationships with individual people. Instead, captured and saddled by force by strangers, then often driven with spurs, quirt (short whip), and yelling, these horses had experiences in captivity that could lead to psychological trauma (balkiness or unpredictability, as horse people knew it) and physical injuries.

The horse population had peaked in the 1910s, then began a steady decline in the 1920s. With the economic collapse of the 1930s, countless people set their equines loose to fend for themselves and the numbers of unowned wild mustangs grew. Relieved of work, free-roaming horses gathered where they could and began having babies. Montanans in particular remembered that there were "horses on every hill" in that state as free-roaming horses multiplied that decade. Many hated the mustangs, complaining that their own working horses, if left unattended in the wrong place, were sometimes lured away by wild herds and could not be retrained if captured again. Ranchers believed that wild or feral horses consumed forage that rightly belonged to cattle. After the passing of the Taylor Grazing Act, critics argued that wild horses complicated the work of the Federal government to manage range health in the interest of cattle growers since government land managers were tasked with measuring and culling horse bands.

In some places, government-sanctioned and -financed horse-eradication programs had begun already in the late 1920s. It was said thereafter that the size of the wild horse population was directly proportional to men's bank accounts. Many men became dedicated to mustanging and the entrepreneurial income it generated, especially in Nevada and Montana.[30] Critics looked at the mustangers not as the storied cattlemen or working cowboys of the West, but as poor rural men who disreputably made a living off a public resource however they could. Once captured, the fortunate among those horses might be sold to farmers if they could be trained to tolerate contact with humans. Others were auctioned off in groups, driven on hoof many miles to a stockyard, then shipped by train to their ultimate destination. Some called the 1930s the "great removal" because horses were systematically captured and destroyed by agents of canning companies, notably the Chappel Brothers company, which sold horsemeat to consumers overseas or used it

---

30 Young and Sparks, *Cattle in the Cold Desert*, 222–23.

to manufacture dog and cat food for the American market.[31] The scale of human poverty in the West guaranteed that there was enormous economic pressure bearing down on western horses. The mustangers and canners, the ranchers who continued to fence land to keep cattle in and horses out, and government restrictions that made horses unwelcome on public grazing lands all caused the US horse population to decline from an early peak estimated at 20 million in 1910 to about 5 million by 1954.[32]

During the 1950s, a question that arose out of these changes was how long unowned horses might live at large in the West before people would agree that they had a right to exist there, even though they were an introduced species. Supporters of wild horses believed they deserved protection like the bison or antelope, and were symbolic of an imagined spirit of the West in their persistence, self-sufficiency, and history of labor and companionship (at times) with people. In a region with an arid environment and fragile plant life, where land was expected to generate capital and sustain human lives, others saw wild horses as competitors and pests—an invasive species even.

A series of legislation would moderate the capture of wild horses over the years but not end it. Most famous was the original Federal Public Law 86-234, popularly named the "Wild Horse Annie" Act after a Nevada horse advocate, which was supported by a national letter-writing and publicity campaign that included many schoolchildren. Passed in 1959, it banned mechanized hunting (i.e., chasing them with helicopters) of wild horses on private (not public) lands in Nevada. The bill was inspired in part by the publication of Gus Bundy's beautiful but tragic photographs of mustangers capturing wild horses in the Nevada desert, which showed horses being chased, roped, and dragged onto trucks. The 1971 Wild and Free-Roaming Horses and Burros Act later addressed wild horses on public lands in the West, although not banning round-ups or slaughter. To this day, ranchers see wild horses as unwelcome pests or worry about them fending for themselves, occasionally starving to death over the winter or living without veterinary care like the deer and coyotes. In response, the Bureau of Land Management has responded to such complaints by collecting wild horses on public lands and, when they can, finding adoptive homes for them, or sending them to long-term holding facilities.

The debate over mustangs was one of many disputes in the second half of the twentieth century over land use. The federal government owned outright a majority of land in the West, which was managed by bureaucracies and on-site staff from the National Park Service, US Forest Service, and Bureau

---

31   Leisl Carr Childers, *The Size of the Risk: Histories of Multiple Use in the Great Basin* (Norman: U of Oklahoma P, 2015), 160; Walker D. Wyman, *Wild Horse of the West* (1945; Lincoln: U of Nebraska P, 1963), 157, 204–08.

32   Childers, *Size of the Risk*, 171.

of Land Management (**BLM**). The Federal Land Policy and Management Act of 1976 reorganized the work of these agencies, but did not make federal control of public lands any less controversial among ranchers and others seeking more private land or at least local state control over public lands. Many such advocates mobilized in the 1970s and 1980s in a short-lived lobbying campaign remembered as the Sage Brush Rebellion. Ultimately they were unsuccessful simply because management of vast federal lands (as much as 75 per cent of total land area in some states) was a responsibility most Western states simply did not have the revenue to afford.

6. RANGE AND CATTLE CONTROVERSIES

The fate of wild horses and the competition over land use in the West, which pitted ranchers against animal advocates with the federal government in the middle, was a mirror image of disputes over land use and cattle ranching that would follow in the second half of the twentieth century. While the public still admired cowboys, cowgirls, and ranching families as timelessly emblematic of the ruggedness and ingenuity of Westerners, the atmosphere became newly politicized. In this last part of the book, we again examine government, academic, and commercially produced primary sources typical of the twentieth century, plus one new element—social media.

As early as 1874, John Wesley Powell's *Report on the Lands of the Arid Region* had recommended federal regulation and restriction of cattle grazing to prevent destruction of rangelands from over-grazing and protect the future of the industry. Instead, the federal government generously subsidized cattle and horse ranching as a way to develop western state economies and national food security. As with the rail system in the late nineteenth century, in the twentieth century access to low-cost forage on Bureau of Land Management and US Forest Service lands was crucial to most ranching outfits. Grazing leases were generally inexpensive and ranchers formed various state Cattle Growers Associations as political lobbies to protect and try to expand such access to public lands by entities that raised cattle, be they corporations or family ranches.

Other examples of "subsidies" for rural living included federally financed national highway systems, tax breaks for the agricultural sector, federal management and repair of public lands such as overgrazed public ranges, construction and maintenance of irrigation and land-reclamation projects, which sparsely populated individual states could never afford. Many ranching operations hired foreign temporary workers as hired hands and, even in the 1990s, those cowboys made only $800 per month cowboying.[33]

To critics, ranching was an essentially consumptive lifestyle in which environmental costs were externalized.[34] Certainly government subsidized technologies and cheap access to federally managed public resources put into question the myth, entertained by plenty of cow hands and ranching families, of westerners as fiercely independent and self-sufficient people who labored to make something productive (in commodity terms) of the vast expanses of the American West. In fact, many ranchers (and farmers) were rural folks living in "next year country," as the popular saying went, that is, a culture of faithful optimism wherein they persevered with modes of making a living that were difficult, unpredictable, and often unprofitable. To critics who did not find that to be a romantic notion, cattle ranching on public lands seemed to be a lot of unnecessary work and environmental destruction—and for what?

Beginning in the 1970s, active and nationally popular environmental and other social justice movements included a minority of rural westerners who saw firsthand the damage cattle herds did to fragile waterways and plant life. One outspoken critic would express ongoing exasperation with the political power of the Stock Growers associations by exclaiming around 1990, "Cows in the West are a stupid tradition. They don't make sense anymore. Cows on our public land are destroying our soil, our water, our wildlife—and we're giving them subsidies to do it! Let's kick them off! Every single one!"[35] Some people complained of "welfare ranchers" to advocate against public lands grazing. They pointed to environmental and range science research that disputed old rancher arguments claiming cattle grazing was sustainable and even beneficial for a healthy range, which to them included natural and man-made waterways, plus a variety of plants and wild animals posing little danger to beef cattle. Critics saw a lack of ecological diversity, noting that the presence of cattle made restoration of late nineteenth-century ecologies essentially impossible, especially since about 70 per cent of western lands were leased for grazing. "To the cowboy, this is good, for the land must be used. You can't eat scenery," explained one observer of the ideological stand-off in the early 1990s.[36] By that logic, land left to exist as part of a larger ecosystem was idle land and thus wasted land. (Recall the point about irrigation of desert and semi-desert regions as land "reclamation" above.) Wild predators

---

33   Sharman Apt Russell, *Kill the Cowboy: A Battle of Mythology in the New West* (Lincoln, NE: U of Nebraska P, 1993), 2.

34   Paul F. Starrs, *Let the Cowboy Ride: Cattle Ranching in the American West* (Baltimore: Johns Hopkins UP, 1998), 73.

35   Denzel Ferguson quoted in Russell, *Kill the Cowboy*, 26.

36   Russell, *Kill the Cowboy*, 3–4.

or competitors for forage needed to be minimized or eliminated to protect ranching and the rural lifestyles it permitted for working-class people, pro-ranching people said. Really, the argument was about the nature of the rural West—was it a preservation area or a workspace?

The Federal Land Policy and Management Act was passed in 1976 to attempt to respond to changing public concerns for the environment, but offered only incremental changes to land use. Many rural people saw even that as an overreach. In the rural West, conservative politics ruled the day—many took heart in the fact that in 1980 President Ronald Reagan was elected after he had campaigned, in part, as a cowboy from California—photographed on horseback in a cowboy hat or doing manual labor on his ranch. Although many western states had a net inflow of federal dollars into their economies over those years, resentment against "government meddling and interference" became perennial political issues in many places due to many rural westerners' belief in themselves as self-sufficient economic actors (although they remained tied for their subsistence to distant commodity markets, subsidized federal lands, and fickle urban meat consumers). They expressed distrust toward federal bureaucracies and "big government," and had a love-hate relationship with federal officials and funding that, in many cases, made possible the rural living those fiercely independent people insisted upon.[37] Social scientists of the rural West have called this late twentieth-century bundle of values and politics "ranch fundamentalism."[38] Nevada rancher Cliven Bundy came to renewed public attention in 2014 after having refused for over 20 years to pay fees for grazing licences to the Bureau of Land Management, which then amounted to more than $1 million, a dispute that led to an armed standoff between Bundy's family and allies and Federal Bureau of Investigation agents, and Cliven Bundy's arrest. The fact that anti–federal government sentiment had not subsided after the Sage Brush Rebellion was clear when Bundy's son, Ammon, led an illegal armed occupation by 24 men of the Malheur National Wildlife Refuge in Oregon two years later, likewise claiming that the federal government had no constitutional power to own or control public lands. These armed actions were part of a revitalized anti-government movement in the years leading up to and during the Trump presidency among far-right voters nationwide.

Readers across the country would find rural settler values and politics portrayed in late twentieth-century Western lifestyle magazines like *Western Horseman*, *True West*, *American Cowboy*, and later *Cowboys and Indians*. Countless tourism advertisements for western states documented rural life with picturesque color photography of horses with manes blowing in the

37 Russell, *Kill the Cowboy*, 15–25.
38 Starrs, *Let the Cowboy Ride*, 76–79.

wind, stoic and rugged-looking people in Western attire, beautiful landscape photography, and behind-the-scenes looks at the trials and victories of famous rodeo competitors. The overarching theme to many of these depictions was of the proposed righteousness and family values–style morality inherent in the rural West. Long-established family ranch businesses were especially celebrated as wholesome and patriotic. All of it helped viewers forget the longer history of the West—the violence of the Indian Wars, chronic poverty among working cowboys, all the ranchers who went broke, the industrial agriculture companies that bought up those ranches, and how often ranching and meat production externalized to the government and taxpayers the environmental costs of grazing, feeding, and shipping.

CHRONOLOGY

1500s	Early Spanish cattle and horse introductions to the Americas.
1598	Self-sustaining herds of and market for horses established in old Mexico (today the US Southwest).
18th c.–early 19th c.	Height of the southwestern and southern great plains Hispanic and Indigenous horse markets
1862	Homestead Act, the first of various pieces of legislation giving private individuals title to lands expropriated from Indigenous peoples by the US government.
1869	Completion of the first transcontinental railroad, the Pacific Railroad.
1870s–80s	Decline of criollo cattle in favor of heavy shorthorn and shorthorn-long cross cattle for beef production under the Midwestern system.
1870s–1885	Beef Bonanza era, the economic bubble in which many absentee speculators drove beef cattle production until prices collapsed during the winter of 1886–87.
1878	Swift & Company begin use of refrigerated rail boxcar designed by Andrew Chase for "dressed" (slaughtered and cut) meat.
1886–87	Big Die-Up on the Great Plains, in which millions of cattle weakened by lack of forage due to years of overgrazing died in record cold and blizzards.
1887	Dawes Severalty Act, which founded the modern reservation system and divided remaining Native American lands into smaller plots for individuals and families, rather than collective tribal ownership.
1889–93	Johnson County War, one of various "fence cutting wars," a period of vigilante violence against small cattle operation ranchers and farmers, and consolidation of large disparities of wealth and power in the West.
1890	Wounded Knee Massacre marking the end of the Indian Wars and armed Indigenous resistance to the US government and military.
1902	Owen Wister's *The Virginian*, early and influential Western novel, published.
1900–20	Competitive community rodeo networks replace traveling Wild West Shows of dramatic vignettes and staged cowboy and cowgirl sports as premier venue for Western sports and entertainment.

1916	Stock-Raising Homestead Act provides individuals and families title to 640-acre plots of public land to encourage the founding of ranching operations.
1930s	Dust Bowl disaster due to destruction of native grasses on Great Plains; wild horse population crashes due to predation by mustangers during decade-long economic crisis.
1934	Taylor Grazing Act authorizes regulation of grazing on public lands by Bureau of Land Management and National Forest Service.
1951	Gus Bundy's controversial photographs of Nevada mustang capture first made public.
1952	Collapse of beef prices coincides with historically high beef consumption in the United States.
1960s–70s	Birth of the modern environmental movement, including critics of extensive ranching.
	Western cities Denver, Houston, and Phoenix grow to over one million inhabitants each.
1971	Wild and Free-Roaming Horses and Burros Act (Wild Horse Annie Act) to regulate federal management of feral, unowned horses on federal lands.
1980	Election of Ronald Reagan, the "Cowboy President," symbolizing resurgence of rural and conservative politics in national politics.
1990s	First substantive public awareness of global warming.

PART 1

Enter Horses and Cattle

DOCUMENT 1:

Pierre Marie François Pagès describes cattle and horse behavior and husbandry in the region of San Antonio: *Travels Round the World, in the Years 1767, 1768, 1769, 1770, 1771* (1791)[1]

François Pagès was a French naval officer and writer who visited the region of San Antonio, today in the US state of Texas and regions south of there into central Mexico. In an age when most Europeans scarcely traveled more than 50 miles from home in their lifetimes, Pagès became known as an explorer for visiting places few in Europe would ever see.

In the eighteenth and nineteenth centuries, published travel narratives such as this one, and the Catlin and James volumes below, were expensive but popular among middle- and upper-class European and American readers curious about the world, considering a move to frontier areas, or speculating on ways to invest or trade there. People of European descent dominated the travel narrative trade, so similar printed accounts by Indigenous people or enslaved people are virtually unknown until the nineteenth century.

e

In the settlement of San Antonio we find a **Spanish colony from the Canary Isles**; whilst all their other stations consist merely of soldiers, and a few **Indians** who have been **seduced from the innocence of savage life**. Their principal employment is to rear horses, mules, cows, and sheep. Their cattle, commonly allowed to roam at large in the woods, are once in two months driven into fields adjoining to the houses of their owners, where every means is used to render them tame and tradable. After having been subjected to hunger and confinement, they receive their liberty, and are succeeded by others, which experience in their turn a similar course of discipline. Such of the inhabitants as are at pains to prevent their herds from running entirely wild, possess five or six thousand head of cattle.

The inhabitants of San Antonio are excellent horsemen, and particularly fond of hunting their wild animals. Having entered the field, and started an animal they mean to take alive, they give him chase at full speed from

Spanish colony from the Canary Isles: Spanish-speaking settlers from the Canary Islands, a colony of the Spanish Empire located just off the west coast of Morocco.

Indians: Probably members of the local Payaya people.

seduced from the innocence of savage life: Pejorative reference to the minority of Indigenous peoples who had converted to Christianity and begun to engage in settled agriculture.

---

1   Vol. 1, 2nd ed. (1791; repr. London: J. Murray, 1793), 103–05, 139–40.

thong: A strip of hide or leather employed as a whip or lasso.

Anson's Voyages: In the 1740s, Commodore George Anson circumnavigated the globe leading a squadron of ships from Britain. Anson's journals of the expedition were published in 1748 as a well-regarded and lucrative travel account, *A Voyage Round the World in the Years 1740, 1741, 1742, 1743, 1744*.

horse or mule: In the eighteenth century, the term "cattle" could indicate any group of livestock, whether including pigs, sheep, horses, or other equines.

savages: From the seventeenth to the early twentieth century, it was common for settlers and later Americans to refer to Indigenous people by this pejorative term, even though many people found it offensive at the time. The idea was grounded in the false belief that Indigenous people were uncivilized because most were not Christians and refused to submit to the Spanish and, later, US government, instead preserving their political, economic, and cultural autonomy.

sward: An eighteenth-century term for an area of short grass or grassland.

Spaniard: Foreign travelers routinely hired local people as guides in order to travel in lands unknown to them.

Sartille: The Mexican town of Saltillo just southwest of Monterrey.

couteau-de-chasse: Hunting knife.

wood to valley, till his fatigue enables the hunter to come within a certain distance of him. Here the rider, holding the running noose of a strong lash or **thong** coiled round his arm in his right hand, throws it with such dexterity, that he seldom fails to catch the game round the neck or horns; and in the same instant, by pulling up his horse, or turning him abruptly from the line of his career, he checks his prey, and obliges him to stop. A custom very similar to this is described in **Anson's Voyages**, and represented by the author as peculiar to the coast of Patagonia.

They have likewise the use of tame animals, which, besides yielding milk, supply them with fat and dried flesh for their extensive peregrinations. Their horses and mules are no sooner a little broken in, than they are offered to sale; but here the market-price is so extremely low, which, indeed, may be imagined, that I have seen a good horse sold for a pair of shoes. Having but one or two keepers for all the cattle of the settlement, even their domestic animals run day and night in the woods.

The keen eye which the habit of close and minute attention has bestowed on those people is truly surprising. Discovering in the morning that one of their cattle has disappeared in the course of the night, they examine the inclined position of the grass over which he must have passed, when they are able to distinguish by the prints of his feet whether he is a **horse or mule**, and whether he quitted his pasture grazing or in flight; nor do they despair of finding him before they have gone fifteen perhaps twenty leagues from home. In their wars with the **savages** this extreme nicety of fight is still of greater consequence; but as each party is on its guard against the discernment of the other, and both have the same motives to conceal the direction of their flight, it is usual to set fire to the **sward** as they retreat, leaving three or four leagues of black desert behind them.

The **Spaniard** whom I hired at **Sartille**, and who succeded [sic] my good Indian of San Antonio, was a man of a bad character. As long as I enjoyed the benefit of the governor's company, from whom I had just parted, I considered myself secure against injury from whatever quarter; but we were now alone, and with the opinion I entertained of this Spaniard, I could not help being a good deal apprehensive of danger. Luckily, however, he seemed to have no arms about his person, while I, as usual, wore a **couteau-de-chasse** at my girdle. My horses and mules had been always kept at grass with those of the governor, and consequently had hitherto cost me neither trouble nor expense; but I was now afraid to trust them in the custody of my Spaniard during night, lest he should decamp, and leave me to make the best of my way on foot in the morning.

As on this route the traveller easily finds a house for his accommodation in the evening, I used the precaution to purchase from my host the provender necessary for my animals over night; but as in these inns there is no such convenience as a stable, I ordered the Spaniard to sleep within doors, while I lay in the field, at the foot of the stake to which my mules were made fast. Besides, as I was always more careful of my beasts than myself, I knew by this means in what manner they fed, and in what condition they were able to travel next day. It is surprising how much they seemed hampered and dissatisfied with their confinement. The three first nights they would eat nothing but a little cut grass; and it was with the utmost difficulty I could make them chew their corn, after taking the pains to moisten it for them in salt water. On the morning subsequent to the first night they passed in this unnatural situation, such was the **benumbed condition of their limbs**, that it was impossible to say from their motions that they had a single joint in their bodies. However, what with pulling them after us by force, and a severe application of the whip, they began at length not to walk but to leap, dragging their hinder legs as if they had been tied in halters; meanwhile, their blood becoming warm, and the circulation accelerated by discipline and exercise, they gradually recovered the ordinary use of their limbs.

On the second day of my journey, I arrived at the celebrated mines of gold and silver at **San Louis Potosi**, the richest of which is that of Serro San Pedro. **Potosi** is a handsome well-built town, large, populous, and situated in the midst of beautiful gardens. The streets are neat, and run in strait lines; the churches magnificent; the people opulent, and in possession of all the comforts and conveniences of life. The Indians, however, appear to be of a melancholy humour all over this province; for, besides the ordinary hardships of a yoke to which they have ever **submitted with reluctance**, the imposition of new taxes, and the abolition of the order of the **Jesuits**, were recent causes of much dissatisfaction. Their chiefs to the distance of **Venau**, mindful of many former injuries, and in resentment of what they considered additional oppression, engaged their vassals in a kind of revolt, which, as the natives are twenty to one Spaniard, without the prompt interference of government, and the severities exercised for its suppression, might have been of serious consequences.

I purchased a horse at Potosi, this country being eminently distinguished for a fine breed of that animal, as well as for rearing cows for the consumption of Mexico. The method employed here to catch wild cattle is, perhaps, peculiar to those people: the cattle are generally permitted to roam at large over the fields; but in case of a sale are hunted down in the following manner: the master coming up to a herd on horseback and at full speed, forces them to a gallop; but in a short time they are worn out with fatigue, and sink to the ground on their knees; he then alights from his horse, and, exerting all his strength, raises the animal obliquely by the

benumbed condition of their limbs: Horses and mules who are confined in stalls or staked for many hours may temporarily have painful stiffness in their legs.

San Louis Potosi: The Mexican state of San Luis Potosí known for seventeenth-century Spanish mining of gold and silver.

Potosi: The town of San Luis Potosí in north central Mexico.

submitted with reluctance: In the Spanish colonial period, Indigenous peoples often were exploited as forced labor by the operators of silver mines and other enterprises.

Jesuits: In a political dispute with the Spanish government, the Jesuit order, which had property and religious missions in Spanish American territories, were expelled in 1767. Local Indigenous peoples favored the Jesuits because the order ran large ranching and farming operations where one could find paid work and a supply of necessary food products.

Venau: Probably the Mexican town today known as Venado (meaning venison or deer), which is about 100 kilometers north of San Luis Potosí, a region in which Spanish colonial authorities had violently suppressed Indigenous resistance.

tail; by which means she loses her balance, and drops upon her nose; an attitude so awkward and confounding to the cow, that she will remain a whole day without attempting to recover her liberty. Selecting therefore such as he can immediately dispose of, the rest are relieved from their confinement.

DOCUMENT 2:

George Catlin reports on Indigenous peoples and their horses: *Letters and Notes on the Manners, Customs, and Conditions of North American Indians* (1844)[2]

George Catlin was a Pennsylvania artist and writer based in St. Louis. From there, he took extended trips west and documented life among dozens of Native American nations. Unlike many of his peers, Catlin had a serious interest in Indigenous peoples and in understanding the ways they lived off the land, especially with horses. Horses had transformed Indigenous people's relationship to the land, wild animals like bison, and one another. Those who owned many horses held an economic and political advantage over rival tribes and nations; indeed, in many places the proliferation of horses increased disparities of wealth and power among Indigenous nations and among people within those nations. For wild horses, who had proliferated since the Spanish first introduced horses to the continent, life could be difficult and dangerous.

e

We had with us about thirty **Osage and Cherokee, Seneca and Delaware Indians**, employed as guides and hunters for the regiment; and with the war-party of ninety or a hundred **Camanchees**, we formed a most picturesque appearance while passing over the green fields, and consequently, sad havoc amongst the herds of **buffaloes**, which we were almost hourly passing. We were now out of the influence and reach of bread stuffs, and subsisted ourselves on buffaloes' meat altogether; and the Indians of the different tribes, emulous to shew their skill in the chase, and prove the mettle of their horses, took infinite pleasure in dashing into every herd that we approached; by which means, the regiment was abundantly supplied from day to day with fresh meat.

In one of those spirited scenes when the regiment were on the march, and the Indians with their bows and arrows were closely plying a band of these affrighted animals, they made a bolt through the line of the dragoons, and a complete breach, through which the whole herd passed, upsetting horses and riders in the most amusing manner, and receiving such shots as came from those guns and pistols that were *aimed*, and not fired off into the empty air.

The buffaloes are very blind animals, and owing, probably in a great measure, to the profuse locks that hang over their eyes, they run chiefly by the nose, and follow in the tracks of each other, seemingly heedless of

Osage and Cherokee, Seneca and Delaware Indians: Members of the Ni-u-kon-ska "People of the Middle Waters" (Osage), Aniyvwiyaʔi (ᎠᏂᏴᏫᏯᎢ) "Principal People" (Cherokee), Onödowá'ga: "Great Hill People" (Seneca), and Lenni Lenape (Delaware) respectively.

Camanchees: An old term for members of what today is known as the Comanche Nation, or Nʉmʉnʉʉ. In the eighteenth century, the nation had expanded its territorial range from what is today Colorado and Kansas south into Texas and New Mexico. People in the region reported that the Nʉmʉnʉʉ often raided neighboring people of horses and other valuables or were engaged in armed conflict with other tribes and Spanish colonists.

buffaloes: American bison (*Bison bison*).

---

2   Vol. 2, 3rd ed. (New York: Wiley and Putnam, 1844), 57–60.

what is about them; and of course, easily disposed to rush in a mass, and the whole tribe or gang to pass in the tracks of those that have first led the way.

The tract of country over which we passed, between the **False Washita** and this place, is stocked, not only with buffaloes, but with numerous bands of wild horses, many of which we saw every day. There is no other animal on the prairies so wild and so sagacious as the horse; and none other so difficult to come up with. So remarkably keen is their eye, that they will generally run "at the sight," when they are a mile distant; being, no doubt, able to distinguish the character of the enemy that is approaching when at that distance; and when in motion, will seldom stop short of three or four miles. I made many attempts to approach them by stealth, when they were grazing and playing their gambols, without ever having been more than once able to succeed. In this instance, I left my horse, and with my friend Chadwick, skulked through a ravine for a couple of miles; until we were at length brought within gun-shot of a fine herd of them, when I used my pencil for some time, while we were under cover of a little hedge of bushes which effectually screened us from their view. In this herd we saw all the colours, nearly, that can be seen in a kennel of English hounds. Some were milk white, some jet black—others were sorrel, and bay, and cream colour— many were of an iron grey; and others were pied, containing a variety of colours on the same animal. Their manes were very profuse, and hanging in the wildest confusion over their necks and faces—and their long tails swept the ground.

After we had satisfied our curiosity in looking at these proud and playful animals we agreed that we would try the experiment of "creasing" one, as it is termed in this country; which is done by shooting them through the gristle on the top of the neck, which stuns them so that they fall, and are secured with the hobbles on the feet; after which they rise again without fatal injury. This is a practice often resorted to by expert hunters, with good rifles, who are not able to take them in any other way. My friend Joe and I

were armed on this occasion, each with a **light fowling-piece**, which have not quite the preciseness in throwing a bullet that a rifle has; and having both levelled our pieces at the withers of a noble, fine-looking iron grey, we pulled trigger, and the poor creature fell, and the rest of the herd were out of sight in a moment. We advanced speedily to him, and had the most inexpressible mortification of finding, that we never had thought of hobbles or halters, to secure him—and in a few moments more, had the still greater mortification, and even anguish, to find that one of our shots had broken the poor creature's neck, and that he was quite dead.

The laments of poor Chadwick for the wicked folly of destroying this noble animal, were such as I never shall forget; and so guilty did we feel that we agreed that when we joined the regiment, we should boast of all the rest of our hunting feats, but never make mention of this.

The usual mode of taking the wild horses, is, by throwing the *laso* whilst pursuing them at full speed, and dropping a noose over their necks, by which their speed is soon checked, and they are "choked down." The laso is a thong of rawhide, some ten or fifteen yards in length, twisted or braided, with a noose fixed at the end of it; which, when the coil of the laso is thrown out, drops with great certainty over the neck of the animal, which is soon conquered.

laso: A lasso.

The Indian, when he starts for a wild horse, mounts one of the fleetest he can get, and coiling his laso on his arm, starts off under the "full whip," till he can enter the band, when he soon gets it over the neck of one of the number; when he instantly dismounts, leaving his own horse, and runs as fast as he can, letting the laso pass out gradually and carefully through his hands, until the horse falls for want of breath, and lies helpless on the ground; at which time the Indian advances slowly towards the horse's head, keeping his laso tight upon its neck, until he fastens a pair of hobbles on the animal's two forefeet, and also loosens the laso (giving the horse chance to breathe), and gives it a noose around the under jaw, by which he gets great power over the affrighted animal, which is rearing and plunging when it gets breath; and by which, as he advances, hand over hand, towards the horse's nose, he is able to hold it down and prevent it from throwing itself over on its back, at the hazard of its limbs. By this means he gradually advances, until he is able to place his hand on the animal's nose, and over its eyes; and at length to breathe in its nostrils, when it soon becomes docile and conquered; so that he has little else to do than to remove the hobbles from its feet, and lead or ride it into camp.

This "breaking down" or taming, however, is not without the most desperate trial on the part of the horse, which rears and plunges in every possible way to effect its escape, until its power is exhausted, and it becomes covered with foam; and at last yields to the power of man, and becomes his willing slave for the rest of its life. By this very rigid treatment, the poor animal seems to be so completely conquered, that it makes no further struggle for its freedom; but submits quietly ever after, and is led or rode away with very little difficulty. Great care is taken, however, in this and in subsequent treatment, not to subdue the spirit of the animal, which is carefully preserved and kept up, although they use them with great severity; being, generally speaking, cruel masters.

The wild horse of these regions is a small, but very powerful animal; with an exceedingly prominent eye, sharp nose, high nostril, small feet and delicate leg; and undoubtedly, have sprung from a stock introduced by the Spaniards, at the time of the invasion of Mexico; which having strayed off upon the prairies, have run wild, and stocked the plains from this to **Lake Winnepeg**, two or three thousand miles to the North.[3]

This useful animal has been of great service to the Indians living on these vast plains, enabling them to take their game more easily, to carry their burdens, &c.; and no doubt, render them better and handier service than if they were of a larger and heavier breed. Vast numbers of them are also killed for food by the Indians, at seasons when buffaloes and other game are scarce. They subsist themselves both in winter and summer by biting at the grass, which they can always get in sufficient quantities for their food.

Whilst on our march we met with many droves of these beautiful animals, and several times had the opportunity of seeing the Indians pursue them, and take them with the laso. The first successful instance of the kind was effected by one of our guides and hunters, by the name of Beatte, a Frenchman, whose parents had lived nearly their whole lives in the Osage village; and who, himself had been reared from infancy amongst them; and in a continual life of Indian modes and amusements, had acquired all the skill and tact of his Indian teachers, and probably a little more; for he is reputed, without exception, the best hunter in these Western regions.

This instance took place one day whilst the regiment was at its usual halt of an hour, in the middle of the day.

When the bugle sounded for a halt, and all were dismounted, Beatte and several others of the hunters asked permission of Col. Dodge to pursue a drove of horses which were then in sight, at a distance of a mile or more from us. The permission was given, and they started off, and by following a ravine, approached near to the unsuspecting animals, when they broke upon them and pursued them for several miles in full view of the regiment. Several of us had good glasses, with which we could plainly see every movement and every manoeuvre. After a race of two or three miles, Beatte was seen with his wild horse down, and the band and the other hunters rapidly leaving him.

Seeing him in this condition, I galloped off to him as rapidly as possible, and had the satisfaction of seeing the whole operation of "breaking down," and bringing in the wild animal. When he had conquered the horse in this way, his brother, who was one of the unsuccessful ones in the chase, came riding back, and leading up the horse of Beatte which he had left behind, and after staying with us a few minutes, assisted Beatte in leading his conquered wild horse towards the regiment, where it was satisfactorily examined and commented upon, as it was trembling and covered with white foam, until the bugle sounded the signal for marching, when all mounted; and with the

---

3   [Catlin's note] There are many very curious traditions about the first appearance of horses amongst the different tribes, and many of which bear striking proof of the above fact. Most of the tribes have some story about the first appearance of horses; and amongst the Sioux, they have beautifully recorded the fact, by giving it the name of Shonka-wakon (the medicine-dog).

rest, Beatte, astride of his wild horse, which had a buffalo skin girted on its back, and a halter, with a cruel noose around the under jaw. In this manner the command resumed its march, and Beatte astride of his wild horse, on which he rode quietly and without difficulty, until night; the whole thing, the capture, and breaking, all having been accomplished within the space of one hour, our usual and daily halt at midday.

Several others of these animals were caught in a similar manner during our march, by others of our hunters, affording us satisfactory instances of this most extraordinary and almost unaccountable feat.

The horses that were caught were by no means very valuable specimens, being rather of an ordinary quality; and I saw to my perfect satisfaction, that the finest of these droves can never be obtained in this way, as they take the lead at once, when they are pursued, and in a few moments will be seen half a mile or more ahead of the bulk of the drove, which they are leading off. There is not a doubt but there are many very fine and valuable horses amongst these herds; but it is impossible for the Indian or other hunter to take them, unless it be done by "creasing" them, as I have before described; which is often done, but always destroys the spirit and character of the animal.

DOCUMENT 3:

Image group: George Catlin's paintings "Wild Horses at Play," "Catching the Wild Horse," "Buffalo Hunt, Chase" (1845)[4]

Catlin's 1830s drawings appeared in his travel account, *Letters and Notes on the Manners, Customs, and Conditions of North American Indians*, and were sold a decade later as color prints. In an era before video or color photography, Catlin's paintings were a revelation to people curious about life out West. Still, like all documentary efforts, Catlin's were not "the truth" but somewhat stylized in order to provide visually pleasing depictions. Here, he shows Ni-u-kon-ska (Osage) men capturing wild horses on the Great Plains and Nʉmʉnʉʉ (Comanche) hunters using horses to hunt bison. The Ni-u-kon-ska originated in the Ohio River valley, then migrated west due to pressure from the Iroquois or Haudenosaunee "People of the Longhouse," eventually controlling lands at the center of the continent intersecting at what is today Kansas, Missouri, Arkansas, and Oklahoma. The Nʉmʉnʉʉ were a dominant nation on the Great Plains to the west and south, were widely respected as horsepeople, and feared as warriors.

"Wild Horses at Play"

---

4   These images are part of a portfolio published in 1845, *Catlin's North American Indian Portfolio: Hunting Scenes and Amusements of the Rocky Mountains*, digitized by the New York Public Library.

"Catching the Wild Horse"

"Buffalo Hunt, Chase"

Thomas James describes horse markets of the 1810s: *Three Years among the Indians and Mexicans* (1846)[5]

American Thomas James traveled through what is today Texas and the American Southwest in 1821, the year Mexico concluded its war for independence from colonial Spain. Mexico was an ethnically diverse nation in that era and home to Mexican nationals and subjects of the Spanish empire, plus a large number of autonomous Indigenous peoples, some of whom were of mixed Indigenous and European ancestry—hence James's reference to "Mexican Indians," for instance. Horses were a crucial form of capital then and the region was known for lucrative horse markets run by Mexican and Indigenous horsemen. James describes the politics and economics of horses there, at times revealing himself to be an imperious racist, in that he reflected the attitudes of quite a few white men in the region who were politically suspicious of some Indigenous tribes while still seeking to trade with them. To finance his travels, James stayed mobile and worked at whatever venture he could. Still, he was frequently in debt or was owed money by people he might or might not ever see again, exposing the precarious financial position of travelers to the region.

❧

I have spoken before in favorable terms of the Mexican Indians. They are a nobler race of people than their masters, the descendants of the conquerors; more courageous and more generous; more faithful to their word and more ingenuous and intellectual than the Spaniards. The men are generally six feet in stature, well formed and of an open, frank, and manly deportment. Their women are very fascinating, and far superior in virtue, as in beauty, to the greater number of the Spanish females. I was informed that all the tribes, the **Utahs**, the **Navahoes**, and others inhabiting the country west of the mountains to the Gulf of California, like those in Mexico lived in comfortable houses, raised wheat and corn, and had good mills for grinding their grain. I saw many specimens of their skill in the useful arts, and brought home with me some blankets and counterpanes of Indian manufacture of exquisite workmanship, which I have used in my family for twenty-five years. They are generally far in advance of the Spaniards around them in all the arts of civilized life, as well as in the virtues that give value to national character.

In the latter part of February I received a deputation of fifty Indians from the Utah tribe on the west side of the mountains. They came riding into the

Utahs: The Ute Nation or *núuchi-u* "the people."

Navahoes: Members of the *Diné* or *Naabeehó* (Navajo) tribe.

---

5   Waterloo, IL: War Eagle, 1846, 71–73.

city and paraded on the public square, all well mounted on the most elegant horses I had ever seen. The animals were of a very superior breed, with their slender tapering legs and short, fine hair, like our best blooded racers. They were of almost every color, some spotted and striped as if painted for ornament. The Indians alighted at the **Council House** and sent a request for me to visit them. On arriving I found them all awaiting me in the Council House, with a company of Spanish officers and gentlemen led hither by curiosity. On entering I was greeted by the chief and his companions, who shook hands with me. The chief, whose name was Lechat, was a young man of about thirty and of a right princely port and bearing. He told me in the Spanish language, which he spoke fluently, that he had come expressly to see me and have a talk with me. "You are Americans, we are told, and you have come from your country afar off to trade with the Spaniards. We want your trade. Come to our country with your goods. Come and trade with the Utahs. We have horses, mules, and sheep, more than we want. We heard that you wanted beaver skins. The beavers in our country are eating up our corn. All our rivers are full of them. Their dams back up the water in the rivers all along their course from the mountains to the **Big Water**. Come over among us and you shall have as many beaver skins as you want."

Turning round and pointing to the Spaniards in most contemptuous manner and with a scornful look, he said: "What can you get from these? They have nothing to trade with you. They have nothing but a few poor horses and mules, a little **puncha**, and a little tola (tobacco and corn meal porridge) not fit for any body to use. They are poor—too poor for you to trade with. Come among the Utahs if you wish to trade with profit. Look at our horses here. Have the Spaniards any such horses? No, they are too poor. Such as these we have in our country by the thousand, and also cattle, sheep, and mules. These Spaniards," said he, turning and pointing his finger at them in a style of contempt which John Randolph would have envied, "What are they? What have they? They won't even give us two loads of powder and lead for a beaver skin, and for a good reason. They have not as much as they want themselves. They have nothing that you want. We have everything that they have, and many things that they have not."

Here a Spaniard cried out: "You have no money." Like a true stump orator, the Utah replied, "and you have very little. You are depicca." In other words, you are poor, miserable devils and we are the true capitalists of the country.

With this and much more of the same purport, he concluded his harangue, which was delivered in the most independent and lordly manner possible. He looked like a king upbraiding his subjects for being poor, when they might be rich, and his whole conduct seemed to me like bearding a wild beast in his den.

Council House: A building housing officials of the Spanish colonial government.

Big Water: The Gulf of California.

puncha: An alcoholic drink of Spanish origin, made locally.

The "talk" being had, Lechat produced the calama or pipe, and we smoked together in the manner of the Indians. I sent to my store and procured six plugs of tobacco and some handkerchiefs which I presented to him and his company, telling them when they smoked the tobacco with their chiefs to remember the Americans, and treat all who visited their country from mine as they would their own brothers. The council now broke up and the chief, reiterating his invitations to me to visit his country, mounted his noble steed and with his company rode out of the city, singing and displaying the hand-kerchiefs I had presented them from the ends of their lances as standards.

They departed without the least show of respect for the Spaniards, but rather with a strong demonstration on the part of Lechat of contempt for them. I noticed them at the council inquiring of this chief with considerable interest what the Navahoes were doing, and whether they were preparing to attack the Spanish settlements. They had been at war with this tribe for several years, and seemed to fear that the Utahs might take part in it as allies of the Navahoes, for which reason they conducted themselves with the utmost respect and forbearance towards Lechat and his band. What was the immediate cause of this war, I did not learn, but I saw and heard enough of it to enlist my sympathies with the Navahoes.

DOCUMENT 5:

Nat Love tells a tall story about his 1877 capture by the Akimel O'odham (Pima): *The Life and Adventures of Nat Love, Better Known in the Cattle Country as "Deadwood Dick"* (1907)[6]

Nat Love was born enslaved in Tennessee in 1854. After emancipation, he worked for wages for a time, then traveled West in about 1870 to find work, like many African American men who cowboyed after the Civil War. His autobiography consists, first, of a narrative about his escape from enslavement, followed by stories of his adventures as a cowboy. Love seldom addresses the racialization of American Blacks directly, instead telling incredible stories that nodded to the market for tales of cowboys as wild men and adventurers[7]— not the underpaid, often-bored working men they usually were. Still, Love's autobiography is an example of how one person of color negotiated the politics of catering to predominantly white settler readers while also finding a way to speak for himself in an age when few Blacks were published authors. While Love's account is certainly in the genre of the cowboy memoir as tall tale, it is also a source on relations between people of color in the West, namely an African American man and the O'odham, or Pima tribe. Additionally, the memoir contains details of how the O'odham people living around the Salt and Gila Rivers (today in Arizona) made use of the land and their horses in order to live in that arid landscape.

ᥱ

It was a bright, clear fall day, October 4, 1876, that quite a large number of us boys started out over the range hunting strays which had been lost for some time. We had scattered over the range and I was riding along alone when all at once I heard the well known Indian war whoop and noticed not far away a large party of Indians making straight for me. They were all well mounted and they were in full **war paint**, which showed me that they were on the war path, and as I was alone and had no wish to be **scalped** by them I decided to run for it. So I headed for Yellow Horse Canyon and gave my horse the rein, but as I had considerable objection to being chased by a lot of painted savages without some remonstrance, I turned in my saddle every once in a while and gave them a shot by way of greeting, and I had the satisfaction of seeing a painted brave tumble from his horse and go rolling in the dust every time my rifle spoke, and the Indians were by no means idle all this time, as their bullets were singing around me rather

war paint: Warrior men from many tribes painted their bodies and faces both to intimidate their adversaries and since many believed the practice provided spiritual protection in battle.

scalped: The practice of removing a portion of a dead person's scalp and hair as a trophy in armed conflict is a global one. Various Indigenous and settler people practiced it over the centuries.

---

6   Los Angeles, CA: Nat Love, 1907, 98–105.

7   Part 2 includes more on this topic.

lively, one of them passing through my thigh, but it did not amount to much. Reaching Yellow Horse Canyon, I had about decided to stop and make a stand when one of their bullets caught me in the leg, passing clear through it and then through my horse, killing him. Quickly falling behind him I used his dead body for a **breast work** and stood the Indians off for a long time, as my aim was so deadly and they had lost so many that they were careful to keep out of range.

But finally my ammunition gave out, and the Indians were quick to find this out, and they at once closed in on me, but I was by no means subdued, wounded as I was and almost out of my head, and I fought with my empty gun until finally overpowered. When I came to my senses I was in the Indians' camp.

My wounds had been dressed with some kind of herbs, the wound in my breast just over the heart was covered thickly with herbs and bound up. My nose had been nearly cut off, also one of my fingers had been nearly cut off. These wounds I received when I was fighting my captors with my empty gun. What caused them to spare my life I cannot tell, but it was I think partly because I had proved myself a brave man, and all savages admire a brave man and when they captured a man whose fighting powers were out of the ordinary they generally kept him if possible as he was needed in the tribe.

Then again **Yellow Dog's tribe** was composed largely of half breeds, and there was a large percentage of **colored blood in the tribe**, and as I was a colored man they wanted to keep me, as they thought I was too good a man to die. Be that as it may, they dressed my wounds and gave me plenty to eat, but the only grub they had was buffalo meat which they cooked over a fire of **buffalo chips**, but of this I had all I wanted to eat. For the first two days after my capture they kept me tied hand and foot. At the end of that time they untied my feet, but kept my hands tied for a couple of days longer, when I was given my freedom, but was always closely watched by members of the tribe. Three days after my capture my ears were pierced and I was adopted into the tribe. The operation of piercing my ears was quite painful, in the method used, as they had a small bone secured from a deer's leg, a small thin bone, rounded at the end and as sharp as a needle. This they used to make the holes, then strings made from the tendons of a deer were inserted in place of thread, of which the Indians had none. Then horn ear rings were placed in my ears and the same kind of salve made from herbs which they placed on my wounds was placed on my ears and they soon healed.

The bullet holes in my leg and breast also healed in a surprisingly short time. That was good salve all right. As soon as I was well enough I took part in the Indian dances. One kind or another was in progress all the time. The war dance and the medicine dance seemed the most popular. When in the war dance the savages danced around me in a circle, making gestures, chanting, with every now and then a blood curdling yell, always keeping time to a sort of music provided by stretching buffalo skins tightly over a hoop.

When I was well enough I joined the dances, and I think I soon made a good dancer. The medicine dance varies from the war dance only that in the medicine dance the Indians danced around a boiling pot, the pot being filled with roots and water and they dance around it while it boils. The medicine dance occurs about daylight.

I very soon learned their ways and to understand them, though our conversation was mostly carried on by means of signs. They soon gave me to understand that I was to marry the chief's daughter, promising me 100 ponies to do so, and she was literally thrown in my arms; as for the lady she seemed perfectly willing if not anxious to become my bride. She was a beautiful woman, or rather girl; in fact all the squaws of this tribe were good looking, out of the ordinary, but I had other notions just then and did not want to get married under such circumstances, but for prudence sake I seemed to enter into their plans, but at the same time keeping a sharp lookout for a chance to escape. I noted where the Indians kept their horses at night, even picking out the handsome and fleet Indian pony which I meant to use should opportunity occur, and I seemed to fall in with the Indians' plans and seemed to them so contented that they gave me more and more freedom and relaxed the strict watch they had kept on me, and finally in about thirty days from the time of my capture my opportunity arrived.

My wounds were now nearly well, and gave me no trouble. It was a dark, cloudy night, and the Indians, grown careless in their fancied security, had relaxed their watchfulness. After they had all thrown themselves on the ground and the quiet of the camp proclaimed them all asleep I got up and crawling on my hands and knees, using the greatest caution for fear of making a noise, I crawled about 250 yards to where the horses were **picketed**, and going to the Indian pony I had already picked out I slipped the skin thong in his mouth which the Indians use for a bridle, one which I had secured and carried in my shirt for some time for this particular purpose, then springing to his back I made for the open prairie in the direction of the home ranch in Texas, one hundred miles away. All that night I rode as fast as my horse could carry me and the next morning, twelve hours after I left the Indians camp I was safe on the home ranch again. And my joy was without bounds, and such a reception as I received from the boys. They said they were just one day late, and if it hadn't been for a fight they had with some of the same tribe, they would have been to my relief. As it was they did not expect to ever see me again alive. But they know that if the Indians did not kill me, and gave me only half a chance I would get away from them, but now that I was safe home again, nothing mattered much and nothing was too good for me.

picketed: When traveling overnight with horses, people often tethered horses to a rope line stretched between two trees, which allowed horses to lie down or stand up and graze on any grass within reach.

It was a mystery to them how I managed to escape death with such wounds as I had received, the marks of which I will carry to my grave and it is as much a mystery to me as the bullet that struck me in the breast just over the heart passed clear through, coming out my back just below the shoulder. Likewise the bullet in my leg passed clear through, then through my horse, killing him.

Those Indians are certainly wonderful doctors, and then I am naturally tough as I carry the marks of fourteen bullet wounds on different parts of my body, most any one of which would be sufficient to kill an ordinary man, but I am not even crippled. It seems to me that if ever a man bore a charm I am the man, as I have had five horses shot from under me and killed, have fought Indians and Mexicans in all sorts of situations, and have been in more tight places than I can number. Yet I have always managed to escape with only the mark of a bullet or knife as a reminder. The fight with the Yellow Dog's tribe is probably the closest call I ever had, and as close a call as I ever want.

The fleet Indian pony which carried me to safety on that memorable hundred mile ride, I kept for about five years. I named him "The Yellow Dog Chief." And he lived on the best the ranch afforded, until his death which occurred in 1881, never having anything to do except an occasional race, as he could run like a deer. I thought too much of him to use him on the trail and he was the especial pet of every one on the home ranch, and for miles around.

persued: A nineteenth-century spelling of pursued.

I heard afterwards that the Indians **persued** me that night for quite a distance, but I had too much the start and besides I had the fastest horse the Indians owned. I have never since met any of my captors of that time. As they knew better than to venture in our neighborhood again. My wound healed nicely, thanks to the good attention the Indians gave me. My captors took everything of value I had on me when captured. My rifle which I especially prized for old associations sake; also my forty fives, saddle and bridle, in fact my whole outfit leaving me only the few clothes I had on at the time.

My comrades did not propose to let this bother me long, however, because they all chipped in and bought me a new outfit, including the best rifle and revolvers that could be secured, and I had my pick of the ranch horses for another mount. During my short stay with the Indians I learned a great deal about them, their ways of living, sports, dances, and mode of warfare which proved of great benefit to me in after years. The oblong shields they carried were made from tanned buffalo skins and so tough were they made that an arrow would not pierce them although I have seen them shoot an arrow clean through a buffalo. Neither will a bullet pierce them unless the ball hits the shield square on, otherwise it glances off.

All of them were exceedingly expert with the bow and arrow, and they are proud of their skill and are always practicing in an effort to excel each other. This rivalry extends even to the children who are seldom without their bows and arrows.

They named me Buffalo Papoose, and we managed to make our wants known by means of signs. As I was not with them a sufficient length of time to learn their language, I learned from them that I had killed five of their number and wounded three while they were chasing me and in the subsequent fight with my empty gun. The wounded men were hit in many places, but they were brought around all right, the same as I was. After my escape and after I arrived home it was some time before I was again called to active duty, as the boys would not hear of me doing anything resembling work, until I was thoroughly well and rested up. But I soon began to long for my saddle and the range.

And when orders were received at the ranch for 2000 head of cattle, to be delivered at Dodge City, Kansas, I insisted on taking the trail again. It was not with any sense of pride or in bravado that I recount here the fate of the men who have fallen at my hand.

It is a terrible thing to kill a man no matter what the cause. But as I am writing a true history of my life, I cannot leave these facts out. But every man who died at my hands was either seeking my life or died in open warfare, when it was a case of killing or being killed.

DOCUMENT 6:

Image group: Apsáalooke (Crow) Tribe members and their horses (ca. 1898–1912)[8]

Like everyone in the pre-automobile age, the Apsáalooke Tribe, or Crow People, depended upon horses to keep their families together and sustain themselves on the land over the course of the nineteenth century. Originating near the Great Lakes, the Apsáalooke contended with environmental change, new diseases, a steady flow of settlers, the power of the US government and, at times, conflict with other Indigenous nations. As populations migrated and jostled for territory and resources, eventually the Apsáalooke landed in central Montana. These early photographs taken at the Crow Reservation show how even young children were expected to be skilled riders. Like all westerners, tribe members acquired horses by capturing them from wild bands they maintained on their own reservation lands or purchasing them from neighbors and nearby dealers. The images below are described by the archival record for each photograph.

"Outdoor portrait of Blanket Bull, his wife, daughter, and son posed in front of tipi. The son sits on horseback. Photograph shot by Fred E. Miller circa 1898–1912 on the Apsáalooke Reservation in Montana."

---

8   Fred E. Miller photograph collection, NMAI.AC.108, National Museum of the American Indian, Smithsonian Online Virtual Archives.

"Photograph depicting a group of men, women, and children on horseback. On the far left is Bull Don't Fall Down. Photograph shot by Fred E. Miller circa 1898–1912 on the Apsáalooke Reservation in Montana."

"Photograph depicting children on horseback in a river. Photograph shot by Fred E. Miller circa 1898–1912 on the Apsáalooke Reservation in Montana."

DISCUSSION QUESTIONS/WRITING PROMPTS

1. What regions, people, animals, and time periods are addressed by the primary sources here?

2. Think about limits of the primary sources here as a representation of the entirety of the eighteenth and nineteenth centuries with respect to horses, cattle, and people in North America. What is here? What might be missing?

3. What might be the potential problems with sources written by white American and European travelers depicting non-Americans for an audience of wealthy readers, speculators, and adventurers?

4. How might whites' and settlers' better access to media, publishing, and recording technology (like cameras and photograph developing equipment) have shaped the sources here? Consider also the power of the creator of a primary source, or an archivist years later, to define primary sources by writing archival descriptors for them. With respect to the photographs here, how and why might we rewrite the archival records for each one?

5. What is the overall impression from these sources about how people regarded horses, or cattle? Do we get any sense from them what it was like to be a horse, a cow, or bull in this era?

PART 2

Beef Bonanza

DOCUMENT 7:

A Geographically Correct County Map of the States Traversed by the Atchison Topeka and the Santa Fé Railroad and Its Connections (ca. 1880)[1]

After the 1860s, migration of people into the West relied upon developing transportation routes, many of which followed old overland trails people had used for centuries to move on foot or horseback. In the railway era, speculators and government officials referred to maps to make countless decisions about where the most valuable land might be, where to invest, or how to lobby a railway company to build a depot in the town one had just founded in a remote district. The Library of Congress says of this map, published in St. Louis around 1880: "Detailed map of the central United States showing relief by hachures, drainage, counties, cities and towns, roads, wagon trails, and the railroad network. This line was chartered by the state of Kansas in 1859; the first 75 miles of line were not completed until 1871." Interestingly, the map offered viewers a depiction of the region's transportation routes, political boundaries, and its landscape.

ℰ

---

1   Published by Woodward, Tiernan, and Hale, St. Louis [1880], Library of Congress.

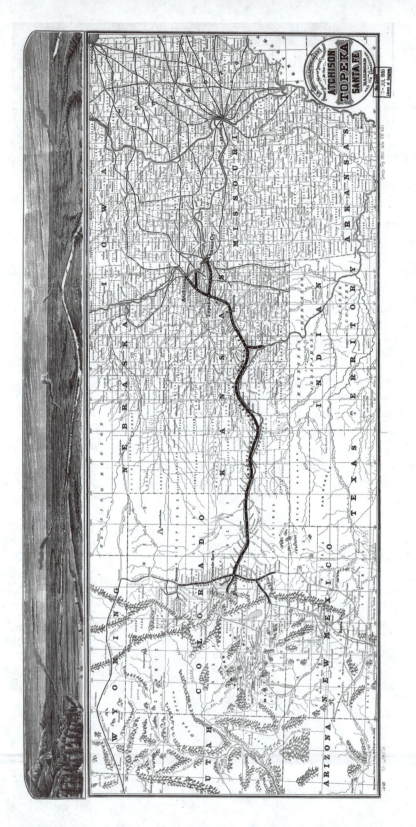

DOCUMENT 8:

James Sanks Brisbin promotes the cattle business: *Beef Bonanza; or, How to Get Rich on the Plains, Cattle Growing, Sheep Farming, Horse Raising and Dairying in the West* (1881)[2]

James Brisbin was a US Army Colonel who was stationed in various parts of the Great Plains in the 1870s and 1880s. A prolific writer and Western booster, he served as an official of the National Cattle and Horse Growers Association. His influential book about the cattle trade, *Beef Bonanza*, advised would-be cattlemen that turning a profit was almost assured because the US population would grow, western lands were vast, and longhorn crillo cattle were uniquely self-sufficient and able to prosper there. Brisbin's book helped attract wealthy men to the West seeking to set up cattle operations and soon many American cattle businesses were owned by such novices or absentee investors, largely from Britain. Equally, thousands more middle-class migrants ventured West looking for land—some would prosper, many would not. It would not be the first or last time people flooded into the West hoping for easy riches.

e

On the atlases of thirty or forty years ago, when the stock of information concerning the territory now comprised in the flourishing States of Kansas and Nebraska, and in Eastern Colorado and Dakota, was exceedingly limited, the whole of it was represented as the "**Great American Desert**." The boy who studied geography then conceived an affection for this desert, a fact which did honor to his patriotism. His country had the highest mountains, the greatest lakes, and the largest rivers in the world, and it flattered his national pride to see on its map a desert which rivalled in size anything the Old World could produce in the same line. There was one natural feature of the Eastern Continent which humbled his pride of country somewhat. This was the terrible **Maelstrom** on the coast of Norway, that furious whirlpool which the Western World had nothing to match. But he has lived to see that unmatched whirlpool robbed of its terrors. It is almost surveyed out of existence, and in its present condition it does not greatly outrank the late **Hell Gate** in New York harbor. With the disappearance of the hated Maelstrom, however, he has had the mortification to see his favorite desert vanish from the map. That barren terra-incognita of his youth is now one of the finest grazing regions on the globe, and a large portion of it is yielding excellent crops to the agriculturist. This ancient desert has been for a long

Great American Desert: Reference to an early nineteenth-century name for the Great Plains. The early American traveler Stephen Harriman Long visited the region in 1820 and described its vast, flat grasslands as a "Great Desert." Thereafter, writers and map makers, believing the region could not be exploited with extant forms of settled agriculture since it was too arid, devoid of timber that could support construction of houses, and covered with native grasses whose root mass was several feet deep so impenetrable to (then unmechanized) plows, called the region the Great American Desert.

Maelstrom: A reference to *Mokstraumen*, tidal whirlpools and eddies of great strength off the coast of Norway, which many Americans discovered from reading the well-known 1841 Edgar Allen Poe short story "A Descent into the Maelström."

Hell Gate: A tidal straight in the East River as it flows through New York City, which was dangerous to shipping and during the 1870s and 1880s was subjected to immense blasts of explosives to widen and deepen the passage.

---

2 Philadelphia: J.B. Lippencott, 1881, 9–11, 13–19.

time the favorite pasturing ground of the buffalo, and it doubtless now contains more domestic cattle than it ever did buffaloes.

The eastern boundary of the old desert was the Missouri River, and it is fresh in the memory of many that when settlement began on the west bank of that river it was supposed its natural limit would be in the immediate vicinity of the stream. Gradually the desert was pushed westward a hundred miles, as far as the **Big Blue**, which was fixed upon as its eastern boundary. But the farmers did not stop here. They continued to plough up the eastern edge of the desert until it was moved another hundred miles west, to **Fort Kearney**, where it was supposed it would forever remain. This frontier was about in the middle of the desert as originally laid out by **Lewis and Clark**, and it was thought that here at least the spirit of innovation would be satisfied. Nevertheless, the farmers continued to push westward, and now the occupants of the remaining portion of the great waste are viewing with alarm the persistent demonstration of the fertility of their desert domain. The great **cattle-kings** claim that the country is utterly unfit for cultivation, to which the farmers reply by ploughing up a strip on its eastern edge every year some ten miles wide, and raising good crops.

The cattle-kings fear the utter destruction of their fine ranges in prospect unless something can be done to establish their desert character. They need have no cause for alarm. There is an American Desert in the far West which can never be used for any other purpose than the raising of great herds. It is of these lands and the cattle upon them the following pages treat.

The plains of the West, instead of being barren and worthless as early geographers supposed, have become one of the richest parts of our public domain. The vast beef reservoir they contain is now the fit subject of an interesting volume....

The West! The mighty West! That land where the buffalo still roams and the wild savage dwells; where the broad rivers flow and the boundless prairie stretches away for thousands of miles; where new States are every year carved out and myriads of people find homes and wealth; where the poor professional young man, flying from the over-crowded East and the tyranny of a moneyed aristocracy, finds honor and wealth; where the young politician, unoppressed by rings and combinations, relying upon his own abilities, may rise to position and fame; where there are lands for the landless, money for the moneyless, briefs for lawyers, patients for doctors, and above all, labor and its reward for every poor man who is willing to work. This is the West as I have known it for twelve years, and learned to love it because of its grateful return to all those who have tried to improve it. Its big-hearted people never push a young man back, but generously help him on, and so, by being great themselves, have learned how to make others great. "Where

Big Blue: The Blue River, which flows in Missouri and Kansas.

Fort Kearney: US Army outpost near what is today Kearny, Nebraska.

Lewis and Clark: Meriwether Lewis and William Clark, leaders of the Corps of Discovery expedition, famously guided by Shoshone woman Sacagawea, sponsored by President Thomas Jefferson to chart territories the US had acquired from France in the 1803 Louisiana Purchase.

cattle-kings: Large-scale cattle ranch owners, often absentee investors in the eastern US and Britain, who controlled stock growers' associations and thus much of the cattle trade.

had I best settle?" "Where can I buy the cheapest and best land?" "Where will I be safe?" "Where can I raise the best stock?" These are questions asked every day by people all over the East. In vain do they look into books and newspapers for answers to their inquiries; they are not to be found; at least, not truthful ones. I do not suppose I can supply all the information required, but I can give my impressions, which shall at least have the merit of being honest. I believe Kansas and Iowa are the best unsettled farming States; Nebraska is the best State for farming and stock-raising combined; Colorado is the best State for sheep-growing, farming, and mining; Wyoming is the best Territory for cattle-growing alone; Montana is the best Territory for cattle-growing and mining.

It does not matter where the emigrant settles in the West, so he comes; and he will almost anywhere soon find himself better off than if he had remained East.

When I visit the Eastern States, it is a matter of astonishment to me to learn how little is known of the advantages, resources, and interests of the West. The masses do not seem to understand what is west of them, and cling to the hilly, stony, and unproductive lands where they were raised rather than move to an unknown country. Often I hear city young men in the East say, "If I had only come here twenty years ago, I might now be a rich man. Land then sold for a few dollars a foot, while now it is worth as many hundreds or even thousands." So, too, the young farmer exclaims, "Land is so high, I can never afford to buy a farm. When my father settled here and bought, it was worth only $10, $20, or $30 per acre, and now it is held at $100, and were I to buy a farm, and pay the purchase-money down, I could not more than raise the interest on the balance; therefore, I can never hope to own a farm of my own." Every one East seems to think the days for speculation are over, and they regret a hundred times a year they had not been born fifty years sooner. To the discouraged let me say, be of good heart and come West, for what has been occurring in the East during the last two hundred years is now occurring in the West, only with tenfold more rapidity. Young men, when your fathers bought the homes and land which they now own, and on which you were raised, there were no railroads, and emigration was necessarily slow. Their property has been thirty, forty, or even fifty years in reaching its present value. Not so the West. Railroads are everywhere, and ten or twenty years at most will do for you what it took your fathers fifty years to accomplish. Millions of people are pressing westward, and settle where you may you will soon find yourself surrounded by neighbors, not in twos and threes as were your fathers, but by hundreds and thousands of newcomers. The growth of this West of ours has been the miracle of the nineteenth century, and its improvement has as yet only fairly begun. The Old World annually pours myriads of people upon our Western shores, and to these we add hundreds of thousands from our native population, who find new homes each year. The increase and development of the West is, therefore, not to be wondered at, for it has the best facilities of any land in the world. In one year 390,000 foreign emigrants landed in the United States, and these did not include 30,000 Chinese and 2000 Canadians. When the emigration from foreign sources, which has been interrupted by domestic war, shall have been restored to its natural flow, the influx will probably reach the following figures: Landing at New York, 350,000; at San Francisco, 100,000; at Philadelphia, 50,000; at Portland, Oregon, 10,000; at New Orleans, 10,000; at Galveston, Texas, 10,000; total, 530,000. Of these fully 300,000 will come West, and the remainder scatter through the South and East. Add to the Western emigration 200,000 from native sources, and we shall have half a million people annually seeking homes in the West. It will not be very long until the annual accessions to our population will equal the whole number of inhabitants living in the United States at the time they achieved their independence from Great Britain.... The result of all this will be to settle up the West and double our population, large as it is. Young men who have polled their first vote will live to see the day when the United States will contain 100,000,000 of people....

A great deal of sport a few years ago was made of Horace Greeley for so often repeating his advice, "Go West, young man; go West and take a farm, and grow up with the country." But after living in the West twelve years, I can safely say that never did any man give better advice to the youth of a nation. No industrious man can make a mistake in moving West, and if I had a son to advise, I should by all means say to him, "Go West as soon as you can; get a good piece of land, and hold on to it."

DOCUMENT 9:

Andy Adams on young male aspirations to the cowboy life: *The Log of a Cowboy: A Narrative of the Old Trail Days* (1903)[3]

Originally from Indiana, Andy Adams worked as a range cowboy in Texas before writing his much-loved novel, *The Log of a Cowboy*. In it, he tells the story of a young man, Tommy Moore, whose family home in Georgia was destroyed during the Civil War. The family, like many from the South, moved to Texas looking to homestead. There, Tommy and his two brothers are irresistibly drawn to range work. Against the backdrop of the essential aridity of the West, Adams in the voice of Moore recounts his experiences in about 1882 working with a crew of men driving a herd of "long-legged, long-horned Southern cattle, pale-colored as a rule, possessed with the running powers of a deer," from Mexico to the what is today the Blackfeet Indian Reservation of the Ampskapi Piikani (Piegan Blackfeet) in northwestern Montana. In this passage, the crew has recently left San Antonio and is traveling north through Texas.

e

The Indian Lakes, some seven in number, were natural reservoirs with rocky bottoms, and about a mile apart. We watered at ten o'clock the next day, and by night camped fifteen miles on our way. There was plenty of good grazing for the cattle and horses, and no trouble was experienced the first night. McCann had filled an extra twenty gallon keg for this trip. Water was too precious an article to be lavish with, so we shook the dust from our clothing and went unwashed. This was no serious deprivation, and no one could be critical of another, for we were all equally dusty and dirty. The next morning by daybreak the cattle were thrown off the bed ground and started grazing before the sun could dry out what little moisture the grass had absorbed during the night. The heat of the past week had been very oppressive, and in order to avoid it as much as possible, we made late and early drives. Before the wagon passed the herd during the morning drive, what few canteens we had were filled with water for the men. The **remuda** was kept with the herd, and four changes of mounts were made during the day, in order not to exhaust any one horse. Several times for an hour or more, the herd was allowed to lie down and rest; but by the middle of the afternoon thirst made them impatient and restless, and the **point men** were compelled to ride steadily in the lead in order to hold the cattle to a walk.

remuda: Also spelled "ramutha," a Spanish vaquero term for the large string of horses employed in rotation by the men on a trail drive or ranching operation. It was more productive to keep a pool of horses since individual horses became injured or exhausted quickly, so needed to be cycled in and out of service.

point men: In a cattle drive, the cowboys who ride at the front of the herd, leading the cattle while controlling their speed and direction.

---

3   Boston and New York: Houghton, Mifflin and Company, 1903, 58–65.

A number of times during the afternoon we attempted to graze them, but not until the twilight of evening was it possible.

After the fourth change of horses was made, Honeyman pushed on ahead with the saddle stock and overtook the wagon. Under Flood's orders he was to tie up all the night horses, for if the cattle could be induced to graze, we would not bed them down before ten that night, and all hands would be required with the herd. McCann had instructions to make camp on the divide, which was known to be twenty-five miles from our camp of the night before, or forty miles from the Indian Lakes. As we expected, the cattle grazed willingly after nightfall, and with a fair moon, we allowed them to scatter freely while grazing forward. The beacon of McCann's fire on the divide was in sight over an hour before the herd grazed up to camp, all hands remaining to bed the thirsty cattle. The herd was given triple the amount of space usually required for bedding, and even then for nearly an hour scarcely half of them lay down.

We were handling the cattle as humanely as possible under the circumstances. The guards for the night were doubled, six men on the first half and the same on the latter, Bob Blades being detailed to assist Honeyman in night-herding the saddle horses. If any of us got more than an hour's sleep that night, he was lucky. Flood, McCann, and the horse wranglers did not even try to rest. To those of us who could find time to eat, our cook kept open house. Our foreman knew that a well-fed man can stand an incredible amount of hardship, and appreciated the fact that on the trail a good cook is a valuable asset. Our outfit therefore was cheerful to a man, and jokes and songs helped to while away the weary hours of the night.

The second guard, under Flood, pushed the cattle off their beds an hour before dawn, and before they were relieved had urged the herd more than five miles on the third day's drive over this waterless mesa. In spite of our economy of water, after breakfast on this third morning there was scarcely enough left to fill the canteens for the day. In view of this, we could promise ourselves no midday meal except a can of tomatoes to the man; so the wagon was ordered to drive through to the expected water ahead, while the saddle horses were held available as on the day before for frequent changing of mounts. The day turned out to be one of torrid heat, and before the middle of the forenoon, the cattle lolled their tongues in despair, while their sullen lowing surged through from rear to lead and back again in piteous yet ominous appeal. The only relief we could offer was to travel them slowly, as they spurned every opportunity offered them either to graze or to lie down.

It was nearly noon when we reached the last divide, and sighted the scattering timber of the expected watercourse. The enforced order of the day before to hold the herd in a walk and prevent exertion and heating now required four men in the lead, while the rear followed over a mile behind, dogged and sullen. Near the middle of the afternoon, McCann returned on one of his mules with the word that it was a question if there was water enough to water even the horse stock. The preceding outfit, so he reported, had dug a shallow well in the bed of the creek, from which he had filled his kegs, but the stock water was a mere **loblolly**. On receipt of this news, we changed mounts for the fifth time that day; and Flood, taking Forrest, the cook, and the horse wrangler, pushed on ahead with the remuda to the waterless stream.

loblolly: Muddy water.

The outlook was anything but encouraging. Flood and Forrest scouted the creek up and down for ten miles in a fruitless search for water. The outfit held the herd back until the twilight of evening, when Flood returned and confirmed McCann's report. It was twenty miles yet to the next water ahead, and if the horse stock could only be watered thoroughly, Flood was determined to make the attempt to nurse the herd through to water. McCann was digging an extra well, and he expressed the belief that by hollowing out a number of holes, enough water could be secured for the saddle stock. Honeyman had corralled the horses and was letting only a few go to the water at a time, while the night horses were being thoroughly watered as fast as the water rose in the well.

Holding the herd this third night required all hands. Only a few men at a time were allowed to go into camp and eat, for the herd refused even to lie down. What few cattle attempted to rest were prevented by the more restless ones. By spells they would mill, until riders were sent through the herd at a break-neck pace to break up the groups. During these milling efforts of the herd, we drifted over a mile from camp; but by the light of moon and stars and the number of riders, scattering was prevented. As the horses were loose for the night, we could not start them on the trail until daybreak gave us a change of mounts, so we lost the early start of the morning before.

Good cloudy weather would have saved us, but in its stead was a sultry morning without a breath of air, which bespoke another day of sizzling heat. We had not been on the trail over two hours before the heat became almost unbearable to man and beast. Had it not been for the condition of the herd, all might yet have gone well; but over three days had now elapsed without water for the cattle, and they became feverish and ungovernable. The lead cattle turned back several times, wandering aimlessly in any direction, and it was with considerable difficulty that the herd could be held on the trail. The rear overtook the lead, and the cattle gradually lost all semblance of a trail herd. Our horses were fresh, however, and after about two hours' work, we once more got the herd strung out in trailing fashion; but before a mile had been covered, the leaders again turned, and the cattle congregated into a mass of unmanageable animals, milling and lowing in their fever and thirst. The milling only intensified their sufferings from the heat, and the outfit split and quartered them again and again, in the hope that this unfortunate out-break might be checked. No sooner was the milling stopped than they would surge hither and yon, sometimes half a mile, as ungovernable as the waves of an ocean. After wasting several hours in this manner, they finally turned back over the trail, and the utmost efforts of every man in the outfit failed to check them. We threw our ropes in their faces, and when this failed, we resorted to shooting; but in defiance of the fusillade and the smoke they walked sullenly through the line of horsemen across their front. Six-shooters were discharged so close to the leaders' faces as to singe their hair, yet, under a noonday sun, they disregarded this and every other device to turn them, and passed wholly out of our control. In a number of instances wild steers deliberately walked against our horses, and then for the first time a fact dawned on us that chilled the marrow in our bones, the herd was going blind.

The bones of men and animals that lie bleaching along the trails abundantly testify that this was not the first instance in which the plain had baffled the determination of man. It was now evident that nothing short of water would stop the herd, and we rode aside and let them pass. As the outfit turned back to the wagon, our foreman seemed dazed by the sudden and unexpected turn of affairs, but rallied and met the emergency.

"There's but one thing left to do," said he, as we rode along, "and that is to hurry the outfit back to Indian Lakes. The herd will travel day and night, and instinct can be depended on to carry them to the only water they know. It's too late to be of any use now, but it's plain why those last two herds turned off at the lakes; someone had gone back and warned them of the very thing we've met. We must beat them to the lakes, for water is the only thing that will check them now. It's a good thing that they are strong, and five or six days without water will hardly kill any. It was no vague statement of the man who said if he owned hell and Texas, he'd rent Texas and live in hell, for if this isn't Billy hell, I'd like to know what you call it."

We spent an hour watering the horses from the wells of our camp of the night before, and about two o'clock started back over the trail for Indian Lakes. We overtook the abandoned herd during the afternoon. They were strung out nearly five miles in length, and were walking about a three-mile gait. Four men were given two extra horses apiece and left to throw in the stragglers in the rear, with instructions to follow them well into the night, and again in the morning as long as their canteens lasted. The remainder of the outfit pushed on without a halt, except to change mounts, and reached the lakes shortly after midnight. There we secured the first good sleep of any consequence for three days.

It was fortunate for us that there were no range cattle at these lakes, and we had only to cover a front of about six miles to catch the drifting herd. It was nearly noon the next day before the cattle began to arrive at the water holes in squads of from twenty to fifty. Pitiful objects as they were, it was a novelty to see them reach the water and **slack** their thirst. Wading out into the lakes until their sides were half covered, they would stand and low in a soft moaning voice, often for half an hour before attempting to drink. Contrary to our expectation, they drank very little at first, but stood in the water for hours. After coming out, they would lie down and rest for hours longer, and then drink again before attempting to graze, their thirst overpowering hunger. That they were blind there was no question, but with the causes that produced it once removed, it was probable their eyesight would gradually return.

slack: Slake.

DOCUMENT 10:

Owen Wister describes cowboys in the voice of an eastern visitor: *The Virginian* (1902)[4]

Owen Wister's famous novel *The Virginian* is an important early example of the modern Western novel, which developed out of the dime novel and magazine Westerns of the nineteenth-century popular press. Wister's work offered readers characters and themes that would reappear in the various movie and television-show iterations of the novel, as well as the Western genre in entertainment more broadly. In Chapter 1, "Enter the Man," Wister's **tenderfoot** narrator describes his first sight of cowboys in Wyoming, including first a horse wrangler and then a transplanted southerner, "The Virginian," a primordial cowboy character that would influence such figures in books, magazine, and graphic novel Western fiction, as well as television, film, and advertising.

tenderfoot: A person from outside the West, often deemed to be naïve and unaccustomed to hard work or outdoor living.

e

Chapter 1. Enter the Man

Some notable sight was drawing the passengers, both men and women, to the window; and therefore I rose and crossed the car to see what it was. I saw near the track an enclosure, and round it some laughing men, and inside it some whirling dust, and amid the dust some horses, plunging, huddling, and dodging. They were cow ponies in a corral, and one of them would not be caught, no matter who threw the rope. We had plenty of time to watch this sport, for our train had stopped that the engine might take water at the tank before it pulled us up beside the station platform of Medicine Bow. We were also six hours late, and starving for entertainment. The pony in the corral was wise, and rapid of limb. Have you seen a skilful boxer watch his antagonist with a quiet, incessant eye? Such an eye as this did the pony keep upon whatever man took the rope. The man might pretend to look at the weather, which was fine; or he might affect earnest conversation with a bystander: it was bootless. The pony saw through it. No feint hoodwinked him. This animal was thoroughly a man of the world. His undistracted eye stayed fixed upon the dissembling foe, and the gravity of his horse-expression made the matter one of high comedy. Then the rope would sail out at him, but he was already elsewhere; and if horses laugh, gayety must have abounded in that corral. Sometimes the pony took a turn alone; next he had slid in a flash among his brothers, and the whole of them like a school

---

4   *The Virginian: A Horseman of the Plains* (New York: Macmillan Company, 1902), 1–8.

of playful fish whipped round the corral, kicking up the fine dust, and (I take it) roaring with laughter. Through the window-glass of our **Pullman** the thud of their mischievous hoofs reached us, and the strong, humorous curses of the cow-boys. Then for the first time I noticed a man who sat on the high gate of the corral, looking on. For he now climbed down with the undulations of a tiger, smooth and easy, as if his muscles flowed beneath his skin. The others had all visibly whirled the rope, some of them even shoulder high. I did not see his arm lift or move. He appeared to hold the rope down low, by his leg. But like a sudden snake I saw the noose go out its length and fall true; and the thing was done. As the captured pony walked in with a sweet, church-door expression, our train moved slowly on to the station, and a passenger remarked, "That man knows his business."

But the passenger's dissertation upon roping I was obliged to lose, for Medicine Bow was my station. I bade my fellow-travellers good-by, and descended, a stranger, into the great cattle land. And here in less than ten minutes I learned news which made me feel a stranger indeed.

My baggage was lost; it had not come on my train; it was adrift somewhere back in the two thousand miles that lay behind me. And by way of comfort, the baggage-man remarked that passengers often got astray from their trunks, but the trunks mostly found them after a while. Having offered me this encouragement, he turned whistling to his affairs and left me planted in the baggage-room at Medicine Bow. I stood deserted among crates and boxes, blankly holding my check, furious and forlorn. I stared out through the door at the sky and the plains; but I did not see the antelope shining among the sage-brush, nor the great sunset light of Wyoming. Annoyance blinded my eyes to all things save my grievance: I saw only a lost trunk. And I was muttering half-aloud, "What a forsaken hole this is!" when suddenly from outside on the platform came a slow voice:

"Off to get married again? Oh, don't!"

The voice was Southern and gentle and drawling; and a second voice came in immediate answer, cracked and querulous:

"It ain't again. Who says it's again? Who told you, anyway?"

And the first voice responded caressingly:

"Why, your Sunday clothes told me, Uncle Hughey. They are speakin mighty loud o nuptials."

"You don t worry me!" snapped Uncle Hughey, with shrill heat.

And the other gently continued, "Ain't them gloves the same yu' wore to your last weddin'?"

"You don't worry me! You don't worry me!" now screamed Uncle Hughey.

Already I had forgotten my trunk; care had left me; I was aware of the sunset, and had no desire but for more of this conversation. For it resembled

Pullman: A Pullman Company rail passenger car.

none that I had heard in my life so far. I stepped to the door and looked out upon the station platform.

Lounging there at ease against the wall was a slim young giant, more beautiful than pictures. His broad, soft hat was pushed back; a loose-knotted, dull-scarlet handkerchief sagged from his throat; and one casual thumb was hooked in the cartridge-belt that slanted across his hips. He had plainly come many miles from somewhere across the vast horizon, as the dust upon him showed. His boots were white with it. His overalls were gray with it. The weather-beaten bloom of his face shone through it duskily, as the ripe peaches look upon their trees in a dry season. But no dinginess of travel or shabbiness of attire could tarnish the splendor that radiated from his youth and strength. The old man upon whose temper his remarks were doing such deadly work was combed and curried to a finish, a bridegroom swept and garnished; but alas for age! Had I been the bride, I should have taken the giant, dust and all.

He had by no means done with the old man.

"Why, yu've hung weddin' gyarments on every limb!" he now drawled, with admiration. "Who is the lucky lady this trip?"

The old man seemed to vibrate. "Tell you there ain't been no other! Call me a **Mormon**, would you?"

"Why, that—"

"Call me a Mormon? Then name some of my wives. Name two. Name one. Dare you!"

"—that Laramie wido' promised you—"

"Shucks!"

"—only her docter suddenly ordered **Southern climate** and—"

"Shucks! You're a false alarm."

"—so nothing but her lungs came between you. And next you'd most got united with **Cattle Kate**, only—"

"Tell you you're a false alarm!"

"—only she got hung."

"Where's the wives in all this? Show the wives! Come now!"

"That corn-fed biscuit-shooter at Rawlins yu' gave the canary—"

"Never married her. Never did marry—"

"But yu' come so near, uncle! She was the one left yu' that letter explaining how she'd got married to a young cyard-player the very day before her ceremony with you was due, and—"

"Oh, you re nothing; you're a kid; you don't amount to—"

"—and how she'd never, never forgot to feed the canary."

"This country's getting full of kids," stated the old man, witheringly. "It's doomed." This crushing assertion plainly satisfied him. And he blinked his

Mormon: Member of the Church of Latter-Day Saints, which in the early to mid nineteenth century became controversial in the US for their practice of polygamy, especially in Utah Territory. The practice was formally outlawed in Utah only when the territory gained statehood in 1896.

Southern climate: In the late nineteenth and early twentieth century, doctors often advised those suffering unduly from asthma or allergies to move to the southwest where the dry, warm air relieved symptoms.

Cattle Kate: Wister's novel refers obliquely here to the case of Ellen Watson. She was a Wyoming settler lynched in 1889 by vigilantes representing big cattlemen in the Wyoming Stock Growers Association, who were seeking to intimidate and push out small cattle raisers in order to monopolize grazing lands. The Watson killing was a precursor to the Johnson County War. See also Document 13, p. 74.

eyes with renewed anticipation. His tall tormentor continued with a face of unchanging gravity, and a voice of gentle solicitude:

"How is the health of that unfortunate—"

"That's right! Pour your insults! Pour 'em on a sick, afflicted woman!" The eyes blinked with combative relish.

"Insults? Oh, no, Uncle Hughey!"

"That's all right! Insults goes!"

"Why, I was mighty relieved when she began to recover her mem'ry. Las' time I heard, they told me she'd got it pretty near all back. Remembered her father, and her mother, and her sisters and brothers, and her friends, and her happy childhood, and all her doin's except only your face. The boys was bettin' she'd get that far too, give her time. But I reckon afteh such a turrable sickness as she had, that would be expectin' most too much."

At this Uncle Hughey jerked out a small parcel. "Shows how much you know!" he cackled. "There! See that! That's my ring she sent me back, being too unstrung for marriage. So she don't remember me, don't she? Ha-ha! Always said you were a false alarm."

The Southerner put more anxiety into his tone. "And so you're a-takin the ring right on to the next one!" he exclaimed. "Oh, don't go to get married again, Uncle Hughey! What's the use o' being married?"

"What's the use?" echoed the bridegroom, with scorn. "Hm! When you grow up you'll think different."

"Course I expect to think different when my age is different. I'm havin' the thoughts proper to twenty-four, and you're havin' the thoughts proper to sixty."

"Fifty!" shrieked Uncle Hughey, jumping in the air.

The Southerner took a tone of self-reproach. "Now, how could I forget you was fifty," he murmured, " when you have been telling it to the boys so careful for the last ten years!"

Have you ever seen a cockatoo—the white kind with the top-knot—enraged by insult? The bird erects every available feather upon its person. So did Uncle Hughey seem to swell, clothes, mustache, and woolly white beard; and without further speech he took himself on board the East-bound train, which now arrived from its siding in time to deliver him.

Yet this was not why he had not gone away before. At any time he could have escaped into the baggage-room or withdrawn to a dignified distance until his train should come up. But the old man had evidently got a sort of joy from this teasing. He had reached that inevitable age when we are tickled to be linked with affairs of gallantry, no matter how.

With him now the East-bound departed slowly into that distance whence I had come. I stared after it as it went its way to the far shores of civilization. It grew small in the unending gulf of space, until all sign of its presence was gone save a faint skein of smoke against the evening sky. And now my lost trunk came back into my thoughts, and Medicine Bow seemed a lonely spot. A sort of ship had left me marooned in a foreign ocean; the Pullman was comfortably steaming home to port, while I—how was I to find Judge Henry's ranch? Where in this unfeatured wilderness was Sunk Creek? No creek or any water at all flowed here that I could perceive. My host had written he should meet me at the station and drive me to his ranch. This was all that I knew. He was not here. The baggage-man had not seen him lately. The ranch was almost certain to be too far to walk to, to-night. My trunk I discovered myself still staring dolefully after the vanished East-bound; and at the same instant I became aware that the tall man was looking gravely at me, as gravely as he had looked at Uncle Hughey throughout their remarkable conversation.

To see his eye thus fixing me and his thumb still hooked in his cartridge-belt, certain tales of travellers from these parts forced themselves disquietingly into my recollection. Now that Uncle Hughey was gone, was I to take his place and be, for instance, invited to dance on the platform to the music of shots nicely aimed?

"I reckon I am looking for you, seh," the tall man now observed.

Charles A. Siringo on the abuse of range horses: *A Texas Cow Boy; or, Fifteen Years on the Hurricane Deck of a Spanish Pony* (1886)[5]

Charles A. Siringo started out as a range cowboy in the 1870s and later became a hired detective and bounty hunter who pursued a number of the most famous "outlaws" in Western history and lore, including **Tom Horn, Billy the Kid, and Butch Cassidy**. He was also a writer and recounted his time as a working cowboy in a memoir of life on the range. In the late-nineteenth and early-twentieth century, range work memoirs constituted a genre of Western literature that was read across the US and beyond, especially in Europe. Like Siringo, the handful of cowboys who became such storytellers were invariably white men who had access to publishers that could facilitate publication of their stories, unlike the vast majority of working cowboys from various backgrounds. Here, Siringo laments the suffering of remuda horses, the half-wild herds of mustangs who lived at large on ranch properties but were periodically captured and put to work.

ev

Tom Horn, Billy the Kid, and Butch Cassidy: Tom Horn was a notorious soldier, scout, and livestock investigator of the 1880s and 1890s, who was hanged in 1903 for killing the teenage son of a Wyoming sheepman. Billy the Kid (Henry McCarty) and Butch Cassidy (Robert LeRoy Parker) were known to have killed at least a dozen people in personal disputes or robberies and traveled in western territories where law enforcement struggled to track them. Like Horn, Billy the Kid became involved with "Regulators" and other armed vigilante groups that threatened and killed small-time ranchers and local law-enforcement officers who attempted to stop them.

The Cow-Pony—And How He Is Abused on the Large Cattle Ranches

It requires at least five ponies to each man, on a large cattle ranch; on a small one, where the amount of work, such as rounding-up, cutting, etc. is less, the number can be cut down.

A cow boy should be allowed to keep the same ponies just as long as he remains on the ranch, as he becomes attached to them, and they to him.

If you want to see a cow boy on the war-path, and have him quit, just take away one of his good ponies. Of course, if he has got one that is "no good" he won't kick, as he thinks he might get a better one in its place.

A cow boy always has one or two, "cutting" horses in his "mount" which he uses only on special occasions—when he wants to "show off." Any of his ponies will do to "cut" cattle on, but this one he dotes on, is so much better than the rest that he keeps him fat and well rested for those special occasions.

To illustrate what the word "cutting" means, I will try and explain:

After all the cattle in a radius of from ten to twenty miles are driven or run into one bunch, it is called a "round-up." I have seen as high as 50,000 head in one of those round-ups.

Now, we will say those 50,000 head belong to at least 50 different owners. And you being one of the owners and wanting to get your cattle home

---

5   Chicago: Siringo and Dobson, 1886, 326–36.

onto your own range you would have to put your men to work cutting them out—one at a time. Of course, once in a while a fellow gets a chance to "cut" two or three or half a dozen at a time—for instance, where a little bunch is standing on the outer edge, where you can dart in and "cut" them out before they realize what's up.

Now to begin, you will send about two men, on good "cutting" horses, into the round-up to begin "cutting" them out, while the rest of you help hold the round-up close together—or into a compact form—and keep the ones that are already "cut" out from getting back. The "cut" is watched, to keep it from getting too far off, by one man. The distance between the "cut" and round-up is from one to three hundred yards. About two *good* men on *quick* horses are generally placed between the "cut" and round-up, so that when the ones who are "cutting" run an animal out *they* take it and keep it going until it reaches the "cut," or at least gets so near that it will go on of its own accord.

A "cutting" pony to be considered a "Joe-dandy" has to be awful quick as well as limber. An old experienced one can be guided with the little finger—that is, by holding the bridle-reins on the end of the little finger. While performing the "cutting" act he will move along as though half asleep, until the animal is near the outer edge, when all at once he will make a spring forward and take the steer or cow out at a break neck gait. No matter how the animal dodges in its mad effort to get back he will be right at its heels or side. Sometimes of course the best of "cutting" ponies will fail to bring the animal out—especially when tired or over heated, or when the animal gets on the war-path and goes to fighting.

The cow-pony is a terribly abused animal, especially in large outfits, where so many different men are at work. It requires treble the number of men on a cow-ranch in the summer than it does in winter, therefore it will be seen that most of the cow-ponies are subject to a new master every season, if not oftener.

For instance; a man goes to work on a large ranch, and is given five or six horses for his regular "mount." Maybe he has just hired for a few months, during the busiest part of the season, and therefore does not care to take the interest in the welfare of his ponies, as if he was going to remain for an indefinite period.

Now this man quits late in the fall, and his ponies are turned loose on the range to rustle a living as best they can until spring, at which time they are caught up again and given to some other new hand, who will put them through the same old mill again all summer.

To give you a faint idea of how some of the poor dumb brutes suffer, I will try and illustrate—that is, dear reader if you will let me use *you* a few moments:

Now to begin with; lean back, shut your eyes and imagine yourself an old knee-sprung, poor, sore-backed pony, whose hips and shoulders are scarred up with Spanish brands and spur gashes.

It is now early spring; the green grass is just beginning to show itself. You are feeling happy after your long rest, and the thoughts of having plenty of green, tender grass to eat, instead of having to root amongst the snow and ice for a few sprigs of dry tasteless herbs.

But your happiness is of short duration; for here comes a crowd of the "old" hands on their fat **corn-fed** ponies to round you in; for spring work is about to commence. You break and run, to try and get away, but you are too weak; they soon overtake you, and start you towards the "home-ranch."

You are driven into the corral with the rest of your bony looking companions. The old last year's sore on your back has healed up and a new coat of hair is just starting to grow over it.

Here comes the boss down to the corral with a lot of new men he has hired for the summer. He is going down to give each man a "mount" out of the herd of extras, of which, patient reader, *you* are supposed to be one.

You are leaning against the fence scratching yourself when a rope is pitched over your head.

"Here 'Curly!' you can take this fellow for one of yours," yells the boss as he drags you towards the gate to meet "Curly," who is coming in a dog-trot to put *his* rope on you.

Now this man "Curly," your new master, has just returned from the east, where he has been spending the winter with the old folks, and telling the boys around town about the fun he had last summer on the staked plains, roping coyotes, etc. A couple of those "new" men who are standing at the gate, are old playmates whom he has persuaded to leave their happy homes and become cow boys too.

After each man has been supplied with a "mount," you are taken out, with the other four or five of "Curly's" ponies and turned loose in the "ramutha"—the herd of ponies which are to accompany the outfit on the "general round-up."

The outfit has now been on the road two days. They have been traveling hard to get to a certain place where all the different outfits, for a hundred miles, north, south, east and west, will meet on a certain day to begin "rounding up."

The place is reached about sundown. The little valley is dotted here and there with white-topped wagons—and still they come; wending their way down ravines from every quarter.

After supper the bosses all meet at one of the camps and lay out plans for work on the following day.

corn-fed: Horses who have their hay supplemented with high-energy grain or corn would run longer and faster than horses forced to subsist on range forage, which has relatively less nutrition and energy.

Next morning at the first peep of day everybody is eating breakfast, in all the different camps.

The morning meal being over, the "ramutha," which has been guarded all night, is driven up to camp and each man ropes the horse he wants for the day's work.

"Curly" catches you for the first time, since turning you loose in the "ramutha" before leaving the ranch.

When he goes to throw his old shell of a saddle on your back, you give a snort and go to **pitching**—like nearly all Spanish ponies, after having rested a few months—which causes Mr. "Curly's" blood to become riled. So he, after you get your spree out, puts a hitch on your nose and begins to tame you, by beating you over the head and back with a doubled rope.

He finally gets you saddled, but when he goes to mount, you let in to pitching again. But he manages to stick onto you.

Everybody being in their saddles the boss tells "Bill," one of the old hands, to take "Curly," "Red Dick" and "Locoed Tom" (Locoed, meaning crazy) and drive down "San Pedro Canyon" to "Buzzard Flat" where the round-up will be.

So "Bill" dashes off on his corn-fed pony for the head of "San Pedro Canyon," a distance of twenty miles, with the other three boys right at his heels.

You finally step in a **badger hole** or stub your toe against a rock and fall, throwing Mr. "Curly" against the ground with a terrible force.

You jump up and stand trembling from the shock you received, while your mad master takes hold of the bridle-reins and goes to abusing you for falling—not only with his tongue, but by jerking the reins, which are attached to the severe Spanish bit, causing your mouth to bleed, and kicking you in the stomach with the toe of his boot.

At last he is satisfied and mounts again, by which time the other boys are a mile or two off. Being such a common occurrence, when you fell they just glanced over their shoulders to see if "Curly" was killed or not. On seeing him jump up they knew he wasn't badly hurt. Hence them keeping right on.

Now you will have to do "**some tall**" running, under **quirt and spur**, to overtake the boys.

Finally the head of "San Pedro Canyon" is reached. Everybody dismounts to "fix" their saddles—that is, move them back in place and tighten the girths. "Bill" looks at his watch and finds that an hour and ten minutes has been spent in coming the twenty miles, over a rough and rocky country. Their ponies are white with sweat, and panting like lizards.

After surveying the surrounding country a few moments, "Bill" gives orders thusly: "Curly, you gallop over yonder," pointing to a large bunch of cattle five miles to the west, "and run those cattle down the Canyon; and

pitching: Kicking and bucking in resistance.

badger hole: Probably the opening of a prairie dogs' tunnel. Prairie dogs, also known colloquially as gophers, lived in complex tunnels under ground in grassland areas. The openings of these tunnels produced holes in the ranges that could trip and even cripple horses who stepped into them.

some tall: Difficult or exhausting.

quirt and spur: The quirt was a short leather whip. Along with sharp, pointed, Spanish-style spurs on the heels of a rider's boots, these tools could be used to force a horse to act. Cowboys would drag the spurs along a horse's shoulders or belly, while whipping the horse's head, a frightening and painful experience for any equine.

you," talking to "Red Dick," "go after that little bunch yonder, while me and 'Locoed Tom' will push everything down the Canyon."

"Curly" starts off by burying both spurs deep into your already bloody sides.

When within half a mile of the cattle, they start at full speed, but in the wrong direction; hence you have got a three or four mile race, under quirt and spur, to run before they are "headed off" and turned down the Canyon.

After getting them turned, and to give them a good "send off," so they won't stop running until they strike the round-up, where men will be on hand to catch and hold them, "Curly" will fire his pistol a few times.

You are almost out of breath now, and should get time to blow awhile, but no, your cruel master, who feels good and wants exercise, after being housed up all winter, spies a coyote off in the distance and **starts after it**. He chases it five miles and then, after firing a few shots to scare it, starts back down the Canyon to help the other boys shove all the cattle down towards the round-up.

About eleven o'clock, the round-up, of several thousand head, is formed and ready for the "cutting" process.

Towards night the days' work is finished; the round-up is turned loose and each outfit starts to their respective camp with the little herd, which will be held night and day, and which will continue to grow larger every day, until too large to conveniently handle, when it will be sent by a few men back to the range, from whence they had drifted during the winter.

Camp is reached, and "Curly," in his great anxiety to get to the steaming "grub" or "chuck," which the cook has just taken from the fire, jerks the saddle off and turns you loose without washing your back—which should be done, especially in hot weather—at the same time giving you a kick with the toe of his number eight boot.

You are by this time a pitiful looking sight as you trot off towards the "ramutha." But the worst part of it is your back. The day has been very hot, causing the old last year's sore to become scalded; consequently, when the saddle was jerked off, the old scab with its new growth of hair, also went, having adhered to the blanket.

We will now drop the curtain a while, as our subject is not very pleasant to dwell upon.

It is morning; and the sun is just peeping over yonder tree-tops, which are alive with little birds whose sweet melodious songs make the air ring with joy.

But there is no joy nor happiness for you. It is your day to be ridden, therefore you are roped and dragged up to where "Curly's" saddle lies. The bridle is put onto you, and then your lazy master picks up the dirty, hard, saddle blankets—which have not been washed for a month—and throws

starts after it: Many rural westerners routinely chased and killed coyotes, wolves, or bears, wild animals deemed detrimental to extensive ranching. Coyotes frequently fed off the carcasses of dead livestock and less often hunted weakened animals.

them over your raw and swollen back. Now for the saddle, which causes you to squirm and twist; and then to add to the pain, imagine a man whose weight, counting pistol, leggings and all, is one hundred and seventy-five pounds, climbing onto that saddle.

You can now wake up, dear reader, for we know you are disgusted playing the role of a sore-backed Spanish cow-pony.

But don't think for an instant that the majority of cow boys are the cruel-hearted wretches, such as we have pictured this man "Curly" to be. There are though, on every range a few who can **discount** my friend Mr. "Curly" for cruelty.

Many a Christian-hearted boy have I seen quit and throw up a paying job rather than ride one of those poor sore-backed brutes.

There should be a law passed in the west making it a penitentiary offence for an owner, or head man of a ranch to allow, or rather compel, a man to ride one of their sore-backed ponies, especially after the sore becomes so large that the saddle won't cover it, as is often the case.

discount: Call out.

DOCUMENT 12:

Bent County Cattle and Horse Growers Association, *Brand Book* of Colorado cattle and horse brand diagrams (1885)[6]

Brand books were a common reference one could find in ranch houses, livestock registry offices, at the stockyards, or in the dusty hands of men and women who worked with cattle and horses on the land. This page from an 1885 brand book displays the various brands of some local horse and cattle owners in Bent County in the southeast corner of Colorado. Here, stock images of meaty, shorthorn cattle and Quarter Horses from the east stood in for the more stringy longhorn-shorthorn cross cattle and the stout mustangs many Coloradans knew.

---

6   *Brand Book, Containing the Brands of the Bent County Cattle and Horse Growers' Association* (West Las Animas, CO: Colorado Leader Newspaper, 1885), 16, 19.

DOCUMENT 13:

The *Cheyenne Daily Leader* (Wyoming) reports on the killings of Ella Watson and Jim Averell: "A Double Lynching" (23 July 1889)

Disputes over brands or unbranded animals could be political and occasionally turn violent. They often came to light as large stockholders accused cowboys, homesteaders, or smaller cattle operations of "rustling" livestock by claiming, rightly or disingenuously, that those individuals had intentionally ignored or misread a brand in order to abscond with others' animals. Of course, large cattle growers did that with regularity. It was also true that often animals were missed on branding day—so called mavericks—and when some small operators found those cattle, they marked them with

their own brands to claim them. The case of Ella Watson, the cowgirl cattle raiser also called "Cattle Kate," and Jim Averell was nationally famous. Although many believed the stories the papers told about them, Watson and Averell were not rustlers but independent operators who simply got in the way of powerful large cattle holders who unofficially governed the territory of Wyoming by way of extra-legal or vigilante justice.

DOCUMENT 14:

Image group: Cowboys and ranching people (1895–1935)

A. The cowboy myth, part 1: Frederick Remington, "The Bronco Buster" (1895)[7]

For many Americans, the image of the cowboy as a daring free spirit was grounded in early depictions of cowboys and horses by artists like Frederick Remington. Born in New York state, Remington was a sketch artist, painter, sculptor, and writer who in his twenties traveled west as a reporter and professional illustrator. His work was favored by Teddy Roosevelt and many others who imagined the West as a space of manly individual freedom, action, and adventure, and Remington became the preeminent Western artist of his time.

Remington's sculpture is an influential example of the broadly popular icon of a cowboy riding a bucking horse. The "bronco buster" figure celebrated

then-current modes of horse breaking in which a cowboy would mount a wild horse, spurring and whipping until the horse became exhausted or otherwise ceased struggling. Although this was traumatic, horses learned that when they became calm, the whipping and spurring stopped, thus learning not to resist riders. In Western lore and popular culture, people interpreted the frightened horse's frantic struggle to escape and the cowboy's determination to stay on board as representative of the challenges and opportunities of the West. Since the 1970s, an original casting of "The Bronco Buster" has usually been on prominent display in the Oval Office at the White House, indicating how its symbolism still resonates with Americans today.

---

7   Metropolitan Museum of Art donation to Wikimedia Commons.

B. Black cowboys at Negro State Fair, Bonham, Texas (ca. 1911–15)[8]

In the American South, black men had long done the ranching and cattle work, first as enslaved people, later as homesteaders and range workers on ranches in Texas. After the US Civil War, freedmen left the South and found cowboy work all over the West. The well-known "cowboy photographer" Erwin E. Smith took this image of a group of men at the Negro State Fair in Bonham, Texas sometime between 1911 and 1915. The fair was an opportunity for people of color to congregate in public as rural westerners proud of their work with horses and cattle.

8   Erwin E. Smith, photographer, "African-American cowboys on their mounts ready to participate in horse race during Negro State Fair, Bonham, Texas," ca. 1911–15, Amon Carter Museum.

C. Charles Belden cowboy photographs[9]

With the demise of the "free grass" era, many of the men who labored as cowboys took whatever work was available, not all of it so glamorous. Traditional cattle work was still common, but also sheep management, and work on dude ranches taking tourists on pack camping trips and trail rides. These photographs were taken in the 1920s by Charles Belden (a San Franciscan transplanted to Wyoming) at the Pitchfork Ranch near Meeteetse, Wyoming. Many of Belden's photographs appeared in magazines like *Saturday Evening Post* and *National Geographic*, which served the middle-class readers who predominated among tourist visitors to the West. They show how westerners and their admirers collaborated to idealize the working cowboy as a mythical western figure, although the lives of these men were often more mundane. The titles of the photographs below are taken from the archival records for them at the American Heritage Center at the University of Wyoming.

"Branding cattle"

---

9   Charles J. Belden Photographs Collection, American Heritage Center, University of Wyoming.

"Sheep camp"

"People riding horses entering a corral"
(Cowboys returning from trail ride with dude ranch clients)

D. Cowboys, cowgirls, and ranchers[10]

Recall that the equipment and techniques of the cowboy emanated from Hispanic cattle people, including the *vaqueros* of Mexico. In the Southwest and Texas, as in many cattle-raising regions, the line between working cowboy, small cattle holder, homesteader with a few head, or the owner of an **estancia** could be blurry.

estancia: A large-scale ranch in Mexico or the Southwest, also known as a *hacienda*.

Luis Romero (left) and cowboy Ramon Ahumada photographed with horse in Arizona, ca. 1890.

---

10 These photographs can be viewed online at the Arizona Historical Society's Arizona Memory Project.

Adelina Ruelas working at a ranch in Box Canyon in the Santa Rita mountains just south of Tucson, Arizona, ca. 1920, when she was about 16 years old. Although it was not common for Mexican or Latina women in the US to work directly with horses and cattle, it did occasionally occur.

Tucson rancher Felix Quiroz and cowpony photographed in Arizona, ca. 1927. The Arizona Historical Society says of Quiroz, "He was born in 1872 at Ranch of Los Reales. He married Luz Fiquera in Carbocha. His father was Preciliano Quiroz and his grandfather was Felix Quiroz, both of whom were born in Tucson."

E . The cowboy myth, part 2: "Working Cowboy," photographer unidentified (1934)[11]

The myth of the cowboy as a picturesque and mysterious lone male figure informed photographers' and other artists' depictions of cowboys in ways that romanticized these low-paid workers and their dangerous labor. This image was captured by a government photographer during the depths of the Great Depression when millions of men struggled with unemployment and a sense of personal failure. What was its meaning then?

11   Library of Congress.

DISCUSSION QUESTIONS/WRITING PROMPTS

1. What regions, people, animals, and time periods are addressed by the primary sources here?

2. The phenomenon of economic boom and bust appears frequently in American economic and environmental history. In what ways did the Beef Bonanza bubble display that pattern? From the primary sources here, what do we learn about why so many people believed they too might strike it rich in the West?

3. What do we learn from the primary sources here about the working conditions of cowboys and horses during the late nineteenth and early twentieth century? Why did so many people idealize the cowboy and western horses as free spirits when they labored for wealthy cattle owners for little reward?

4. According to the historical sources here, who was a cowboy or cowgirl? What kind of person was he or she?

5. What is the role of contemporary creative works like Remington's *The Bronco Buster*, Wister's *The Virginian*, and Adams' *Log of a Cowboy* in enhancing or complicating our understanding of both the lives of historical cowboys versus their popular reputation as a (white male) hero to young men and some young women?

PART 3

Fattening, Shipping, Slaughtering, Selling

DOCUMENT 15:

Image group: Abilene, Kansas, and the early cattle trade from Joseph McCoy's *Historic Sketches of the Cattle Trade of the West and Southwest* (1874)[1]

Joseph McCoy was a cattle trader and booster of the railhead town of Abilene, Kansas. His illustrated narrative about the early years of the cattle trade explained how he and other investors facilitated the sale of longhorn criollo cattle, and later shorthorn and their crosses, from Texas's **Chisholm Trail** to local and distant packing houses in Kansas City, Chicago, and beyond. McCoy wrote with humor and optimism about well-known fellow cattlemen, cowboys, cattle, and the environmental and economic conditions through which many men made and lost fortunes, small and large. Within five years of its founding Abilene would be surpassed by other railhead towns, reflecting the boom and bust nature of the cattle business.

Chisholm Trail: The dirt trail stretching from near Austin, Texas, north to Kansas and the first route by which cowboys drove herds of cattle north for sale at railheads in the 1860s and 1870s.

ABILENE IN ITS GLORY.

Abilene in Its Glory

---

1   Kansas City, MO: Ramsey, Millett, & Hudson, 1874.

Premium Texas Cattle Fed by John B. Hunter

Herd of Short-Horns—Property of A. Wilson

Joseph McCoy explains land, cattle fattening, and packing in Kansas:
Historic Sketches of the Cattle Trade of the West and Southwest (1874)[2]

❧

The Abilene enterprise opened up, or was the precursor to many lucrative avocations, one of which was the business of buying, late in the fall, the thin unmarketable cattle, and holding them over winter and fattening them during the following summer upon the native grasses. This operation was found to be very profitable and in due time many engaged in it.

Among the first, if not the first, was Maj. J.S. Smith, of Springfield, Ill., who was the first northern cattle man or buyer that came to Abilene in 1867, and bought cattle for his Illinois pastures and feed-lots; and whilst at Abilene was induced to buy a small lot of **scalawag** cattle and to put them into winter quarters in Kansas as an experiment. Everyone was astonished the following spring to see how well the cattle had wintered. They had actually gained in flesh and general condition during the winter. In a few months after spring opened and grass was abundant, the small herd was in sufficiently good condition to go to the eastern market. This experiment was sufficient to demonstrate the practicability as well as the profit of wintering **Texan cattle** in Kansas. The following fall many engaged in it. This of course created a demand for hay.

The wild grasses of the valleys of Kansas, when mowed and properly cured in the months of July and August, make hay of equally good quality to the best timothy and clover hay of the Middle States. Many young men of energy found lucrative employment in putting up hay to sell to cattle men desirous of wintering stock.

No eastern meadow has so smooth a surface as the valleys of Western Kansas. In many places the mowing machine can be driven for miles without meeting an obstruction or running over a single rod of rough or uneven ground. The Major was not slow to see the prospective profit in the operation of wintering cattle, and to engage in it extensively. Besides sending to his Illinois farm about five hundred cattle annually—to depasture his bluegrass fields, and consume his corn crops, after which but a few months grazing upon tame grass pastures would fit them for the New York markets—he has for five successive winters held from one thousand to two thousand head in Kansas, over winter.

scalawag: Steer who had not grown to "market weight," that is, the minimum weight of one head of cattle that stock buyers demanded so that it would be profitable to ship an animal to slaughter.

Texan cattle: Texas Longhorn and other criollo cattle that had spread across Texas, the American southwest, and Mexico.

---

2   McCoy, *Historic Sketches of the Cattle Trade*, 214–23, 309–15.

Wintering Texan cattle in Kansas has some peculiar features worthy perhaps of definite description, more from the magnitude of the business, the great numbers annually wintered, rather than from the scientific manner in which it is done.

The cattle man who undertakes to winter a herd of cattle, secures about one ton of hay to each head he desires to winter. This he provides at his permanent ranch, if he has any, sometimes cutting the grass, curing, and putting it up in long ricks, from forty to one hundred feet in length, and from ten to twenty feet in breadth—on his own account. At other times he secures his hay by contracting with hay-making parties, or buys it of those who have put it up on purpose to sell it. Often in the latter case he will establish a temporary ranch in the immediate vicinity of the hay, by improvising temporary camps, sometimes mere tents, other times rude "dug-outs" in the banks of some ravine, will be constructed for the comfort and convenience of the men.

A large adjacent tract of land, embracing many thousands of acres, will be "fire-guarded," in order to secure a winter range from the ravages of prairie fires, so common, and often so destructive in prairie countries. To guard against such contingencies two or more plow furrows, about four rods apart, are run around the tract of land desired to be "fire-guarded," and then upon some quiet, breezeless evening, the intervening strip is set fire and closely watched until it is consumed. Thus it will be seen that an impassable barrier would be created between the unburned grass within the encircled tract, and that upon the outside of the "fire-guard."

Unless the "fire-guard" is perfect, and of ample width it is worthless as a protection against the great fires, fanned and driven by high winds, which invariably sweep over large prairie countries.

Sometimes the fire-guard is made during the summer when the grasses are green and inflammable, by mowing two swaths a few rods apart, instead of plowing, and after the mown grass has lain in the hot sun a few days it will burn without igniting the adjoining standing grass. Then when frost has come and the prairie grass is deadened, the intervening strip of grass between the two burned swaths is burned off much in the same manner as in the case of the plow furrows.

It is customary with cautious operators to burn circumscribed fire-guards around their ricks of hay and camp, as a precaution against accidents. So long as there is no snow, and the weather is fine, the cattle will get ample food on the range upon which they are allowed to graze in the day time, but are usually corralled, or rounded up near the camp at night much in the same fashion as in summer herding. But when stormy weather occurs, or there is much snow or ice upon the ground, the cattle are held near camp, and hay given them to eat. One or two yokes of oxen attached to a wagon upon which is a rude hay rack or frame, usually constitutes a feeder's outfit, upon which the hay is loaded, and then scattered off in a circle upon the ground, to be eagerly devoured by the hungry Texans.

Hay made from wild grass, such as is found in the valleys of central and western Kansas in great abundance, is very good and contains a great amount of nutriment. Texan cattle eat it with avidity and without any trouble learning them to take hold of it. It will keep in good heart and flesh any Texan bovine that can get enough of it, and will in many cases, increase their weight and condition during the winter.

The experienced cattle man usually chooses or prefers a wintering situation which has good running water, with considerable timber and underbrush; or one that has near the location of the hay, a tract of rough broken country in the gulches, and behind the hills of which the cattle can find shelter from the piercing winds and driving storms to which western Kansas, in common with other prairie countries, is subject.

Many cattle men prefer to winter in eastern Kansas, where they turn their herds upon fields of cornstalks from which the corn has been previously gathered, and in February and March give them a few bushels of corn to strengthen them up so they will take the new grasses and improve rapidly. Whilst in extreme western Kansas many herds are put through the winter with little or no other feed than the **Buffalo grass**, which, cured up during the previous summer, contains a great amount of nutriment. So long as the cattle can get a sufficient amount of the dry Buffalo grass they will thrive finely. Many thousands are wintered in that manner annually. But it is liable to serious objection as a method of wintering, inasmuch as when the snow or sleet falls deep, as it sometimes does, the cattle are compelled to fast longer than is profitable to the owner, or consistent with the laws of life, and the poor brutes starve to death or stray away in quest of food. When the cattle are wintered upon the range it is customary to place them in some suitable district and then herd or outride the country daily, turning back any that may be found going beyond the prescribed limits. In all styles of wintering, the inevitable and necessary cow-ponies are used, which in addition to the grass or hay they get whilst picketed out are fed corn, oats, or other grain. This is done to give them strength requisite for riding service, and to enable them to withstand the rigors of the climate, for the Texan cow pony cannot withstand the cold of northern winters hardly so well as Texan cattle, besides he is daily ridden more or less....

The manner of fattening cattle at a **still-house** is one differing altogether from all other methods of feeding in the northwest. Each particular bullock is tied up by a chain around the neck, in a separate stall, the front of which is a manger or platform for hay. A box to receive the allowance of **swill** is also

Buffalo grass: One of a number of perennial grasses native to the Great Plains, in this case probably *Bouteloua dactyloides*.

still-house: A distillery.

swill: Waste plant materials left over from the distilling process.

provided and placed where the bullock can reach it easily; into which the slop is conducted by pipes, running from an immense tank or cooler, which is kept constantly full of slop, fresh from the still-house, which stands at some distance from the cattle stables. Behind the stall is a trench or gutter provided to receive all the filth and offal from the cattle, and is daily cleaned out. The slop is the refuse arising from distilling or manufacturing grain into liquors, and would, without something to eat it, become an entire loss. The stalls are arranged in long rows and the platform in front serves to place hay on daily to be consumed by the stalled ox, which, by the economy of his nature must have some rough coarse food, or else he would soon lose his appetite after becoming gorged upon rich concentrated food.

Cattle are usually still-fed for from six months to two hundred days, and in that time become very fat, and are considered as good beef as if fatted in any other manner.

Being long tied up, they become clumsy and almost lose the use of their limbs. So it is common to let them out in an enclosure once or twice during the two or three weeks previous to shipping them to market, and let them run about and recover the proper use of themselves. It is amusing then to see the dumb brute, rejoiced at regaining his liberty, and to get once more into the sunshine. He attempts to kick up his heels, which usually results in falling headlong on his nose; then he will look foolish, and walk about the yard carefully but awkwardly, until he regains self confidence, when he will spurt off at some tangent only to be again hopelessly discomfited by tumbling down.

Little trouble is experienced in getting every bullock to learn to eat the slop, and they usually get very fat. Inasmuch as they become mature before grass fatted cattle can be had, and at a time when the supply of corn-fed cattle is almost exhausted, they invariably command good prices and generally make large profits to the feeder.

It is the cheapest way to fatten cattle on feed during the winter, from the fact that the slop would be a waste if stock was not provided. This the still operator does not care, or have time to do. Hence he sells the slop at low figures, say from three to eight cents per diem, per bullock, which is much cheaper than the animal could be fed on corn....

Cattle packing is chiefly done in the late fall and early winter months, when a supply of grass-fatted stock can be had, and the weather is sufficiently cold to thoroughly cool the meat. It is only grass-fatted cattle that can be had at prices sufficiently low to justify packing. For this reason, corn-fatted cattle are seldom, if ever, packed. Hence a point near the plains where cattle are cheaply bred and fatted, at which a supply of hogs can also be had, is the one most likely to do the principal portion of cattle packing. Such a point Kansas City rightly claims to be.

When a herd of cattle is placed in the yards adjoining a packing establishment for the purpose of being packed, they are separated into squads of two or three and driven through a long narrow lane, and forced into a small box pen, the gate being securely fastened behind them. A dozen or more of those box pens are located side by side, all connected with the main lane, or drive way, so that the men in the yards always have empty pens to fill. So soon as a pen is filled, a man standing upon a narrow gangway, just above the cattle's heads, with a rifle loaded with fixed ammunition, shoots the bullocks in the head. The ball ranges down into or through the brain, producing instant death. Of course the bullock instantly drops, only to receive the falling body of his comrade.

Formerly a long pike was used, with which the brute was speared just behind the horns, or forehead, upon the top of the neck, where the vertebrae joins the head. But this method of killing was abandoned, as being less humane than the rifle. Often when good aim was not taken, or the animal, at the critical moment moved its head, it would be mangled horribly, but not killed without repeated blows.

So soon as all are shot down in any one pen, a rising door, which divides the pen from the inner portion of the establishment, is hoisted, and a man enters from within the house dragging a long chain with a noose formed at the end thereof. This chain extends back and around certain pulleys and up to a revolving drum, or windlass, which is driven by steam and governed by means of a lever in the hands of a person whose sole duty is to manage the machine, stopping and starting it instantly at the call of the man who handles the chain. This he drops over the bullock's head, around his neck, or horns, as may be convenient, then calls for power, which the man at the lever at once applies, and the bullock is drawn out on a narrow floor, inclining toward a gutter, or drain, near to which the head of the bullock is stopped. The chain loosened, the drawing out operation is repeated upon the comrade, which is left lying beside him. Then the chain man shifts his chain into the next pully and enters the next pen. So soon as the bullock is stopped upon the narrow inclining floor, a butcher opens the skin on the under side of the neck and cuts both jugular veins, thus letting the hot blood run freely upon the floor, thence into the drain, which conducts it from the building and empties it into the river. Even before the blood is done flowing, and before the bullock is quiet in death, the butchers begin dressing it, one taking off its head, first denuding it of the skin, another peels the hide down the legs to the knees, then adroitly separates the joint, throwing the feet and shins upon the floor, from whence an **urchin** removes them to the proper room. The bullock is then turned upon its back, being propped by a short pointed brace, and another pair of butchers take it in charge, and whilst the first two are beheading and unlimbing the next bullock, they quickly strip

urchin: A young boy employed at the slaughterhouse.

the hide from belly, quarters, and sides of the animal. Then comes one or more men and insert a strong **gammon**, of four or more feet in length, in the hocks beneath the hamstrings of the hinder legs. In the middle of the gammon stick a flat iron hook is adjusted, which is attached to a strong rope running over a pully aloft, and is wound up on a windlass so rigged and geared, that a muscular man can raise slowly upward the carcass of the bullock, which is fast relieved of its hide and entrails, whilst so moving. So soon as the hide, is off and the innards taken out, the carcass is split in twain, dividing the back bone with a broad-bladed ax, save a small portion of muscle at the back of the neck. The hide is dragged off to a small hole in the floor, through which it is tumbled to the salting cellar below. The paunch and entrails are dragged with hooks of steel to their proper rooms, whilst the lungs are thrown into the drain with the blood and other filthy waste, and passes out of the building. In the meantime the carcass is windlassed to a height which brings it clear off the floor and the gammon level with a series of skids, a distance apart equal to the length of the gammon; the ends of which groove into smooth slots. The hook and rope being relaxed, the carcass rests upon the skids, which run parallel the entire length of the cooling room, at right angles to the dressing floor. Upon the skids the carcasses are permitted to hang in close proximity until they are thoroughly cooled and the fatty parts become hard and firm, which occurs as soon as all animal heat is out.

When the reader bears in mind that of the four score or more of men engaged, each one has a certain part only, which he performs, and then passes to the next bullock—one assisting, some throwing feet, others dragging off heads, others scraping and cleaning the floor, whilst others are doing various duties,—and that the space over which the work is done is more than one hundred feet in length, and that a score or more of bullocks are being operated upon at the same time, he may rightly conclude that the scene of cattle dressing is one of entirely too great activity, life, and space, for one illustration to do ample justice.

When the carcasses are properly cooled, the work of cutting up may begin. This requires a large number of men to do the work expeditiously. However, of late years, the saw, propelled by steam, is largely substituted for the cleaver and knife. A full complement of saws to do all the different styles of cuts, comprises five, each of which is operated in a separate frame, and driven by a belt which receives its motion, or power, from a shaft and pulley overhead, which is driven by steam power. These saw frames stand in position describing a flat-iron, the first one being next to the hanging carcasses, at the opposite end of the large cooling-room from which the cattle are dressed; the other saw frames stand two and two, just opposite to each other, and behind the first frame; still farther back the remaining pair of saw frames are stationed; trimming tables are near, and also suspended platform scales for weighing of each barrel or **tierce** of beef, care being taken to have as near the same pieces and the exact weight in each package as possible. Near by the barrels are brought, and a given amount of salt provided to each. Meats for certain brands and markets are cut in uniform shape and size, and from certain portions of the carcass.

Quite a large number of men are required to operate all the saws, to bring the carcasses, handle the meat on the frames, trim on the tables, weigh up and pack in barrels, bring up salt, empty barrels and take away full ones. The quarters of beef are brought one at a time and thrown upon the first saw frame where two men adjust the quarter and pass it up to the saw, which divides flesh and bone in a jiffy and the pieces pass on to the next saw, and over trimming tables, and then to the scales, thence to the barrel.

tierce: A 42-gallon barrel.

Philadelphia Times reporter describes cattle lands of South Dakota in a Texas newspaper: "In the Bad Lands," *Galveston Daily News* (27 July 1884)[3]

Stories like this one appeared in newspapers around the country and patched together environmental, social, and economic information about the West for the public. This item written by a correspondent for the *Philadelphia Times*, was reprinted, sometimes in abridged form, in various papers including the *Galveston Daily News* in Texas. It appeared just a few years before the horrific losses of the Big Die-Up (1886–87) and described the atypical career of a wealthy French immigrant, the Marquis de Mores, who had arrived in the US with plenty of capital to invest in the growing continental food network. The reporter describes South Dakota's badlands, marked by multicolored rock, soil, buttes, and other beautiful geographic features juxtaposed with vast expanses of level grassland. Like many such stories about the West, it portrayed the region as a land of the incredible—landscape, people, and opportunity.

e

Swedenborg: Swedish theologian Emanuel Swedenborg (1688–1772), known for his writings on the nature of the afterlife.

red, black and blue cliffs: Here the author refers to the badlands in what today is South Dakota.

Have I been transported in spirit to some other planet, as **Swedenborg** went to heaven and saw the landscapes and the dwellings of the inhabitants? These **red, black and blue cliffs**, with their pinnacles and encampments, do not seem to belong to any earthly scenery. The face of the country appears to have been scourged and tormented by extramundane forces. Are these enormous battlements on the horizon the fortifications of some strange race? This river in the background has an unnatural look, with its golden-brown water. The sky is almost white, and the sun pours down a flood of intolerably fierce rays. The air is thin and exhilarating. Here are flowers, but they are all unfamiliar. This must be the moon. It looks singularly like the magnified telescopic photographs of that satellite, which show a ridged and corrugated country full of bare, sun-scorched mountains, and dark holes and hollows. So I mused last evening, sitting on the piazza of the Marquis de Mores's house in the Bad Lands. The white light changed to roseate and plush tints as the sun went down behind a big butte, and the fancy about the unnatural character of the surroundings was dispelled by the marquis's valet announcing that dinner was served.

3   Page 10.

An Adventurous Frenchman

This handsome young French nobleman, who has left Paris clubs and boulevards to become a prince of cowboys and a manager of slaughter-houses and refrigerator cars is a picturesque character. When he came here the herders of the Bad Lands thought at first that he was an adventurous crank, who would leave after he had secured a few hunting trophies to take back to Paris. He built a shanty, secured large tracts of **government land**, and bought herds of cattle. Then they hated him because he had a servant and wore clean clothes. He was a monopolist, they said, who was going to fence in the country. They tried to scare him away, but they found he had been a soldier, and did not scare easily. One day last summer, a party of the more desperate among his enemies set out to kill him. In the fracas he **killed one of the cowboys**. Since then there has been peace on the **Little Missouri**. The marquis has gained a footing in the country. The cowboys are now his friends. His enterprises prosper. He has slaughterhouses and ice-houses at several points in Western Dakota and Eastern Montana, and supplies with beef the chief towns between St. Paul and Portland. He has begun shipping fresh salmon in refrigerator cars from Portland to New York. A carload of salmon costs $900 in Portland, the transportation expenses are $1100, and the fish bring about $3000 in New York.

The business of shipping dressed beef to eastern markets is evidently destined to grow to large proportions. It is manifestly a great improvement on the old method of transporting the live animal, packed in cars so closely that they cannot lie down, and tortured by fatigue, hunger and thirst. The beeves are driven from the neighboring ranges to the slaughtering establishments on the line of the Northern Pacific railroad, and their carcasses, when packed in the refrigerator cars, are in the best possible condition to serve as healthful food. A steak from a Montana steer, eaten where the animal built up his juicy fiber from the bunch grass of the ranges, is altogether another thing from a steak from the same sort of a steer after he has been tormented by a journey of 2000 miles. In fact, the system of shipping dressed beef has everything to recommend it, health, economy and humanity being on its side. It is making slow progress, because of the opposition of the great stock-yard interests, especially in Chicago, where millions of capital, now profitably invested, would be wiped out if the old method of shipping cattle on the hoof should suddenly be abandoned.

government land: Keep in mind that such land had been confiscated from local Indigenous peoples just a decade earlier, yet many among settler communities imagined it as public lands that should be sold off to private interests.

killed one of the cowboys: Although this episode may or may not have occurred as described here, the author is nonetheless referring to the fence-cutting wars and other armed conflict around land use of the period, about which many non-westerners held romantic ideas.

Little Missouri: The Little Missouri River, running through what is today Wyoming, Montana, North and South Dakota.

The *Chicago Tribune* on "Cruelty to Cattle" at stockyards and during transport, with rebuttal by a stockyard promoter (1887)[4]

Articles like this one appeared regularly in newspapers, often reprinted simultaneously across the country. They confronted readers with the many welfare problems created by the growing consumer demand for North American beef. Editors at the *Chicago Tribune* and beyond gauged public interest in such reports and often set up debates wherein critics named problems in the industry, and a response from industry spokesmen or participants followed. Here, the well-known animal advocate **Henry Bergh** discusses his work to urge men at the Chicago stockyards to be more conscious of the needs and experience of cattle who arrived by rail after many days travel in crowded cars without food, water, or rest. Thereafter follows a pro-industry rebuttal from Samuel W. Allerton, banker and stockyard owner, later mayoral candidate in Chicago. The picture he paints of cattle traders as more humane than their critics is an old one, portraying critics as uninformed, self-interested, and too alarmist. One can still see such simplifications today in public debates between animal agriculture advocates and their critics. Then, as now, the arguments revolved around how the welfare and needs of animals came into conflict with the profit motive.

Henry Bergh: Bergh was the founder of the Association for the Society for the Prevention of Cruelty to Animals (ASPCA) in New York and one of the most admired and notorious (depending upon one's point of view at the time) advocates for animals in the nineteenth century. The ASPCA was one of dozens of humane societies, local SPCAs, and other organizations that allowed for human uses of animals for agriculture, labor, entertainment, and scientific research, but sought to make those uses less frightening, painful, and deadly for animals, not least beef cattle. Bergh and the officers of other humane organizations were often granted police powers by local governments to inspect sites of animal use and report violations of anti-cruelty laws.

CRUELTY TO CATTLE

What the Humane Society Has Done at the Stock-Yards

How to Secure Better Treatment of Live Stock While in Transit

The New York Tribune of the 15th inst. containing a long article headed "Brutal Cattle-Shippers," wherein an account was given of the cruelty to animals at the Chicago Stock-Yards and while in transit to New York.

"There is undoubtedly a great deal of cruelty," said Officer Mitchell, of the Illinois Humane Society, to a Tribune reporter yesterday, "but it is mostly on the road—not at the Stock-Yards here. The greatest trouble we have to contend with there now is the separation of calves from their mothers."

"A train comes to the yards, and I find the cows in one car and the calves in another; and when the animals are unloaded the calves are not

---

4   "Cruelty to Cattle," and "Denial of New York 'Tribune' and Bergh's Statements by a Cattle-Shipper," *Chicago Tribune*, 20 May 1882, 11.

allowed to go with their mothers if I don't happen to be around. The cows are **bagged up** and actually suffer because they are not milked, and the calves become weak for lack of food. On the 11th inst. I found eleven calves belonging to a man named Patrick Kelly locked up in a small shed, while their mothers were in another part of the yards. The next day I found three other calves which were suffering for want of food, and arrested James Fitzgerald, the owner, and he was fined $5 by Justice Heath. We can't prevent this separation when it is done before the cattle reach here, but we control the matter at the Stock-Yards, and there is not as much of that work at present as there used to be."

"As to feeding salt to cattle and not giving them water until after they are sold, it is not a 'universal practice' here. There is but one man we know of who does it. His name is Heath. He is a cripple, having lost both legs while trying to steal a ride on a locomotive. He has a good deal of money, but is very close. It is said of him when a man was gathering up his legs at the time of the accident a quarter dropped out of Heath's pocket and a fellow picked it up and was going off with it. Heath saw him and shouted out, 'Hold on, I want that quarter.' He is one of the worst men at the yards—will bring cattle in and feed them on salt, making them very thirsty, and will not water them until after they are sold. If a purchaser comes along and asks him to do it, he makes some excuse. As soon as they are sold, however, and the buyer is gone, he gives them water, and thus adds about forty pounds to the weight of each; and then the animals are weighed. We have cautioned him and have been watching him, and others are also, for the purpose of getting a case on him."

"The prodding out of eyes was stopped by the arrest of James Kelley, who was held in $300 bail for trial, and of Nelse Morris, **spearer**, who was fined $25. It is very seldom that we see a prod even in the yards now. If we do, they are taken from the drovers. Hogs are still marked, but not as of old by splitting the nose and cutting off an ear or the tail. They are scratched now behind the ear—just the skin, so that the mark will be there after the hair is taken off at the slaughter-houses. And the tying of a calf's nose with very fine wire so that it couldn't suck has been stopped. The object of that was to convey the impression to the buyer that the mother had a great quantity of milk—more than the calf needed."

"Regarding the overloading of cars, we watch that closely, and have decreased it to a considerable extent; but there are so many trains out every day that the State Agent and myself cannot see them all. I have so much to do down-town that I can't visit the yards more than two or three times a week. The railroad men are more careful in that respect than they used to be. I remember one instance where fifty out of eighty hogs that came in on a Northwestern car were dead when they reached the yards. Crippled

bagged up: Carrying enlarged udders due to heavy milk production from having recently borne a calf, which become painful if the cow is not nursing or being milked.

spearer: A man employed to usher cattle through chutes and pens in the stock yards by prodding them with a pole, board, or other tool.

cattle are not allowed to remain on the platforms longer than four hours. If they seem to be suffering much we shoot them. Now and then the cattle in the pens go a long time without water, but several arrests have checked that cruelty. Our presence in the yards has a good effect. What we need are some United States agents who can travel on the stock-trains and watch the drovers, and arrest them at any point where they abuse the animals. And the State ought to have another man at the yards, for there is plenty for three to do there."

"I do not doubt," said President Shortall, "that stock is badly treated on the road, but our society cannot prevent that."

"There should be a general law covering the transportation of cattle, and it should be enforced. The cruelty cannot be controlled without good legislation and proper officers, who should be under the direction of the Humane Societies in the States where they work. There is considerable cruelty in the Stock-Yards here, but we are fighting it all the time, and have checked it by arresting the guilty ones and enforcing the laws as far as our limited means will allow. The State Agent, Mr. Doty, is conscientious and earnest, and altogether the best man Gov. Cullom has had here up to this time. If the Governor, however, would appoint men recommended by the society we would be responsible for the performance of their duties, and, having them under our control, we could accomplish more than can be accomplished with a divided authority, and indeed no authority on our part to direct. The remedy for overloading, which is the cause of great cruelty, can only be applied by the railroad companies charging by weight, or so much a head, instead of by the car."

Denial of New York "Tribune" and Bergh's Statements by a Cattle-Shipper.

To the Editor of The Chicago Tribune.

Chicago, May 18.—I read the article copied from the New York *Tribune*, "Cruelties of Cattle Transportation." Feeling sure that the writer had been employed by the **Palace Stock-Car Company** to galvanize the worthless stock into life, it was not worthy of notice, but when I find *The Chicago Tribune* containing editorials to aid in giving life to an exploded company it is time that the facts should be known. In reading this article one would be led to suppose that cruelty to cattle commenced at Chicago and ended in New York, and that all the cattle-shippers out of Chicago were brutes, besides being fools, for it must be clear to any man that the shipper who would be humane and take good care of his cattle would save at least twenty pounds in shrinkage and deliver his cattle in New York without being bruised, and thereby save on a shipment of 1,000 cattle in shrinkage 20,000 pounds of

Palace Stock-Car Company: One of the producers of several types of rail cars designed specifically for shipping livestock, with slatted or otherwise ventilated sides or an open top. Although railroad companies disliked the cars since only cattle could be shipped in them (not other goods nor passengers), many observers believed the cars reduced the suffering of cattle riding inside them over a period of days from a midwestern railhead to the live cattle markets in the Midwest and further east.

beef, as cattle are all sold at live weight in New York, the price being on an average 7½ cents per pound. The humane men would save over the brutes $1,500 on his 1,000 cattle; besides, if cattle are badly bruised the butcher comes back the next week for a reduction, and if he does not get it he will not buy.

As to the gross amount of cattle received in Chicago compared with the gross received in New York, there is a much larger amount of dead and bruised received in Chicago. The real reason is this: from country points to Chicago cattle are all shipped by the carload, so much per car, the shipper putting in all he can. The cattle shipped from the country to Chicago are generally full of feed and not used to the cars, and are very uneasy and restless, while the cattle shipped from Chicago to New York are all carried by the pound, so the shipper has no object to overload his cattle, but, upon the other hand, loads as near the maximum weight as possible. Nine-tenths of the bruises the cattle receive are in the first shipment from the country to Chicago.

There was a syndicate formed last fall to buy up the old Palace Stock-Car stock and see if, through false statements and the Humane Societies, Congress could not be prevailed upon to pass a law that would make cattle-shippers use the palace stock-cars. As the Palace Stock-Car Company have offered them free for the past ten years to shippers, who, after one trial, would not use them again, because it is the nature of a steer, when full of water and corn, to lay down, and when cattle are loaded in a palace stock-car, fed and watered, they will lay down, and when they all lay down they get rolled and bruised and in so bad a condition that they must be washed and scrubbed at the end of their journey before they can be sold, and the butchers come back for damages. The shippers say, "D—n the palace stock-cars," and when tied up or put in a box-stall their sides are bruised to a jelly, and they lay on their knees so long that they become paralyzed at the end of the journey. As for what Bergh says, I have heard his statements before a committee in Congress; they were so far from the truth that the committee concluded that he must be interested in the palace stock-cars, or that he wished to get his thousand spies and detectives appointed for his own aggrandizement.

Knowing personally, as I do, most of the men who handle cattle at the Union Stock-Yards, I do not believe there is one but that would whip at sight the man that would treat cattle as the writer in the New York *Tribune* reports. If there is on the face of the earth a body of better, more humane, or charitable men, I do not know them.

If the history of Bergh was written the world would have a better chance to know him. I think, Mr. Editor, before you write any more editorials in regard to this matter you had better visit the Union Stock-Yards and the slaughter-houses, and ask yourself Where do I get the best beef, in New York or Chicago?

Chinook: A warm wind, formally known as a föhn wind, that blows on the downwind, eastern side of the Rocky Mountains and brings unseasonably warm temperatures in winter that last for a few days or less.

DOCUMENT 19:

The "cowboy artist" Charles M. Russell's *Waiting for a Chinook* (1886)[5]

Charles M. Russell, "the cowboy artist," became one of the most famous and successful illustrators to depict the "Old West," both as he experienced it as a cowboy and as the public wished to imagine it. This famous and much-reproduced work depicts an emaciated Montana cow surrounded by wolves. Wild canines like coyotes and wolves multiplied briefly in the 1880s by preying upon the many weakened cattle on over-stocked ranges. The image originated in a letter Russell sent to his employer while working as a cowboy managing a herd of 5,000 head during the Big Die-Up (1886–87). As Russell told the story, when his employers asked him about their stock, he replied simply with a drawing of a starving cow and prowling wolves that later served as the model for this painting.

---

5   Amon Carter Museum, Fort Worth, Texas.

DOCUMENT 20:

Edward Abbott recounts winter range work during the Big Die-Up: *We Pointed Them North: Recollections of a Cowpuncher* (1939)[6]

Edward Charles Abbott came to the United States from England as a child with his family. Later known as "Teddy Blue," in his late twenties he worked as a cowboy during the winter of the Big Die-Up. In 1939 the journalist Helena Huntington Smith facilitated the publication of Abbott's memories from those years, an era when many North Americans and Europeans were curious and decidedly nostalgic about the "free grass" era of extensive ranching in the West.

e

I always got along with [Pike Landusky] all right. He was a good partner, because he had been on the frontier a long time and knew how to take advantage of everything. He used to carry pine splinters soaked in coal oil for starting fires—you'd touch a match to them, and they would flare right up. Another trick he taught me was how to ward off snow blindness, though I didn't pay attention to him in time. There was snow on the ground from one end of that winter to the other and the glare was terrible. Pike cut out the black lining out of his coat and made a mask out of it. He said: "Christ Jesus! When you get her, you'll know her!" And I got her, the very next year. I went snow-blind and had to lie in bed for five days with salt poultices over my eyes, not able to sleep or eat or think from the pain.

Another thing he told me was: "You've got to dress so if you break your leg and have to lay out on the prairie you won't freeze to death." So here were the clothes I wore. I wore two pairs of wool socks, a pair of moccasins, a pair of Dutch socks that came up to the knees, a pair of government overshoes, two suits of heavy underwear, pants, overalls, chaps, and a big heavy shirt. I got a pair of woman's stockings and cut the feet out and made sleeves. I wore wool gloves, and great big heavy mittens, a blanket-lined **sourdough overcoat**, and a great big sealskin cap.

That way I kept warm enough. But not any too warm. For that was the celebrated winter of '86–'87 that broke the back of the range cattle business. In Wyoming and Montana the settlers had run all the big outfits off the plains, so they had moved up close to the mountains, causing the range to be overstocked. Then, too, the summer had been very dry, so what grass we had was eaten off before the first snow fell. In November we had several

sourdough overcoat: A long canvas waterproof canvas coat lined with blankets.

6   Norman: U of Oklahoma P, 1955, 174–77.

snowstorms, and I saw the first white owls I have ever seen. The Indians said they were a bad sign, heavy snow coming, very cold, and they sure hit it right.

We had two weeks of nice weather just before Christmas. But on Christmas Eve it started to storm and never really let up for sixty days. It got colder and colder. I have a cutting from the post paper at **Fort Keogh** that reads that on January 14 it was sixty below zero at that place and snow two feet deep. The latter part of January it started a chinook—just enough to melt the snow on top. But it turned cold, and on February 3 and 4 the worst blizzard I ever saw set in. The snow crusted and it was hell without the heat.

The cattle stood it fairly well for thirty days. When the chinook started in January, I wrote to **Granville Stuart**, telling him I thought the loss would not be over 10 per cent. In ten days I know it was 75 per cent. The cattle drifted down on all the rivers, and untold thousands went down the air holes. On the Missouri [River] we lost I don't know how many that way. They would walk out on the ice, and the ones behind would push the front ones in. The cowpunchers worked like slaves to move them back in the hills, but as all the outfits cut their forces down every winter, they were shorthanded. No one knows how they worked but themselves. They saved thousands of cattle. Think of riding all day in a blinding snowstorm, the temperature fifty and sixty below zero, and no dinner. You'd get one bunch of cattle up the hill and another one would be coming down behind you, and it was all so slow, plunging after them through the deep snow that way; you'd have to fight every step in the road. The horses' feet were cut and bleeding from the heavy crust, and the cattle had the hair and hide wore off their legs to the knees and hocks. It was surely hell to see big four-year-old steers just able to stagger along. It was the same all over Wyoming, Montana, and Colorado, western Nebraska and western Kansas.

Pike had a cabin right close to the Rockies where he lived with his wife and family. Mrs. Pike was a Frenchwoman from Louisiana, and as far as I know she was the only white woman in that country, because north of the river was all Blackfoot reservation at that time. She and five children had left her husband and married Pike in Maiden, Montana, a few years back, and she had two children by Pike. He was a good provider and very good to the whole family while I was there. She was a good housekeeper and a real nice little woman when she wasn't stirred up about something, and the only human being I ever met who was a match for Pike.

I lived with him that winter and [Stuart's] company paid him for my keep, but we was riding most of the time. I rode Grant, Mr. Stuart's old war horse, and one of the best horses I ever had my saddle on. December 24, we left our camp at the foot of the mountains and started home to Pike's for Christmas. I remember it was a beautiful day, clear and sunny, as we rode along Pike kept showing me the different landmarks. At sundown

Fort Keogh: The United States Army post near the modern town of Miles City in southeastern Montana.

Granville Stuart: Montana gold prospector, settler, political figure, and 1880s cattleman who employed Abbott as a cowboy. Stuart was known to have hired men to pursue and, in some cases, kill landless people squatting on rangelands, as well as small-scale cattle raisers whom wealthy stock-growers perceived as "rustlers." Stuart is believed to have overseen the killing of about 20 men either through gun fights or lynching. Abbott eventually married Granville Stuart's daughter, Mary Stuart.

we camped close to Tuckers' cabin at the north end of the Little Rockies, expecting to be home in time for Christmas dinner the next day. But after dark it began to snow.

We made our beds down and Pike got in, but I sat by the campfire smoking and watching the snowflakes fall around me. That fall while we was shipping beef on the Northern Pacific I heard a girl singing a song at a dance hall in Junction; all I could remember was the tune and a line or two, that went: "Fair, fair with golden hair, Sang a fond mother while weeping." So I kept singing that over and over, till all at once Pike raised his elbow and roared out: "Christ Jesus! Can't you let her weep?" Then I taken off my overshoes and went to bed.

Next day the storm was so bad we didn't try to make it home, but rode over to John Healy's ranch on Lodge Pole because it was nearer. We found three men there, so we put our horses in by a haystack and all cooked a Christmas dinner of deer meat and **son-of-a-gun-in-a-sack (plum duff)**. We stayed there two days, but the storm kept getting worse, so we pulled out for home December 27. Healy's cabin was in a sheltered place, but when we got over the hill the wind and snow hit us so hard we could not see fifty feet ahead or hardly breathe. We tried to make Tucker's cabin again but missed it. That night we rode into a narrow canyon where we were out of the wind, but we got off our horses in snow up to our waist. We built a fire and made coffee, and held our meat on sticks until it thawed out, and ate it hot and raw. We never took the bridles off the horses, because there was nothing for them to eat.

Next morning we lit out for home and it was a fight for life. We had to ride sideways to the wind, and horses hate that. The wind blew the breath right out of our bodies and the snow cut like a knife. We got home nearly all in. We got off our horses and started to unpack, but the ropes were froze and our fingers so numb we could hardly untie them; when Mrs. Landusky run out of the house and begun giving us hell. She said: Where was we; and why didn't we come home; and this was a fine Christmas for her, with **Indians all around** and her alone here with all these children; and she had cooked us a big dinner, and so on and so forth. Pike never said a word at first, while she kept on calling us everything she could lay her tongue to because we didn't come home to Christmas dinner, when we like to have froze to death in that awful blizzard and it was a wonder we ever got there. And finally he turned to me and he says: "Christ Jesus! She was sure in the lead when tongues was give out."

And I laughed till I fell over in the snow.

son-of-a-gun-in-a-sack (plum duff): A kind of spiced plum pudding containing dried berries or fruit, sometimes known as "cowboy pudding."

Indians all around: On remote ranches and homesteads, settlers often worried they were exposed to any ill-intentioned person traveling through the area, including local Indigenous men, although such opportunistic attacks were not common.

DOCUMENT 21:

Image group: Consumers and beef

A. Swift & Company Packers, Union Stockyards, Chicago, trade card (1893)[7]

Businesses like Swift & Company Packers sold themselves as trusted mediators between livestock producers and shoppers by way of marketing that emphasized their products' supposed purity and wholesomeness. This folding trade card was given away at Swift's refrigeration technology display at the 1893 World's Columbian Exposition, where meat was presented in a stylized glass rail car to give consumers some of idea of how Swift products traveled. The interior of the card featured a graphic of an aerial view of Swift & Company's packing plants in Chicago.

7   Chromolithographed trade card (7 x 5 7/8 in), American Antiquarian Society.

***B. Livestock pens of "The great Union Stock Yards, the greatest Live Stock
Market in the World, Chicago" (1903)[8]***

This image is one half of a stereograph card reproducing two nearly identical
photographs taken at Chicago's enormous Union Stock Yards. Stereo cards
were a consumer novelty of the turn of the century. One placed the card
in a viewer then spied it through special glasses such that each eye saw
a slightly differently angled image, producing the appearance of a three-
dimensional view. People purchased and viewed all sorts of images as stereo
cards, including scenes like this that spoke to public interest in the growing
industries of the period. Note in the background of the image the vertical
ramp designed for driving live animals under their own power into the
slaughterhouse.

8   Library of Congress.

C. Corrals and slaughterhouse at the Crow Agency Reservation, Montana (1905)[9]

Indian reservations were often situated on unproductive lands where subsistence was nearly impossible. In places, instead of contracting for beef deliveries at inflated prices, government reservation agents and residents encouraged on-site beef production. Here Apsáalooke Crow Agency Reservation residents wait on a slaughter day for butchered meat from the local herd to be released from the barn-shaped slaughterhouse in the background of the image.

---

9   Montana Historical Society, Montana Memory Project.

D. D.D. Collins Meat Counter, Washington, DC (late 1910s)[10]

Before the advent of the supermarket, city- and town-dwelling shoppers purchased meat from butcher shops and market counters where one could often inspect whole carcasses and speak to a butcher to verify the health of the animal before agreeing to make a purchase. Here shoppers crowd a meat counter in Washington, DC. Note the ubiquity of hams in the image; pork would continue to be the most-consumed meat in the US until after World War II when beef and, later, chicken took prominence.

---

10   Library of Congress.

E. "New! Self-Serve Meats Make Shopping Quicker, Easier," DuPont Cellophane advertisement (1949)[11]

Many consumers ate only modest amounts of meat during the Depression and World War II years. Then, in the 1950s beef consumption would begin to rise sharply and steaks became a convenient, everyday luxury. Beef was often marketed to women who tended to do family grocery shopping, although steak-eating and outdoor barbequing were perceived and promoted as masculine hobbies. Many hundreds of companies and industries had a stake in the growing demand for beef and prospered from it, including industrial chemical companies like DuPont that made inexpensive plastic wrap that allowed for more sanitary display of pre-cut meat in stores.

11   dpads_1803-00325, Series 1, Box 43, Folder 27, E.I. du Pont de Nemours & Company Advertising Department records (Accession 1803), Manuscripts and Archives Department, Hagley Museum and Library, Wilmington, DE 19807.

DISCUSSION QUESTIONS/WRITING PROMPTS

1. What regions, people, animals, and time periods are addressed by the primary sources here?

2. Why might people, and which people, around the continent have wanted to read and learn about the cattle trade even if they were not personally invested or working in the business? What did they learn from these books about cowboying and the cattle trade?

3. Is it apparent from the historical sources here what consumers wanted to eat and when or why they ate beef? To what degree can we detect in these sources the process by which most consumers became alienated from the animals who provided their food?

4. What do we learn from these sources about how the food system in the United States developed once settlers had gained firm political control in the West?

PART 4

Twentieth-Century Ranch Life, Imagined and Real

DOCUMENT 22:

"Old Smith County Song," *Smith County Pioneer* (1914)[1]

Early settlers, both cowboys and homesteaders, created folk songs, stories, and humor that explored the hope that the West would be a land of abundance and independence for common people. In the twentieth century, white Americans interested in the early settlement period and cowboy lore talked about a poem by Brewster Higley (1823–1911), known as "My Western Home," among other names. Although Higley wrote the piece while homesteading in a cabin in rural Kansas, in the interwar years the poem and the song derived from it were reinterpreted as a cowboy song entitled "Home on the Range"— imagine a guitar-playing cowboy in fancy Western dress singing to his horse. Higley's original poem is at the root of a whole genre of cowboy poetry and music that is still flourishing today, notably at the yearly National Cowboy Poetry Gathering at Elko, Nevada.

ev

Old Smith County Song

A few days ago there appeared in the Kansas City Star, a poem furnished by Elsie Perkins, of Kirwin, Kansas, entitled "Oh, Give Me a Home Where the Buffalo Roam," which she learned in 1874, but did not know the author. The writer well remembers when this song first came out and was well and intimately acquainted with the author. It was written by Dr. B. Higley, who was an early settler in Smith county, having homesteaded in section 1, Pleasant township, the land being now owned by Mrs. L.C. Ahlborn. The poem was published in The Pioneer in the fall of 1873 and soon attained popularity among the younger people of that time; a tune was arranged for it and no doubt it was sung at every gathering in those early days. Its

---

1   W.H. Nelson, "Old Smith County Song," *Smith County Pioneer* (Smith Center, Kansas), 19 February 1914.

cheering words helped to dispel the gloom of the "**Grasshopper Days**" and the writer can remember humming the fascinating words while travelling over the desolate prairies and at the same time wishing there was some way of getting back to the pleasant Pennsylvania home we had so recently left, but the fates were all against us and we are glad of it now.

Dr. Brewster Higley was an eccentric character, rough and uncouth in appearance, but with a heart filled with poetry and compassion for suffering humanity. As a doctor, and there were few of this profession in those early days, no night was too dark or trail too dim to deter him from answering a demand for service and there are no doubt many yet living in Smith County who owe a debt of never ending gratitude for his timely medical attention. He left this country sometime in the early eighties, going we think to Arkansas, well along in years at that time. After a lapse of more than forty years we again offer to the readers of The Pioneer the good, old time song it first published in 1873.—W.H. Nelson

Oh, Give Me a Home Where the Buffalo Roam

Oh, give me a home where the buffalo roam,
　Where the deer and antelope play,
Where never is heard a discouraging word
　And the sky is not clouded all day.

　　Chorus—
A home, a home where the deer and antelope play,
　Where never is heard a discouraging word
And the sky is not clouded all day.

Oh, give me the gale of the **Solomon vale**,
　Where light streams with buoyancy flow,
On the banks of the **Beaver**, where seldom if ever,
　Any poisonous herbage doth grow.

　　Chorus—

Oh, give me the land where the bright diamond sand
　Throws light from its glittering stream,
Where glideth along the graceful white swan
　Like a maid in her heavenly dream

　　Chorus—

I love these wild flowers in this bright land of ours,
    I love, too, the curlew's wild scream,
The bluffs of white rocks and antelope flocks
    That graze on our hillsides so green.

        Chorus—

How often at night, when the heavens are bright
    By the light of the glittering stars,
Have I stood there amazed and asked as I gazed
    If their beauty exceeds this of ours.

        Chorus—

The air is so pure the breezes so light,
    The zephyrs so balmy at night,
I would not exchange my home here to range
    Forever in asure so bright.

        Chorus—

DOCUMENT 23:

Image group: Western style and modern consumerism (1900–60)

A. *"Typical Cowboys waiting their turn at the Bucking Contest" postcard (ca. 1900)*[2]

Around the turn of the twentieth century, when working cowboys competed in rodeos—then known as cowboy tournaments—they often wore their best work clothes embellished by a special sombrero or cowboy hat, colorful neckerchiefs, silver trimmed belts and pistol holsters, silver spurs, sheepskin chaps, or perhaps a new pair of boots.

5085. Typical Cowboys waiting their turn at Bucking Contest.

---

2   H.H. Tamman Co. postcard, Dickenson Research Center of the National Cowboy and Western Heritage Museum.

B. "Fancy Cowboy Bit and Spur Outfit" advertisement, The Billboard
(2 October 1915)

Professional entertainers, some of whom had been working cowboys or had grown up on ranches, appropriated cowboy styles. One could find fancy cowboy accessories advertised in entertainment industry trade journals, like *The Billboard*, which served people working in the tent show trade, including Wild West shows and early community rodeos, on vaudeville stages and in the burgeoning film industry.

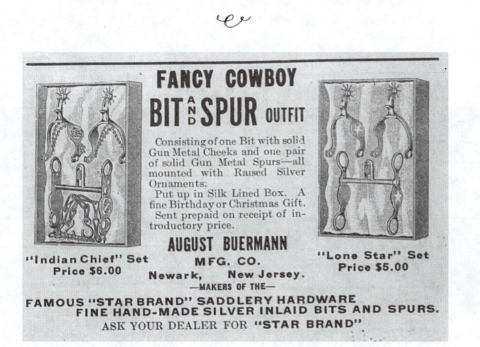

C. "Some Chickens?" postcard featuring female rodeo performers (1921)[3]

Before World War II, women competed in all rodeo events, including bull and bronc riding, and appeared in Wild West shows, which featured non-competitive demonstrations of rodeo contests. Many of these women became nationally famous. Images of them in magazines and newspapers helped popularize western attire, including embroidered shirts, cowboy boots, and the then-fashionable "ten gallon" cowboy hat. This postcard pictured some of the most famous female rodeo and Wild West show performers of the era, satirically referred to as "chickens" (i.e., chicks): Bea Kirnan, Prairie Rose, Mable Strickland, Princis Mohawk, Ruth Roach, Kittie Canutt, and Prairie Lillie Allan.

---

3   Doubleday Co. postcard, Ralph Russell, photographer, Denver Public Library.

D. Tom Mix and Tony "The Wonder Horse" theatrical release film poster for* The Drifter *(1929)

Beginning in the 1910s, Hollywood produced hundreds of cowboy movies and audiences loved them, driving a craze for western-style clothes and toys for kids. Tom Mix and his trained horses, Tony and Tony, Jr., made dozens of such films and Mix pioneered the genre as the first big cowboy star. Tony, Mix's first trained horse, was as famous as Mix himself and amazed film directors by performing complicated series of movements and choreography for the camera without Mix or anyone in the shot to cue or lead him.

Hollywood's early cowboy movies drew on popular ideas about cowboys as gun-toting men of adventure, left over from nineteenth-century dime novels, but reimagined the lone cowboy figure and his loyal horse as community guardians. Mix's films were precursors to mid-century television and film Westerns in which actors like John Wayne and characters like the Lone Ranger rescued working-class white settlers—homesteaders, widows, small-time ranchers, schoolteachers—from criminals, fraudsters, railway agents, or corrupt cattlemen. Ignoring the trials of actual working cowboys, Hollywood cowboys did little actual work, instead persuading many Americans that the West was a meritocracy after all.

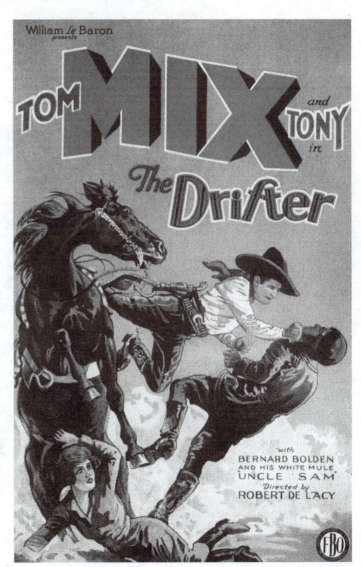

E. Levi's advertisement, "Fit for Action," Rodeo Sports News (1957)[4]

Hat, boot, and other Western apparel manufacturers, especially denim brands like Lee, Levi's, and Wrangler, advertised to local consumers and sponsored rodeo events across the West. Their clothes were central to Western style because practical and durable. In the first half of the twentieth century, many ranch people wore a cowboy hat, boots, jeans, and long-sleeved collared shirt while at work, although in the later part of the century T-shirts and baseball caps would become common workwear on ranches. *Rodeo Sports News*, founded in 1951 by the Professional Rodeo Cowboys Association, was the main periodical documenting the world of elite (white men's) rodeo competitions.

---

4   *Rodeo Sports News*, 15 May 1957, National Cowboy and Western Heritage Museum, Oklahoma City, OK.

F. Rodeo day photographs by Russell Lee and Marion Post Walcott (1939–41)[5]

Many rural westerners saved newer, more expensive, and more ornate Western-styled clothes for special events like rodeo day. For rural westerners, town-dwellers, and tourists alike, rodeo day was an opportunity for conscious self-fashioning through Western-styled clothing, which people could find at the ubiquitous Western outfitter shops. Rodeos were popular with people from all backgrounds, but were often monopolized by settlers—as sponsors and producers, as competitors, and with respect to prize money. Indigenous and Hispanic people might find themselves excluded in particular towns if settlers refused to serve them at restaurants, bars, and hotels, or by corrupt judging in competition (rodeo judges could be notoriously unskilled or partisan). Still, whether as organizer, competitor, or spectator, many westerners saw rodeo day as an opportunity to come together and demonstrate an appreciation for horsemanship and rural labor.

Russell Lee was one of a number of photographers hired by the federal government to document American life during the Great Depression and World War II. Lee did so as an employee of the Farm Security Administration, which was a federal agency mandated to study rural poverty. Among the many places and events Lee captured with his camera are small-town rodeos visited mostly by locals, perhaps a few tourists, and the cowboys who came in to compete. The Bean Day Rodeo, visited by Lee in September 1939, took place in Wagon Mound, New Mexico and was representative of hundreds of locally organized community rodeos that replaced the Wild · West shows at the turn of the century. Competitors were generally settlers, although the audience included members of the Hispanic community long resident in that part of the continent. In March 1940, Lee also photographed the San Angelo Fat Stock Show and Rodeo, which was a larger event that included an agricultural fair. The captions below are drawn from the Library of Congress records for these photographs.

ev

---

5   Library of Congress.

"Spectators at Bean Day Rodeo, Wagon Mound, New Mexico."

Audience, competitors, and horses, Bean Day Rodeo.

Spectators eating lunch.

"Show window in department store in San Angelo, Texas, during the San Angelo Fat Stock Show.
Townspeople adopt rodeo and ranchmen styles during the stock show."

"Youngster in Cowboy Costume watching the rodeo at the San Angelo Fat Stock Show."

"Girl Rodeo Performer."

"Cowboys in the hotel lobby during the San Angelo Fat Stock Show," possibly after having competed earlier in the day.

Marion Post Wolcott was another government photographer who worked for the Farm Security Administration. In September 1941, she captured scenes from the Apsáalooke Crow Agency Fair and Rodeo at the Crow Agency Reservation in Big Horn County, Montana. Founded in 1904 and still a major yearly event in central Montana, the fair includes world-famous Indigenous dance performances and competitions, as well as a rodeo.

"Indians watching the Crow fair at Crow Agency."

"Indians and spectators at annual fair, Crow Agency."

"Dudes from Quarter Circle U Ranch at Crow Fair," with Indigenous spectators in background.

Dudes: Non-ranching people, in this case, tourists visiting a local dude ranch.

Ranching entrepreneur Harold L. Oppenheimer explains the business of cattle: *Cowboy Economics: Rural Land as an Investment* (1966)[6]

By mid-century, many ranchers and their adult sons (and some daughters) earned degrees in agricultural economics or agricultural science from American land-grant universities to bolster their practical knowledge of ranch work. By contrast, Harold L. Oppenheimer's *Cowboy Economics* was a book, not for those ranch kids at university, but for potential investors with no direct experience in the business. Oppenheimer was chairman of a company offering management services to absentee ranch investors. As a staunch opponent of government efforts to control production (of cattle and feed crops in order to keep prices high and protect small producers), Oppenheimer explains the cattle business to wealthy outsiders. His book was published in a period of great volatility and capital accumulation in the industry by big players who would push out many smaller operations.

e

We had better review terms so that we are sure that we are talking about the same thing. For example, the term "yearling" might mean three different animals, depending on whether you are a Californian, a Missourian, or a Texan. A large grass rancher, a small corn farmer, and a commercial feed-lot operator are not thinking of the same animal when you use the term. The animal might be 9 months, 12 months, or 20 months old. It might weigh 400 pounds, 600 pounds, or 900 pounds.

For the purpose of this chapter and with the certainty of boring the majority of my readers, it will be assumed that your knowledge of the cattle industry is limited to ordering steak at your favorite restaurant and that your knowledge of agriculture is limited to a vague feeling that it is better to get dandelions out of your front lawn *before* they go to seed....

A. The Life Cycle of a Cow

1. On a small midwestern farm with lush grass and feed conditions, one bull could service 35 to 40 cows in a season; on an arid, rocky, rough open range, one bull might be required for every 15 cows.

2. The period of gestation of a cow is slightly over nine months.

---

6   Danville, IL: Interstate Publishers, 1966.

3. A calf is normally weaned at seven months but can be given supplementary feed from about two months of age, with an earlier weaning period. "Creep feeding" refers to feeding calves grain while they are nursing by means of some mechanical device that protects the feed from the cows.

4. To be eligible for registration in the Hereford Association, the calf must be out of a cow that was not under 15 months old when bred and must be sired by a bull not under 12 months old at the time of breeding. There is a considerable controversy on the advantages and disadvantages of breeding at this age or a year later. This will be discussed fully in a subsequent chapter.

5. There is some variation around the country, but the following terminology will be used in this book. A young animal is called a "calf" for the first year, after which it is called a "yearling." A female is a "heifer calf"; a male is a "bull calf" until it is castrated, after which it is called a "steer calf." Animals slightly over a year old are called "long yearlings"; slightly under a year, "short yearlings." Up to two years a female is called a "heifer." After she has had a calf, she is called a "first calf heifer." After the first calf is weaned, she is a full-fledged "cow."

6. The following weight schedules, plus or minus 20%, are normal for animals in good, healthy condition but not fattened for market: new born calf, 90 pounds; weaned six-month calf, 400 pounds; yearling, 650 pounds; eighteen-month heifer, 800 pounds; two-year-old cow, 950 pounds; three-year-old cow, 1,050 pounds. In the case of animals fattened for the show ring to create a better appearance, you can add 300 pounds to the preceding figures for all animals over eight months of age. This additional weight in no way improves the cattle's breeding qualities. In fact, you have to go to a lot of trouble and take the animals off feed slowly to reduce this weight before you put them back in the breeding herd.

7. Cows normally come in heat about every 21 days for a period of about 12 to 18 hours. Successful breeding must take place during that short period of time. Artificial insemination is common for dairy animals but rare for beef herds. "Hand breeding" is used for registered show animals but practically never for grade breeding herds. ("Hand breeding" refers to the practice of keeping the bulls penned separately and bringing individual cows that are in heat to be bred under close supervision.)

8. "Calf crop percentage" refers to the number of calves successfully weaned from a given number of cows. This is the pay-off on a cattle breeding operation and is the best criterion for judging the efficiency of the operation. The national average runs around 70%. A good operation would hit 80%. An outstanding operation would reach 90%. A small herd on a small farm can normally do 10% better than an open range operation.

9. The government formerly gave a breeding cow an "8-year useful life" for tax depreciation purposes. The **1962 "Guidelines"** reduced this to 7. Both

1962 "Guidelines": A July 1962 policy from the US Treasury Department that put forward new procedures for evaluating the "capital depreciation" of individual cattle used for breeding. Stockgrowers and others engaged in commercial agriculture used such Internal Revenue Service rules to file business taxes in ways that minimized tax obligations.

are based on averages and take into consideration the diseased or barren animal that might have to be culled at 4 or 5. Actually, once an animal has hit the age of 7, producing a good calf every year and milking it properly, she might very well go on until 10 or 11.

10. Generally at the age of 11, the teeth of cattle begin to go bad. This could happen earlier in sandy country. Under small farm conditions where grain and silage are fed, a valuable registered cow could still be kept for a number of years. As in humans, there is a big individual variation.

11. Cows are usually "aged" or "mouthed" by inspecting the condition of the lower incisors (front teeth). Differing from a horse, a cow does not have upper incisors but nips grass by having the lower incisors press against the upper bony, hard pan. The lower incisors develop and wear out in the pattern shown by Dr. M.E. Ensminger's "Handy Guide for Determining the Age of Cattle by the Teeth." When the incisors are gone, the animals get a "square jaw" appearance. They are also referred to as "gummers."

This does not mean that the molars are not functioning but only that the cattle cannot graze so efficiently and will have to get supplementary feed if they are going to maintain their weight and milk production.

12. A "wet cow" is one that is nursing a calf or has just had her calf weaned and is still in milk. A "dry cow" is one that is not in milk. Generally in the beef industry a "dry" refers to one that was never bred or to a cow that lost the calf early in pregnancy. At the end of the summer, "drys" will outweigh "wets" that have been "pulled down" by big calves by as much as 200 pounds.

13. A "springer" is a cow that is about to calve. A "free martin" is a cow with a genetic malformation in which the reproductive organs never develop. That cow can never breed.

14. Twins occur about once in 200 births. Sometimes the mother has enough milk for both and sometimes not. Sometimes she might abandon one.

15. Dairy breeds, such as Holstein, Jersey, and Guernsey, as opposed to the beef breeds of Hereford, Angus, and Shorthorn, have sufficient milk to raise two or three calves.

16. "Bumming" is the term used when a calf learns to steal milk from other cows when its own mother does not give enough milk or has died. Most cows will kick away any calf that tries to nurse other than her own. Dairy cows are more amenable to accepting "bums" than are beef cows.

F. A Hypothetical 1,000-Head Ranch Pro Forma

Financial Statement

Assets		Liabilities	
10,000 acres @ $60	$600,000	Ranch mortgage @ 6%	$300,000
1,000 cows @ $240	240,000	Cattle mortgages @ 6%	150,000
50 bulls @ $600	30,000	Accounts payable	7,000
100 replacement yearling heifers @ $170	17,000	Value of equity	500,000
Hay and feeding equipment	10,000		
Trucks and cars	10,000		
Feed on hand	30,000		
Miscellaneous	20,000		
	$957,000		$957,000

Annual Income Statement

	Income	Expenses
800 calves @ $120	$ 96,000	
100 miscellaneous culls @ $140	14,000	
Miscellaneous income	2,000	
Protein and grain purchases (ranch produces own hay)		$10,000
Supplementary pasture leases		3,000
Real Estate taxes		4,000
Personal property taxes		2,000
2 men @ $4,000/year		8,000
Manager @ $8,000/year		8,000
Special part-time labor (hay crews)		3,000
Depreciation on improvements and equipment (none on cattle because of **replacement program**)		15,000
Gasoline, supplies, repairs		10,000
Interest on ranch mortgage		18,000
Interest on cattle mortgage		9,000
Miscellaneous		7,000
Totals	$112,000	$97,000
Net return or profit on equity of 3%		$15,000

Cash flow before depreciation and mortgage amortization: $30,000

replacement program: A cattle replacement program is a plan to replace expended cows with new heifers, either by breeding them on site or purchasing them from a breeder. Ideally, ranchers chose whichever option was least expensive, depending upon the costs of future feed, the size of their herd versus land and feed on hand, and veterinary costs for breeding procedures.

Ranching as a Way to Make Money

If one made a survey of the wealthy ranchers in the United States, one would find that nearly every one of them got where he is by one or a combination of the following methods:

1. Had a great-grandfather who bought the land for 10 cents an acre before the Civil War.

2. Discovered oil or uranium on the land.

3. Owned land adjacent to the suburban growth of Dallas or Omaha ten years before the expansion occurred.

4. Bought the property when it was 100 miles from the nearest railroad or highway and had one of the new super-highways go right through the middle of it, not only greatly increasing its value, but giving a big condemnation award at the same time.

5. Bought large herds on a 10% down payment on a distressed market and then had cattle prices double over the next year. There is the old saying, "On a rising market, everybody is a genius."

6. Had a family of ten children, all of whom were sons and all of whom worked for room and board until such time as they married. If your wife can time her pregnancies properly, this procedure guarantees a free labor supply for about 30 years and gives you a tremendous head start on your neighbors.

Corollaries of the particularly fortunate states of affairs just listed involve ranchers who *think* they are making money hand over fist because of peculiarities in their methods of accounting. Some of the important things a rancher should take in to consideration include the following:

1. He should not disregard the "rents" as an element of his cost because he either bought the land cheap many years ago or inherited it from his great-grandfather, as mentioned before. If he considers as a fair operating cost what he could rent his land for, this changes his entire picture. The picture becomes even more unfavorable if he considers what he could sell his land for, figures this potential acquisition of capital as being worth 5% interest, and then charges this figure of potential but unrealized income as an operation cost to the ranch.

2. Even though he is getting the use of his son's labor for nothing, he should consider that it is worth at least $1 per hour and that any realistic appraisal of the operation should include this as a legitimate cost whether or not he paid it.

3. On the assumption that the owner and operator himself is a reasonably competent, intelligent executive and his wife, who is doing the bookkeeping, is also reasonably intelligent, their joint services as "top management" are certainly worth $10,000 per year. Even though this also is not paid out in

cash, it should be considered a legitimate operating cost in any realistic appraisal of the operation of the ranch.

4. Any income being derived from oil or mineral leases certainly should not be grouped with the agricultural income and should be considered as earnings from an entirely separate business.

5. The same line of thinking should also be applied to the sale of timber or to the sale of residential or commercial acreage along the highways, even if these sales are made repeatedly every year. These are sales of capital assets having nothing to do with the cattle operation.

DOCUMENT 25:

Judy Blunt remembers the gender politics of mid-century family ranching businesses: *Breaking Clean* (2002)[7]

Judy Blunt was born in 1954 to a ranching family in eastern Montana, near the tiny community of Malta. In her memoir, she writes of her childhood and life as a young married woman absorbed into an incorporated family ranch business headed by her husband John's father, Frank, and stepmother, Rose. For years living and working there she struggled with depression. In time, she came to question and ultimately abandon her difficult, isolated, and at times dangerous life, as well as the ethos underlying it—"the choice we made to live where we lived, the quarrel we took up with the land and passed along" to the children.[8]

Judy Blunt's memoir documents her life in an eastern Montana ranching family in the 1960s, 1970s, and 1980s. Along with her personal struggles as a woman and mother in a place and time rooted in male authority and land ownership, Blunt recounts how her family persevered in the face of blizzards, rainstorms, drought, brushfires, mud that made roads impassable, and limited access to veterinarians and doctors. Eventually she came to question her role in this tradition, and she gave up her marriage and ranch life to live in Missoula. This was not a typical response, however. Most ranching women lived their whole lives working with cattle and raising their families and, despite the hardships and inequalities they experienced, were grateful for the lives they led. (See Document 38 in Part 6 for more.)

❧

Memories of my grandfather's death were tied to another small death, the day I discovered that as a girl, I would never own my childhood ranch. In retrospect, it seemed I should have always known this, but I didn't. Grandpa Blunt's funeral was held in the same small nondenominational church where I planned to be married. The building dated back to the first years of the town's history, a steepled square with a foyer, dressed in spotless white clapboard except for the wide double doors in the front, and aptly named the Little White Church. Capable of seating perhaps fifty people in its double row of pews, the church had been too small to hold the county full of friends and neighbors who attended Grandpa's funeral. Mourners spilled into the adjoining funeral hall to listen to the service via loudspeaker. I remember a thick damp in the hall, the muggy crush of bodies, the extra

---

7   New York: Vintage, 2002, 210–11, 218–20.

8   Blunt, *Breaking Clean*, 272–73.

folding chairs set up between the rows. Uncle Junior, the eldest son who had worked Grandpa's ranch since returning from the Korean War—I remember him crying. And I remember Aunt Marie scolding a pack of us same-sized cousins for being too noisy at the potluck that followed. But more clearly than all that, more clearly than the sunken, icy face of my grandfather in its unlikely nest of tucked satin, I remember the talk my parents had with us children a few weeks later. We were lined up on the smooth red-vinyl benches built into the walls on two sides of our kitchen table. After the death of her husband, Grandma Pansy had elected to sell the ranch to the boys, my dad and Junior. In a family of seven remaining children, this decision left the five sisters high and dry, and apparently some of them had complained and threatened to challenge her. Dad had stubbed the table with one thick finger, emphasizing there would be no such fight when it came our turn to bury him. In our family the sons would follow the father; Kenny, the elder, would have first refusal. We girls would be left with something of value, but we should know at the outset that we would never inherit the land....

The stove had been warm to the touch, the air still perfumed with garlic, when I moved to the Loving U Ranch the first week in June. John's step-mother, Rose, and his father, Frank, had surprised us the week we married with their decision to turn over the main ranch buildings to us, while they set up housekeeping ten miles from headquarters. It was time, Frank reasoned, for them to get away from the grind of chores and **hired men**. A newer ranch house, vacant since they acquired more land in 1970, took little preparation to ready for occupation, and they had moved the bulk of their belongings over while John and I were on our honeymoon. The main ranch house, which John and I took over, stood at the base of one steep hill facing south to another, with the bunkhouse, out-buildings and corrals taking up the flat ground at the bottom of the pocket. Driving down the lane toward our ranch felt like aiming at the ends of the earth—nothing but hardpan and the suggestion of pines in the distance—when suddenly you popped over a steep hill and the ranch buildings spread out below, cradled in a bend of Fourchette Creek.

Recently removed from this hub of activity, Rose fought the boredom of her new, quiet life by gradually relinquishing her house, her kitchen and her role in bits and pieces. Within days of our return, I would discover that in all these thousands of acres, there existed one oasis, one room that my in-laws and the hired men could not enter with a perfunctory rap, and that was our bedroom. Even Rose drew the line at that threshold.

I changed out of my riding clothes, then sat on the edge of the unmade bed, groping in the dusky light for a cleaner pair of jeans. One low east window faced the bunkhouse, the other looked out to the road, right where

hired men: Men hired to do ranch work on a permanent or seasonal basis to supplement the labor of ranch owners, if living on site, or to run a ranch entirely for operations with absentee proprietor or corporate owners. Hired hands were routinely served meals and provided with temporary housing to facilitate their work on remote properties.

vehicles popped over the hill on their way to the barnyard. I raised the bedroom shades only when I was cleaning the room, changing sheets. The rest of the time they were pulled tight to the sill. The room stayed cool in the muted light, the fuzzy outlines of bed and dresser, lamp and mirror soft as welcoming arms.

Flopping back on the bed, I zipped my jeans and rested a moment, the muscles in my back and neck softening against the loose blankets. So much easier to think my way through supper than get up and start it. What would it be tonight? Frank went home to Rose around six, so the evening meal was as close to private as John and I ever got. Just two hired men and us. If John came in first, I would get a hug, maybe a quick kiss before the hired men trailed in to wash up. If they all came in together, it would be business as usual. John would ask the men what they'd seen that day, what they'd gotten done, any trouble with machinery. Fried meat. Boiled potatoes. Canned beans, I worked my way down the list, counting with slow blinks. I could make Jell-O, set it up with ice cubes. Maybe biscuits. My eyelids shot open and I sat up so fast a gray fog roared through my head. Bent over my knees, I waited as flashes of color gradually gave way to vision, then peered at my watch. Half an hour lost. I worked my neck and shoulders, driving off the last of the dizziness. Forcing myself to rise, I stretched against the ache in my hips and knees.

Our honeymoon had ended just as haying season began, and John arrived home to a relentless grind of fourteen-hour days and seven-day weeks. The men left for the hayfields at dawn, returning for lunch and again for the evening meal. After supper, after the cows were milked and the barn chores done, John started on the shop work, tuning and tinkering and welding on one of the fleet of hard-used **balers, swathers, and tractors**. Something was always breaking down, it seemed....

balers, swathers, and tractors: Motorized equipment for cutting and arranging hay to be baled and stored.

In my first dealings with them, I sensed that [Rose] and Frank shared an Old World view of family. As modern as ranching corporations were with respect to tax and inheritance laws, their structure reflected an ancient patriarchal model. In every case it seemed, the father and son became the president and vice president, Mom was named secretary, and all generations worked for the common good of the ranch. They could deduct the costs of doing business, with income derived from the division of profits based on ownership of shares. The extreme example would be one multigeneration household where Papa directed the sons in working the land and Mama directed the wives in preparing communal meals, and the earnings all funneled into a common purse. That sort of lifestyle was not unknown during the settlement days, when immigrant families worked together to establish their footing in the New World, and later Depression days when a couple might live with one set of parents or the other while they saved for a place of their own. A few of the country's larger ranches still supported two or three generations of family headed by the patriarch of the clan. But more familiar to me were the husband–wife partnerships like that of my parents, couples who bought **improved land** in the forties and fifties and worked it together, an arrangement that often rewarded a woman's strength and independence. It was left to young women of my generation to discover the vast difference between entering a marriage partnership like our mothers had and becoming the daughter-in-law in a ranching corporation.

improved land: Land that has already been prepared for a particular use, in this case having electricity and water available, as well as dirt or paved road access.

I was not caught totally unaware. With Frank and Rose as the major shareholders, I assumed they would control the purse strings to a certain extent. John would draw wages, the bulk of our expenses would be paid by the corporation. But never in my wildest dreams had I expected to run my life as an extension of Frank and Rose's. We were married in 1973, not 1873, I assured myself. Somehow I pictured a corporation as just like a marriage partnership, but with two households serving as the members of the team, both sides working respectfully and cooperatively, but separately.

After allowing us the first week to "get settled," Rose had arrived on my doorstep one morning without warning, her round face beaming, eager to caution and advise my first steps on her old stomping ground. She had arrived nearly every morning since on the pretext of packing, though the cartons often sat unused in the porch while she addressed the arrangement of my cupboards. I was nearly a foot taller than she and tended to use the high shelves for storing everyday items. She seemed determined to break me of the dangerous habit of placing glasses and heavy pots where she had to stand on tip-toe to reach them. I listened patiently as she shifted items from shelf to shelf, victim of an upbringing that allowed no sassing of elders. After she left, I would move everything back. A day or two later she would open the cupboard doors and stand with her plump hands on her hips, tsk-tsking. She must have thought me terribly slow. As the days progressed, the sound of her car pulling up filled me with dread.

Stung by Frank's words that morning and confused by his silence at lunch, I warily poured Rose coffee from the still-warm pot, watching her closely. Her usual cheerful greeting had been dampened. She pulled out one of the new kitchen chairs, hefting it in her hand, then lowered herself toward the seat with exaggerated caution, as though testing the heat of a bath. When it held her satisfactorily, she leaned back and squinted through the living-room doorway at the brown-plaid couch, her mouth a moue of disapproval. She hoped I wouldn't have trouble keeping the couch clean. It was pretty now, but the fabric didn't look practical. She rummaged through her purse while I talked about the new soil-guard treatment, the lifetime warranty, my voice trailing off as she drew out the long receipt from the grocery warehouse.

She spread it on the table and settled herself more firmly. So here it is, I thought wearily. From where I stood braced against the counter, I could see several of the items had been circled. Beer. Cigarettes. Kotex. Soda pop. Five pounds of bacon. A gallon can of pie cherries. My throat tightened with humiliation. I took my time pausing a second with my eyes closed, hoping to hear truck or tractor approaching from down the creek. Where the hell was John in all this, I wondered. He had helped pick out every stick of furniture, had trooped down the grocery aisle adding to the pile on the huge cart and had written the checks without a murmur.

We went through the list item by item as Rose pointed out which of my purchases could be had for less in other stores and the rash of brand-name products I had wasted money on instead of opting for less-expensive store brands. Her manner was serious but sincere, not angry as much as disappointed that I had managed to triple their food bill in one trip to the store. After all, she said as though reciting a clever saying from memory, my joining the family added only one more mouth to feed and we all expected the grocery bill to reflect that. I waited for her to finish, careful not to interrupt, though I was fuming. "We" meant Frank. Frank expected the grocery bill for two households to be almost the same as for one. Frank, the man who bragged that he'd never cooked a meal for himself since he settled on this place. Lord, the injustice. I sputtered. I flushed. I explained, voice shaking, that the bill reflected the cost of setting up a kitchen, not replenishing a pantry. I had had to purchase some of everything all in the same bill, rather than spaced out over months. Like spices—here I pointed to the list—you have to have them to bake, but they last forever.

She studied the circled items around my fingertip as I rambled on, the pleasant smile on her face never dimming. When I stopped, she went on as though I had never spoken. Some, like the breakfast meats and that strawberry jam, were a waste of money to feed hired men. Pancakes and eggs were good enough. My eyes must have widened at that, as she went on for some time about the economic wisdom of pancakes and eggs. I bit my tongue and focused on the list, as though reading it one more time might offer enlightenment. John. It had been John, victim of that same breakfast menu for a year, who had selected the jam and bacon. Some items she'd both circled and checked—the gallon of cherries, the case of soda pop—as too indulgent. One item, a carton of cigarettes, she had crossed off all together. I was, she explained calmly, forbidden to buy these with corporation money.

I waited for her to make her way to the end of the list, conscious of the pent-up thump at the base of my skull, the wash of self-pity that pushed me to the brink of tears. She must have mistaken my mood for remorse, for she patted my hand and smiled her understanding. I would do fine, she said kindly. I just had to use my common sense. She finished her coffee, tucked the receipt back into her purse and left without packing a single box. I waved her to her car, then dropped into my chair at the kitchen table and gazed at the neat list of items she'd written on a sheet of notebook paper. Crib notes for grocery shopping, the mustn't-dos and can't-haves, the good-enoughs. At a complete loss, I sat in the silence of the ranch kitchen, trying to read the lay of the land. Where did I fit? Where was my place in this business, in this kitchen? How could it be that the one person expected to make most of the household purchases for the ranch was the one person not allowed to write checks, the one person with no say in budgeting or bank drafts?

DOCUMENT 26:

Hispanic men and women explain *vaquero* and ranch work at a famous ranch in south Texas: *Voices of the Wild Horse Desert: Vaquero Families of the King and Kenedy Ranches* (1997)[9]

Researchers Jane Clements Monday and Betty Bailey Colley interviewed families and staff at the Kenedy and King Ranches, two well-known south Texas businesses located on the Gulf of Mexico coast between Brownsville and Corpus Christi. This *mestizo* region was only absorbed into the United States in the 1840s after several centuries of Spanish imperial, then Mexican, then Texas Republican government. The Mexican-American family and staff there have defied the fate of many family ranching operations to prosper continuously for generations on an ecologically diverse but arid landscape producing market cattle, including the noted Santa Gertrudis cattle as well as award-winning American Quarter Horses.

ev

*Narrator: While the Ranch owners conceptualized the direction the Ranches would take, the vaqueros executed the expert techniques necessary to accomplish these goals. Julian Buentello married into one of the oldest **Kineño** families, the Quintanillas, and went to work with them at Laureles. He became one of the best at handling horses. Leonard Stiles remembered how Julian knew all of the horses:*

Kineño: A Spanish term for the extended group of family and staff who work at the King Ranch.

Each man would ride twelve to fifteen horses each. If you were out and couldn't find your horse, Julian would whistle in just a minute, and he had found the horse you were looking for. If you roped the wrong horse, Julian would tell you [that] you had someone else's horse. He was the remuda boss, and he was expert at his job. When important people would come, Mr. Bob [Kleberg] or Mr. Dick [Kleberg Jr.] would ask Julian to choose the horse for them because he knew the horses so well. No one rode Mr. Bob's horse but him, unless it was Julian. He would ask Julian to get the "kinks" out, and Julian would say "Why?" and Mr. Bob would say, "If someone is going to be bucked off, I want it to be you." One time he told Mr. Bob to be careful of a particular horse because that horse did not like paper. While riding with the herd, Mr. Bob was looking for certain bloodlines that he had written on paper, and he kept the paper tucked in his boot. He forgot one day, and pulled the paper out of his boot while he was still on the horse and nearly got bucked off.

---

9   Jane Clements Monday and Betty Bailey Colley, *Voices from the Wild Horse Desert: The Vaquero Families of the King and Kenedy Ranches* (Austin: U of Texas P, 1997), 66–70, 102–07.

Narrator: Martín Mendietta Jr. is a fifth-generation vaquero on King Ranch who worked for years with the horse operation. His family members have been leaders in each generation: "My father, Martín Sr., came from Curida, Mexico, in the 1880s. He was a caporal at Santa Gertrudis. Javier Mendietta, his brother, was the next caporal, then my cousin Valentín Quintanilla Jr., then Sixto, another cousin, and I was caporal from 1963 to 1985. Alfredo 'Chito' Mendietta, my cousin, is a caporal today." The Mendietta name on King Ranch is synonymous with expert knowledge of horses. Martín Jr., who worked on both the Kenedy and King Ranches, described his father's work:

Mr. Bob [Kleberg] sent the horses to the mare barn to be trained, and my father and his brothers trained them. They started by riding them bareback, then father trained them to the buggy. As a kid, I rode on the backs of the buggy horses to get them used to having somebody on them before they were broken to the saddle. This type mare was used to pull the carriage that took Mr. Bob's daughter, Helenita, to her wedding. These were Quarter Horses from the Ranch.

Narrator: As an added detail, Miguel Muñiz recalled, "I drove the carriage of Helenita to her wedding. While I was taming that horse, I was kicked, and it broke my leg." Martín Jr. also had the uncanny ability to accurately identify horses through his almost perfect powers of observation and memory. This ability became invaluable, because accurate, intricate records were critical during the upbreeding period. According to Leonard Stiles:

Mr. Dick [Kleberg Jr.] could get his secretary to write down the descriptions of the mare and the type of markings and what stallion they were bred to. Martín could go out in the pasture and locate the colt. Every horse had a registration name and a nickname, and Martín knew both. Mr. Dick would say, "What horse is Chino [Gonzales] riding?" and Martín would tell him … what mare and stallion [had produced that horse]. He knows features and colors. Some people can remember and tell a man's son because he [the son] looks like him. Well, Martín could do that with horses.

Narrator: Martín was an expert at breaking horses. He described the process vaqueros used when the numbers that needed to be broken escalated:

We would take the one-year-olds and halter break [them], lead [them], [and] pick up their feet to get them used to people. Then we branded them and took them off their mother. Next, we put them with old horses with bells on them—the males with an old male horse, and the females with an old female horse. At two years old, we brought them back in. We had handled them a couple of times a year, trimming hooves and grooming, again to get them used to people. At three years old, we actually broke them. Many of the men already had their favorites by then. We ran the horses in the corral for a few days, then mounted them. The old men would spread out in front and back, and we would trot, then lope the colts. The faster you got them to lope, the less chance of them bucking. We loped them from the corral to the bump gate—about a mile—and back. While they were winded, we stopped, started, got on and off. The next step was to work them a half day. We did this every spring about April.

Narrator: Martín also described an earlier method of breaking horses:

We would have an old vaquero stand in the center of the corral with a rope. After the men had the horses used to the bridle, blanket, and saddle, they would put their horses in the corral, about five at a time. Upon signal from the vaquero in the center, who would say, "Riders Up," they would mount their horses and ride them in a circle around the corral with an older vaquero on a gentle horse in front and back. If a horse tried to buck, the vaquero in the center would rope his hind feet to distract him. Vaqueros stopped breaking horses at about forty-five or fifty [years of age]. The old men always had respect and had the pick of the horse they wanted.

Narrator: The vaqueros were highly skilled at gentling these animals, and each had his own special way of accomplishing the task. Enemorio Serna of the Kenedy Ranch described a slightly different method: "We would rope him, tie one foot up, pet him, lead him, and ride him. Then we would work him for a week in the pen and turn him loose. We used different bits. The Thoroughbreds were easier to train, more intelligent. But they were too skinny and tired too quickly." No matter the method, breaking horses was a hazardous business. According to Villarreal, "Jesse Salazar remembers being dragged by a horse on two different occasions in his eight-year career. He escaped serious injury both times, but other vaqueros were not as lucky. Augustin Cavazos, who was working on the adjacent Armstrong Ranch, was kicked to death by a horse he was trying to break.... Augustin's death occurred even though he was working under controlled conditions. He was breaking a horse inside a corral while his father and several other vaqueros watched from the fence" (1972, 43). In addition to his expert training and showmanship with cattle, Beto Maldonado also worked with King Ranch Quarter Horses. He worked as assistant to Dr. Northway, the veterinarian, and had extensive knowledge of the breeding program. Beto recalled:

I remember Old Sorrel very well. We were still hand-breeding him at the age of twenty-six. I still have a picture of Old Sorrel in my head. He was purchased in 1915 from George Clegg. He was the foundation of the Quarter Horse family here at the Ranch today.... Mr. Bob was a very smart, intelligent man, and had a good idea what a horse was going to be when he bought him. In 1941, Wimpy was the number one horse registered by the [American] Quarter Horse Association. He was the grandson of Old Sorrel. In 1984, the two-millionth Quarter Horse was registered, and it was a filly from King Ranch, a descendant of Old Sorrel and Wimpy.

Narrator: Another famous King Ranch horse was Peppy. Beto was also attached to him:

I would ride Peppy before Dr. Northway was going to show him to people [in the 1940s]. It was like riding in a Cadillac. I can compare it to riding in the El Kineño, which was the family hunting car; one time Mr. Dick [Sr.] picked me up on the Ranch road and I rode in it. It was like riding Peppy, with the gentle rock and taking the bumps so easily. Dr. Northway would give Peppy peppermint sticks and when people knew this, they would send him peppermint sticks from all over. I always loved candy and would share with Peppy. He had a good disposition. He was broad, heavy, strong, powerful, turned on a dime and easy to rein. There was a twenty-five-pound flour sack that had the picture of Peppy on it.

Narrator: Beto was responsible for the daily, routine care of the these Quarter Horses:

I had three thousand Quarter Horses that I had to vaccinate, take care of, and keep records on. At first, they got four shots, one week apart. I vaccinated five hundred horses in one day. We ran them through the chute and vaccinated them with a 1 cc vial in a small syringe. I refilled it for each horse and used the same needle. I clipped the hair, used alcohol to clean the animal and the needle, refilled the syringe, picked up the hide, and drove the needle in. If it was a good vaccination, it would develop a nodule. I did the same thing with the mules at Santa Cruz—they were mean. The horses were identified by the names of pens and pastures. When I first started identifying and vaccinating horses we had to vaccinate four times a year. When we got finished with the last group, it was time to start over again. Later they just got two a year. Now it's one. I also helped with the auctions. At first the Quarter Horses would go for $500, and later the highest price paid for a stallion was $125,000.[10] ...

---

10 Monday and Colley, *Voices*, locations 1968–2068.

Narrator: In only a few instances did women on the Ranches work in the same capacity as vaqueros. The traditional woman's role was centered around home and family, and for a woman to work in the corrida was most unusual. There were a few exceptions, however, and Josefina Robles Adrián of King Ranch was one of them. Josefina, who was born in 1923, is the granddaughter of Luis Robles, one of the first vaqueros on King Ranch. Luis is listed as Captain Richard King's bodyguard, thus documenting the Robles family as vaqueros at the beginning of the Ranch (Account Book of Employee Wages, October 1, 1889–October 1, 1892, King Ranch Archives). Josefina's father was Ramón Robles (Luis's son) of the Caesar Pen area on the Santa Gertrudis Division. He was a caporal in charge of livestock. Josefina recounted how she learned to work like the vaqueros. Although she was not a vaquera for King Ranch, she learned the skills and helped her father on the ranchito, but she was not allowed to work in the ranch roundups:

I was trained as a vaquera by my father. Maybe it's because he did not have too many children, but I did all my brother did, and my father taught me. I started riding at seven. My daddy taught me to ride. I would bring the cattle in from the brush with him, and then he would let me do it by myself under his direction. I wore a brush jacket, khakis, men's boots, and used chaps in the pen. My sister, Carolina, also rode and worked the ranchito, while my other sister, Aurora, did not. I also rode the fences.

I was taught to rope, and my father taught me. I started at about seven and began by roping posts, then hogs, then turkeys. I would also rope calves away from the dairy cows. Each afternoon, I would help to bring the calves and cows in, and I would have to separate the calves from their mothers, and sometimes I would have to rope them.

The rope I used was a big one. I did not start with a little rope. I helped them brand, too, by getting the irons hot and handing them the irons.

Narrator: María Luisa Montalvo Silva and her sister, Lupe, who both grew up on the Laureles Division of King Ranch, also learned to ride and work cattle. María Luisa related:

I loved horses from the very first and learned to ride at about nine years old. I would help my father bring in the cows and separate the cows from the calves. We would do this about 3:00 or 4:00 in the afternoon.

Narrator: Girls followed after their mothers and learned from them in much the same way as boys learned boy jobs from their fathers. In the early 1900s, a young Manuela Mayorga, with her mother, Antonia, and her grandmother, Virginia, prepared special meals for guests at the Main House on King Ranch:

Ms. Alice [East] and Mr. Tom East would send out and have rabbits killed for mother to make tamales. The recipe came through the family. The chauffeur would skin the jack rabbits and cut them up. Then we would boil them and grind them up and spice the meat. We would fix masa up with shortening, salt, and soup broth left over from cooking the meat. Mr. Robert Kleberg Jr.'s mother liked for mother to boil the fresh corn and use an antique hand grinder to make the tortillas.

We also made enchiladas for Mrs. King. We would fix big wash tubs full of both for the Big House. We made two kinds of tortillas: plain and, for the ones to be used in enchiladas, we used chili powder in them. To make enchiladas, we made gravy with flour, chili powder, salt, ground yellow cheese from town, and onions. We soaked the tortillas in gravy 'til soft, rolled while hot with cheese, onions, and meat. We always used King Ranch beef.

I helped my mother, and since the school was across the street from our house, at recess I didn't get to play. I went home and helped mother grind corn.

I started working at seven years old. I helped wash. I helped Mom fix breakfast by 5:00 in the morning. I made beds and made the fire. I chopped wood for it. For breakfast we had tortillas with sausage, egg, or potato, and egg or tortillas with chocolate. We drank chocolate or coffee. We didn't have [drink] milk. After breakfast we washed.

Narrator: Sometimes the women worked outside the home to supplement income, and often the young girls helped their mothers with this work. Manuela described working in one of the households on the Ranch:

Mother did housework for the Larry Cavazos [Sr.] family. We washed and ironed their clothes. We washed the clothes outside in tubs. We had water faucets outside. We hung the clothes on the line to dry. We ironed outside on the porch; sometimes we would iron 'til midnight. Mr. Cavazos had five children so we did wash for seven and were paid $6 a month. The irons we heated on the fire, and I still remember all the pleats and ruffles.

Narrator: Manuela also added to the family income by helping her father:

When it was cotton picking time, I helped pick cotton. I would leave at 4:00 in the morning with my dad. We walked toward Bishop along the railroad tracks to the cotton fields. I was very fast. I would pick two hundred pounds of cotton by 5:00 in the afternoon. I was paid $1.25 for every one hundred pounds. I went every day with my dad.[11]

---

11   Monday and Colley, *Voices*, locations 2489–2583.

DOCUMENT 27:

Image group: Buckaroos in Paradise—the ethnography of ranching in Nevada (1978–80)[12]

These photographs are drawn from Buckaroos in Paradise, a 1981 ethnographic exhibition by the American Folklife Center at the Library of Congress. A team of historians, anthropologists, folklorists, archaeologists, and photographers visited Nevada's Paradise Valley between 1978 and 1980 to document "the Nevada cowboy, the buckaroo, presenting a realistic vignette of the cowboy in American social history," as the collection description explains. The team especially focused on labor issues, taking many photographs and conducting interviews with ranchers and their hired men. They also created detailed drawings and photographic studies of tools and workspaces, such as the inside of the ranch house or the equipment at a far-flung bunkhouse where men stayed when working on remote sections of range for extended periods. The collection portrays a diverse and inter-reliant ranching community of Basque immigrants and their descendants, members of Northern Paiute and Western Shoshone tribes, and other Nevadans, while speaking to many Americans' romantic fascination with the cowboy as a symbol of rugged independence, nonetheless.

e

---

12 "Buckaroos in Paradise" exhibition, American Folklife Center, Library of Congress (1981).

"Buckaroos at Cabin," October 1979. Pictured: Tex Northrup, Carl Fleischhauer (the photographer, top right), Myron Smart, Theodore Brown, Mel Winslow, Leslie Stewart, Fred Steward, Henry Taylor, William Smock, Clay Taylor.

"Branding, Grayson Ranch," June 1978. Pictured: Bruno McErquiaga, Ray Morgan, Dennis Brown, Dave Jones, Pete Bishop, Dan Martinez.

"Cattle and **Newly-Wattled** Calves," June 1978.

Newly-Wattled: Along with being ear-tagged, castrated, branded, and possibly dehorned by ranch cowboys, in their first spring cattle are marked for identification with a notch cut to the wattle, or fleshy flap of skin under the neck.

"At the Branding," June 1978. Pictured: Dennis Brown, Maryjo Stephens, Alfonso Marcuerquiaga, Ray Morgan, Pete Bishop, Bruno McErquiaga, Dave Jones.

DISCUSSION QUESTIONS/WRITING PROMPTS

1. What regions, people, animals, and time periods are addressed by the primary sources here?
2. What are the problems and opportunities presented by the different types of primary sources in this section? Prescriptive literature versus memoir versus oral history? Textual sources versus photographs?
3. When we consider the day-to-day life of cattle people, what historical realities of ranching have been obscured by the myth of the cowboy as a figure of white male independence?
4. In what ways did gender and ethnicity shape ranch life? Why is it important to seek out historical primary sources authored by a diverse group of people to understand family ranching businesses in the twentieth century?

PART 5

The Cultures and Politics of Horses

DOCUMENT 28:

Fay E. Ward explains cowboy mustanging techniques: *The Cowboy at Work* (1958)[1]

Fay Ward was born in Iowa and left home at the age of 14 to work as a cowboy. Although he started out with little formal education, he became a talented writer and illustrator. His book, *The Cowboy at Work,* is a classic and trusted account of range work practices. Yet, like most prescriptive literature, it undoubtedly offers readers a best-case scenario about how men worked with horses and cattle, or, according to Ward, how men *should* work with horses and cattle in the modern West. Although it was not Ward's main intention, his account reveals much about how cowboys actually captured horses for ranch work and how they understood wild horses' abilities, needs, and experiences of people.

There are many factors to be taken into consideration if any measure of success is to be attained in the business of catching wild horses, or mustangs, as they are generally called. A great deal of work and a lot of hard riding, combined with a lot of luck, are necessary to achieve profitable results in such work. In wild horse country watering places are few and far between and it is necessary to locate such places in order to plan out the work of catching horses.

When the horses that are to be run are located, the next thing is to locate where they are watering so that a favorable spot can be selected for the construction of a trap. The trap consists of corrals so arranged that it will be difficult for a horse to escape once he is inside the enclosure. The trap must be located in a place where it will be well concealed, as, for instance, in a canyon, where the horses will not be aware of the trap until they are practically in it. The trap, naturally, is more easily concealed in a deep draw

---

1   Fay E. Ward, *The Cowboy at Work: All about His Job and How He Does It* (New York: Hastings House, 1958), 101–05, 128.

or canyon than out in the open. The deeper the canyon the better, for it will serve as a sort of chute that helps prevent the wise ones of the bunch from breaking out and making their getaway. A trap located in a sharp bend of a canyon is better than one in a canyon that has no bend, because then the horses can be forced into the trap before they catch on to where it is. A trap that has been used with good results by mustangers is shown on Plate 27.

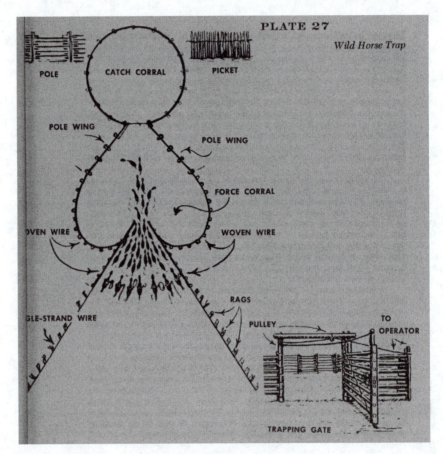

Plate 27

The trap shown is an elaborate arrangement designed for country where it is difficult to find a depression deep enough to prevent the horses from getting away when they are being forced into the trap. The more natural the enclosure appears, the less suspicious the mustangs will be. This is a point which must be taken into consideration. The mustang is much wiser than he is given credit for. The more the horses have been run, the wiser they become, so they will be on the quedow (alert) for anything that doesn't look natural. Once they sense something is wrong, they are pretty sure to make a break, and once they start back, nothing but lead or a well-placed loop will stop 'em from high-tailing it back for the high spots. The trap shown on Plate 27 has a round catch corral constructed of poles or pickets set into the ground close together and fastened together with wires twisted around each post (see the drawing of a section of picket fence at the top of the Plate). A pole corral is best, but where it is difficult to secure timber, heavy woven wire is used instead, reinforced at the top, center and bottom to break the strain the fence will be subjected to when a horse hits it head on. The catch corral is generally from forty to fifty feet in diameter and from eight to nine feet high, and sometimes higher. Horses have been known to go over some pretty tall corrals when they took a notion.

Pole wings are shown on Plate 27 extending out away from the gate of the catch corral, forming the point of the heart-shaped forcing corral; they are necessary when the mustangs are being run into the catch corral. The material used in the construction of the forcing corral is heavy woven wire, doubled, to form a fence eight to nine feet high. Heavy posts, twelve to fourteen feet long, are set three to five feet into the ground and are placed about six feet apart; the woven wire is fastened to and supported by these posts. The wire is on the inside of the posts, which makes for strength and eliminates chances of injury to the stock. The woven wire is attached to the ends of the pole wings running out from the catch corral, as indicated in the drawing.

A second set of wings, running out from the entrance to the force corral, is constructed of the same woven wire as the corral. These wings are extended out some forty to fifty feet from the entrance and are spread out to a considerable width so the horses can be run between them without crowding. They should be about forty-five yards apart at the outer extremities to give ample room to push 'em into the trap.

Booger wings, which consist of a single strand of smooth wire, are attached to the ends of the woven-wire wings and run still further out, for a distance of five or six hundred yards, to form a very wide V. The wire is placed up about five feet from the ground and is fastened to posts and trees wherever possible. Rags consisting of old clothes and sacks torn into wide strips about three feet long are fastened to the wire and placed about six feet apart. The rags will swing and flap in the wind and will help booger the mustangs away from the fence when they head toward it. The posts of the force corral are camouflaged by placing limbs cut from trees on them to make them look like trees. The more the enclosure can be made to look like the natural surroundings the horse is used to, the better. All trace of a sign showing where work has been done in the vicinity of the trap should be removed or concealed and as many precautions taken in placing and arranging the trap as would be used in making a set for a coyote. A wise old mustang can read signs, at times, as well as a wolf, and if that fact is not taken into account, the consequences may turn out to be costly.

Where horses are run in rough country, it is best to place booger wires across the trails and draws forking off the main trail that leads to the trap. This will keep the horses from turning off the trail in an attempt to make a getaway. Traps can be well concealed in timbered territory and in that kind of country it is not necessary to place them in very deep canyons. They can be located in between hills near the head of a creek or draw—often good locations for a trap. The less a human circulates around the scenery where the mustangs run, the better. Precaution must be taken when constructing a trap not to put it too close to where the horses range; any activity taking place near them will cause 'em to get suspicious and quit the country for a new range. The trap should be some distance from the main trail leading to the water hole, which is a trail the mustangs travel every day. If the trap is set up too close to the trail, they will probably notice what is going on before the trap is ready to use, which will never do. The traps have to be some three or four miles away from the locality where the horses circulate if they are to be kept from coming in contact with the work that is going on.

grain fed: Horses who forage on grasses will be weaker and thinner than horses who eat grasses and hay supplemented with grain, which is a more energy rich feed and more easily digested.

broomies: Range horses, especially mares.

The saddle horses used by the mustangers are generally **grain fed** to put 'em in condition to stand up under the hard riding they have to do in running the mustangs. From five to seven riders are needed to handle a bunch of real mustangs. It often takes three or four days hard running to get a bunch of **broomies** simmered down to where a rider can make connections with 'em. The main idea in mustanging is to keep the horses away from water and to run them until they are pretty well played out. Then they will not be able to do much running when they are headed for the trap. Water holes are often guarded at night to keep the horses from drinking. This helps to take the sap out of 'em a lot sooner and saves time and labor.

In starting a run, the riders are stationed around the territory the horses will be run in—that is, around both the area the horses are in and the land between the trap and the horses. The riders are stationed at intervals of two and a half to three miles, on high ground where they will be able to see what is going on. The mustangs are run in a wide circle and are relayed from one mustanger to the next. The riders generally get off their horses and lie down on the ground if there are no trees or brush to conceal them on horseback. The idea is to keep out of sight so that the mustangs will come up close to the rider and give him a chance to get a good run on them. The rider bends 'em back in the direction of the nearest mustanger who, in his turn, will give 'em a run. The mustangs are kept on the jump all day and generally cover from seventy-five to a hundred miles in that time. At the end of the day the mustangers go to camp. They are out early the next morning, mounted on fresh horses, to start the mustangs to running again. The mustangers generally take up new positions each day to keep the mustangs from knowing where the riders are.

When the horses are ready to be corralled, two riders are located at the trap to help lane the mustangs into the mouth of the force corral. The riders are stationed about seventy-five yards back from the ends of the force-corral wings and are cached so the mustangs won't see anything suspicious until the riders dash out alongside them. In corralling mustangs, good timing must be used so the horses will not have a chance to plan a getaway. As the mustangs are run into the booger wings, the riders charge 'em and walk on their hocks until the critters are in the trap. Ropes and hats are put into action and this, combined with a few panther squalls (cowboy yells), helps divert the mustangs' attention from the trap they are headed for. No room or time is given the horses to stop or turn around and no opening is left for them to break through if everybody is at the right place at the right time.

Once the horses are corralled in the catch corral, they are left there for a day or so to get them used to a fence. This makes it easier to hold them in a horse trap (pasture) later on—which is what they will be put in when they are taken to the ranch. Before taking the horses out of the corral, they are forefooted (roped by the forefoot) and thrown in order to sideline them, as shown in the illustrations for the Section entitled "Bronc Busting."[2] The side line is put on to prevent the horse from traveling too fast, so he can be kept in the herd. He cannot step ahead with the foot tied, but he can draw it up into the position shown in Figure J on Plate 33. When all the horses are sidelined, they are turned out into the force corral to circulate around for a while. Some gentle horses are generally thrown in with 'em to help lead the bunch to camp. After the horses are drove into the corral at the ranch, the side lines are often left on them for a few days till they become used to the fence and are a bit more docile. Then they are caught and the side lines are taken off. When the mustangs are turned loose, they are not allowed to drink all they want the first time they make connections with water. A little at a time is best, as they are apt to overdo the thing if left to themselves. Safety first is a good maxim to be guided by.

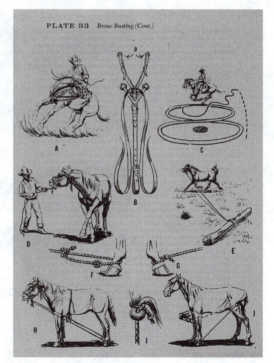

Plate 33

---

2   An illustrated chapter of Ward's book in which he discusses breaking and training range horses for work as saddle horses in detail.

DOCUMENT 29:

Image group: Gus Bundy's photographs of wild horse round-ups in Nevada (1946–51)[3]

Beginning in 1958, photographs of Nevada wild horse round-ups taken earlier by the photographer Gus Bundy appeared in a series of popular magazines and newspapers. The images showed mustangers chasing down wild horses with airplanes and trucks (far easier than days-long round-ups on horseback), roping them to old tires until exhausted, tying them, and dragging them onto trucks to be sent to slaughter. The men who did this work were not the much-romanticized cattlemen or working cowboys of the West, Americans discovered, but men who captured and sold wild horses seasonally or when they needed quick cash. They did not collect horses for use on a ranch or other work, as Fay Ward explains above, but for sale as "canners," that is for manufacture into canned pet foods or for sale as horsemeat overseas in Asia or Europe.

Wild Horses, 1951

---

3 All these photographs are in the Gus Bundy Collection, Special Collections, University of Nevada, Reno.

Roping a Wild Horse, 1946

Wild Horse Roped to Tires, 1946

Men Putting Wild Horse in Trailer, 1946

DOCUMENT 30:

Velma Johnston (a.k.a. "Wild Horse Annie") testifies in Washington, DC, about airplane and truck mustang round-ups (1959)[4]

Velma Johnston, famously known as "Wild Horse Annie," was a dude ranch owner from Nevada who became a national figure as a wild horse advocate when she discovered how freelance mustangers captured horses for slaughter. Johnston called them "airborne cowboys" because they hunted horses in haste with trucks and airplanes. In advocating for laws to protect these horses, Johnston and others would explain that they were not wholly opposed to the capture and even killing of wild horses. Many believed the mustangs had a right to exist at large in the West *as a population*, even if some individuals among them would be killed to avoid overpopulation. Johnston's 1959 Congressional testimony was part of a years-long process to work out more comprehensive plans and funding for the active "management" and protection from extinction of wild horses and burros on federal lands by the Bureau of Land Management, which appeared as the **Wild and Free-Roaming Horses and Burros Act of 1971.**

Wild and Free-Roaming Horses and Burros Act of 1971: This law was substantially weakened by a 2004 amendment that once again allowed authorized agents of the Federal government to kill wild burros and horses.

༄

Mrs. Johnston. There was a time in the early history of Nevada, when the mustangs overran the ranges to the extent that they seriously jeopardized what limited grazing was available. Every mouthful of range grass was needed for the growing herds of cattle and sheep, and the ranchers took matters into their own hands; thousands of mustangs were captured and killed, and the remainder of the wild horses were driven into the rocky and barren desert hills where they learned to eke out a living.

However, the actual turning point in the history of the wild horse came with the rise of the canned pet food business, and the demand for fresh horse meat sold in pet shops. Once the big slaughter got under way, the wild horse was doomed—for now his extermination served two purposes: a vast amount of range clearance was accomplished, and his carcass provided cheap meat for the processors. With this in mind, professional hunters moved in, for it was a lucrative business. In the years immediately following the end of World War II, more than 100,000 of the animals were removed from the state. The old technique of rounding up horses with crews of hard-riding cowboys was too slow and too costly, so the airborne cowboy came into

---

4   Velma B. Johnston, *Statement of Mrs. Velma B. Johnston, The Johnstons' Ranch, Reno, Nevada*, Subcommittee No. 2 of the Committee on the Judiciary regarding H.R. 343–H.R. 2725–H.R. 4289–H.R. 7531 Treatment of Wild Horses and Burros on Land Belonging to the United States, House of Representatives, Washington, DC, July 15, 1959, 86th Cong., 1st sess., 1959.

rimrock: The sheer stone
face at the upper edge of a
canyon.

heavy and terrifying
devices: For instance,
weighted down by a rope
tied to old truck tires.

being. The mustangs are driven at breakneck speed by planes from their meagre refuge in the rough and barren **rimrock** onto flatlands or dry lake beds, where the chase is taken up by hunters on fast-moving trucks and the mustangs are pursued to exhaustion. Sometimes they are burdened with **heavy and terrifying devices** which are attached to them by skillful ropers operating from the trucks.

Sometimes they are driven into box-canyons from which there is no escape—other times into fan-shaped trapping corrals, where the violent contact with the enclosing wires have caused serious and painful injuries occasionally resulting in death from loss of blood.

The horses are sometimes tied and left where they lie until sufficient are driven in to begin loading operations. Sidelining is one method of tying—a front and hind foot are tied together, and when the horse fights, because he will fight his confinement savagely, the legs are rope-burned until there is no hide left on them. To load them, they are dragged up a ramp by saddle horses, in any position in which the mustang drags best. Colts are left behind because they do not weigh enough to warrant their long haul to the processing centers. They have little chance of survival.

The requirements of the market are simple: the animals must be ambulatory and in quantity. The suppliers are paid by the pound—thus the more horses, the more money. Crowded into trucks for the long haul, loaded without regard to size, fighting as they will for release from their confinement, casualties are numerous, and their condition reflects the roughness of their treatment....

The necessity for wide-scale range clearance operations is behind us now, and the one point upon which we are all possibly in agreement is that, except in widely remote instances, the mustangs are no longer a threat to the ranges. Private interests have again won in their demands for the monopolistic use of the ranges to the exclusion of everything not commercially profitable. Because so few of the animals are left, it is now that we should not only pass legislation for their protection, but plan for their control as well, so that there will never again be an excuse for the mass extermination programs as heretofore.

Today's wild horse is not the glamorous mustang of long ago—the fiercely proud, valiant and beautiful animal that roamed our Western country when this century was young. He is, for the most part, underfed, scrubby and inbred. Since he has become the target for wholesale mechanized roundups, he has been driven almost from the face of the earth, and has had to split up into small bands, and live where forage is scarce. He has been pushed to environments where no horse should be able to endure, yet he has adapted to that environment and, with barely a fighting chance, has survived. His habitat is high in remote areas where other livestock does not run, and he comes down only when driven by lack of feed and water. For this, he is pursued and captured.

In the past, the **wild horse bands** furnished virtually the only supply of animals for ranch use, and even in recent years, many of the ribbon winners in stock horse contests have come from mustang bunches. They respond rapidly to good care, and although they do not become very large, they do become efficient, handsome, hardy all-around useful animals. They are alert and intelligent, besides being fast and strong. Their adaptation to their rigorous environment has given them the ability to fend for themselves on the open range during bitterly cold winters and hot dry summers. They can and do buck hard when the occasion warrants it, but they make good **cow ponies** or saddle horses with treated with kindness....

I have discussed at length, with a man who has done considerable work in range management and research, this matter of what to do with the mustangs. He has suggested a plan which was submitted in the original material, and which I outline here:

That the horses be placed under the strict ownership and control of the government, with skilled custodians to periodically dispose of the inferior animals by shooting. They must know horses thoroughly and be excellent marksmen to insure humane handling and treatment of the horses. He feels that in time, a fine specimen of horse will be the result, proving to be an outstanding asset to the country. With ample feed and water, and lack of harassment, a mustang will respond remarkably fast in appearance and disposition.

When the herds are built up into the fine animals they once were, before their constant harassment and pursuit by the airplanes, upon application to the agency responsible for them, individuals may acquire them for their own use—periodically the custodians round up a number of the horses from which the applicants may make their selections. He does not feel that they should be hunted by any individual whatsoever, except under strict supervision of the professional custodians of the herds, and they should be at all times under the complete control of the government agency responsible for them. It is his opinion, also, that it will be a long time before their numbers will increase to the point where they will present any threat to the ranges. He submits this also, for inclusion in protective legislation for the mustangs, and I heartily endorse it.

That the same regulations, protection and control be made to apply to the burros of the Western ranges, and that any law include horses, mares, colts and burros. The little burros, offspring of the early-day prospectors' faithful animals which were turned out into the hills when they were no longer of use, have been the victims of **widespread abuse and wanton destruction** in many of the Western States in recent years....

wild horse bands: Family grouping consisting of a dominant stallion, a "harem" of mares, their young offspring, and related "bachelor" stallions who lurk nearby.

cow ponies: Small horses employed in ranching and close work with cattle herds.

widespread abuse and wanton destruction: As with wild horses, wild populations of burros developed from escaped and abandoned donkeys, a common work animal in arid regions. Federal land management agencies targeted wild burros for culling as a competitor for cattle forage and also a nuisance species on military bases. Similarly to the mustangs, various people advocated for the right of feral burros to live at large on public land due to their ancestors' service to prospectors and other settlers in the American southwest before and after annexation in the 1840s and 1850s.

Because they cannot be successfully kept in enclosed areas, they will naturally roam, and it is possible that there will be individuals who, for purely selfish, financial or sadistic reasons, will take matters into their own hands and in their own way dispose of any trespassers on the ranges. We can only hope that those individuals will be in the minority, and in any event, the abolishing of the comparatively easy means of airplane and other mechanized methods now employed will cut down the percentage against them.

To delude ourselves with the thought that all of this is past history and won't happen again, I have this to say: Even in the past few months when **mustang fever** has been raging at high temperatures throughout the United States, and in the face of strong public opinion, there have been innumerable roundups—possibly in an endeavor to get all of the animals possible before the practice is stopped.

Another bloody chapter was written on February 28, 1959 a few miles from Reno, Nevada. Twenty-five or more of the animals were rounded up by a professional horse hunter from Wyoming, together with some local operators, in a remote public range area upon which the grazing rights belong to a prominent cattle rancher. A witness to the handling of the animals reported that the cruelty was extreme. The operators were apprehended, but the sheriff released them because there had been a permit granted by the Bureau of Land Management to the cattle rancher to have the horses rounded up in the area, and the roundup took place on public lands. The horses were kept for several days in a corral for shipment out of Reno, and one of the men from the sheriff's office, and some individual witnesses, took pictures of them for me. These pictures are included in "Mustang Presentation—Part II" handed to you today, and some of the injuries to the animals are plainly visible. No treatment for the injuries was administered.

I would like to digress a moment here and tell you that in one of those pictures is a **yearling colt** with his entire chest open where he had come in violent contact with [barbed] wires. That wound was never cared for, and the pictures were taken on the sixth day and it is very apparent in the picture the condition in which that yearling colt is. There are innumerable other injuries apparent on the other horses.

Left in the area of approximately 200 square miles where the roundup occurred, were a stallion, a colt and the carcass of a horse that did not survive the rounding up process. Three other roundups were averted by individual intervention....

Mr. Lane. Would you ... tell me now, if you will, please, after those horses are taken from the range, where are they taken to, how far, what is done with them?

mustang fever: The public outcry by way of letter-writing campaigns and calls to elected officials to advocate against mechanized mustang round-ups as a result of the Gus Bundy photographs and other publicity about the trade, including consumer boycotts of canned pet foods containing horse meat.

yearling colt: A male horse between one and two years of age.

Mr. Lane: Representative Thomas J. Lane (D-MA), Chairman, Subcommittee No. 2 of the Committee on the Judiciary.

Mrs. Johnston. Most of them are taken to Santa Rosa, California, which is in the interior of California, and I would say those horses taken from Western Nevada are transported approximately 200 miles. Those taken from further east naturally have the width of the state. Those coming from Idaho, Wyoming, Montana are put off at a range about some miles from where I live and are left there and then picked up by proper truck facilities that come in from California to pick them up. So I don't believe they are ever transported with a non-stop haul clear across the entire state into California. But those caught in Nevada are taken all the way into Santa Rosa, California.

Mr. Lane. So they have a reason for keeping them alive all that distance?

Mrs. Johnston. There are two reasons. One, refrigeration facilities are non-existent in those remote areas to take care of the dead meat. Two, a horse that can walk even on three legs is much easier to handle than a dead carcass that has to be loaded and unloaded with mechanized cranes or derricks.

Mr. Lane. And there is a stink that goes with the dead horse and so forth, and they have to combat it.

Mrs. Johnston. The slaughter takes place at processing centers and it is fresh meat then, of course.

Mr. Lane. You say now there are about how many horses left?

Mrs. Johnston. I have a report from Dr. Tom McKnight of the University of California in which he gives the overall figure for the entire United States as 20,000. I wrote to Dr. McKnight and asked him how he arrived at that figure. He told me he had contacted Bureaus of Land Management, the Department of Indian Affairs, the various agencies of that type and had in addition written to about 900 individuals of whom I was one, individuals who live in the area, to obtain their opinion. From those individual inquiries he received 400 answers. He took the figures, the estimates in those, and through the other sources from which he had obtained his information and came up with a figure of 20,000 for the United States. Mr. Chairman, it is broken down by state in the testimony which I will give you.

Mr. Lane. How many were there originally?

Mrs. Johnston. Out of Nevada alone, well, in a 4-year period, according to one of our former Bureau of Land Management supervisors, in a 4-year period alone 100,000 were removed from the State of Nevada.

Mr. Lane. How long ago was that?

Mrs. Johnston. Immediately following World War II.

Mr. Lane. So they are diminishing rapidly?

Mrs. Johnston. Very rapidly. Not only this diminishment is it alarming, because of the actual physical removal, it is the condition under which the animals have to exist because of this constant pursuit. They will have their own deterioration within their own bands and become **inbred** and frankly, for the most part they are pretty bad looking right now.

Mr. Lane. Would you say in spite of the rough terrain there?

Mrs. Johnston. They still exist.

Mr. Lane. And they still exist.

Mr. Lane. And they still can be captured by these people.

Mrs. Johnston. The airplanes, yes. They flush them out of the canyons. They flush them out of hiding when they are in the planes, you know, when the pilots operate. And it is my opinion that if the terrain is that rugged that they cannot do that horseback, then surely there are no sheep and cattle grazing up in those areas. Therefore, from a standpoint of range depredation they would be not a nuisance or a danger.

Mr. Lane. How much a pound are those horses sold for?

Mrs. Johnston. I think a fairly conservative figure that would be approximately an average over the years is 6-1/2 cents a pound, live weight on hoof.

Mr. Lane. How much do they weigh as an average?

Mrs. Johnston. An 850 or 900 pound horse is considered a big mustang. They go from 500, 600, 700, 750 but you see through this over the years they have bred down in size.

Now, on this particular horse that I mentioned that my husband and I own, he **came out of** a mustang mare that frankly, she was the rattiest looking little thing you ever saw. We liked the characteristics of the mustang, its hardiness, its ability to travel long distances. My husband weighs nearly 200 pounds and we can go out a day's ride horseback. He will ride this half

inbred: Many westerners believed that, due to the social and power dynamics of stallion harems among wild horses, when one stallion became dominant, he would breed with mares, then his own daughters and granddaughters from those mares. As a result, often wild horses tended to become less vigorous and suffer more from genetic disease that reduced overall herd health and the size of individual animals.

came out of: Was birthed by.

mustang horse that is his and come back home and there is not a mark under its saddle blanket, no evidence that it had ever been ridden. Whereas my horse, carrying much lighter weight will have sweat a bit under the saddle blanket. Even knowing that the mother was a scrubby looking little mare, to get that mustang strain we bred her to a blooded stallion and the horse is beautiful. He will go 950, almost white, or it is a very pale cream color with black mane and tail and dark stockings and a very finely shaped head, extremely finely shaped. Many people prefer horses that have the mustang strain for their hardiness and their surefootedness. They are like a mountain goat.

Mr. Lane. How many of those horses can they load onto a truck at a time?

Mrs. Johnston. Mr. Chairman, you have me there. They bring them from the scene of the operation in small trucks that have iron racks to a center, to this ranch that I mentioned, then they are rucked out of there by the big **livestock transportation type trucks,** where there is the big truck and the trailer. I don't know if any of you gentlemen have seen them. In the west that is the way they transport cattle and the horses are transported in these. However, they are brought down from the areas in which they are captured in much smaller trucks. They are packed in there quite solidly. And rather uncomfortably, I would imagine. Sometimes a horse will lose its footing in those conditions and the others in their terror have trampled it. My husband saw that happen. He stopped at a filling station for gasoline and ahead of him was a truck, one of the trucks, and the carcass of the horse was in the bottom of the truck where it had slipped and the others had trampled it to death.

livestock transportation type trucks: Commercial livestock trailer.

DOCUMENT 31:

Emil Her Many Horses (Oglala Lakota) talks about Lakota history and her views about horses: "Remembering Lakota Ways" (2006)[5]

Indigenous peoples helped create and enact the various kinds of relationships that westerners had with horses as workers, rodeo animals, pets, and prey. Many nations still keep herds of wild horses on reservation or other private land, horses who belong to particular people or families but are often feral. Like their non-Indigenous neighbors, Native Americans used horses as a cultural resource as well as a material or financial resource. Here Emil Her Many Horses explains the history of horse gifting and how some family members employed horses to enact identities that were American, but also distinctly Indigenous, as horse people with deep connections to particular regions and land. This is a common story among rural westerners from various backgrounds.

e

My last name, Her Many Horses, is the Lakota name of my paternal great-grandmother. A more accurate English translation of her name is Many Horses Woman, meaning that she owned many horses. Among Lakota people, horses were a means of measuring wealth, but a far more important demonstration of wealth was the gesture of giving away horses in honor of a family member. Generosity is more important than possession.

"The Fourth of July used to be a good time," Grace Pourier, my maternal grandmother, recalled. I liked to listen to her stories about what Lakota life was like in the early 1900s. She knew her Lakota ways as they had been passed on to her by her relatives. Born in 1907 on **Pine Ridge Reservation** and raised on Horse Head Ranch in Manderson, South Dakota, she remembered how community members and extended family gathered to celebrate with giveaways, traditional dances, parades, and feasts. Later in life, she said she wished her grandmother had made her pay more attention to the events surrounding her, but at the time, she was just a kid having fun.

Much of traditional Lakota culture was threatened in the early 1900s. After the Lakota people were placed on reservations in the late 1800s, the U.S. government forbade their language and ceremonial life. Lakota people continued their traditions by incorporating traditional dances and giveaways into the Independence Day (and other American holiday) festivities in

Pine Ridge Reservation: The large Oglala Lakota reservation in southwest South Dakota.

---

5 Emil Her Many Horses, "Remembering Lakota Ways," in *A Song for the Horse Nation: Horses in Native American Nations*, ed. George P. Horse Capture and Emil Her Many Horses (Washington, DC, and New York: National Museum of the American Indian and Smithsonian Institution, 2006), 11–13.

which they were encouraged to participate. For this reason, Fourth of July celebrations became something to look forward to. After Lakota men joined the military to fight World War I, the use of the U.S. flag in beadwork and quillwork took on a new meaning. Today, if a bead worker uses the flag design, he or she is probably a veteran or a family member of someone who has served in the military.

In the early years of my grandmother's youth, horses still played an important role in the lives of the Oglala Lakota people. Since their introduction to the region in the early 1700s, horses had revolutionized Plains cultures. But they were more than work animals; horses were, and still are, cherished. The Pourier family was known for its racehorses. During the **reservation period** of the early 1900s, beautiful beaded horse head covers, saddle blankets, and saddlebags were made to decorate favorite horses on special occasions, such as the Fourth of July parades. Horses were often given away at naming ceremonies, memorial ceremonies (held a year after a family member's death), and giveaways (which might celebrate a returning veteran or honor a graduating student). Traditional giveaways centered on the giving away of horses, money, clothing, blankets, and other material objects. Hosting a giveaway today involves tremendous preparation, including the gathering of gifts, such as brightly colored star quilts, **Pendleton blankets**, and handmade shawls, as well as feeding the whole community.

Grandma Grace once told me that her grandmother really knew Indian ways: "Grandpa Pourier would have been a rich man, but Grandma Pourier kept giving the horses away." A horse to be given away would be brought into the Fourth of July dance arbor or other community gathering, while men on horseback waited outside. The horse was shown to the people or paraded inside the arbor, then taken outside, given a slap on the rump, and released. The man on horseback fortunate enough to catch the freed horse became its proud new owner....

Emily Her Many Horses, my paternal grandmother, remembered receiving her Lakota name at about age ten. She wore a wool dress embellished with many elk teeth, valuable because only two of each elk's teeth—the incisors—are used for decoration. They are natural ivory. Along with this dress, she wore beaded moccasins and leggings, and after the naming ceremony, she was told to give away the dress, moccasins, and leggings. She struggled to keep the dress, but her parents made her part with it—at such a young age, she did not understand what this act of generosity meant, and she wondered why her grandfather had her shoes, which were tied together by their shoestrings and thrown over his saddle horn. Her grandfather gave away five horses that day in her honor.

Leo Her Many Horses, my father, was given a horse at a Hunka Lowanpi, a naming ceremony held during a Sun Dance. He received a wooden stick

reservation period: The years following the 2 March 1889 founding of the Pine Ridge Indian Reservation in South Dakota wherein Oglala Lakota members relinquished claims on other regions in exchange for a territory allowing for limited· self-governance.

Pendleton blankets: Wool blankets manufactured by the Pendleton Woolen Mills company of Oregon, which was founded in the early 1900s.

that had attached to it a rawhide cutout of a horse. This meant that he would later receive the actual horse. The Hunka Lowanpi is a Lakota naming/adoption ceremony. It creates a kinship relationship that is respected by all the family members involved, and it is at this ceremony that Lakota names are given. The family of the person receiving the name will ask a well-respected individual to name its relative. The person naming the individual will pray with an eagle feather and then tie the feather in that person's hair. The names given at a Hunka Lowanpi are used only on special occasions—to have one's name sung publicly in a song is considered a great honor. The person whose name was sung or his or her family members will give away money, horses, or blankets for this honor.

Often on Memorial Day or after a death, people will place articles of clothing, bowls of fruit, packs of cigarettes, or other such items on the grave of a family member. These things are put out with the idea that other people are welcome to come by and take them. This act is performed to honor the deceased family member. My father said that one method of giving a horse away was to place the horse outside the cemetery with the reins left hanging loose to signify that anyone was welcome to take it.

In the collection of the National Museum of the American Indian, there is a beautiful, elaborately beaded horse head cover used at a 1904 Fourth of July parade at Pine Ridge, where my grandmother would be born three years later. The catalog information states that this horse head cover was collected by J.W. Good and was "used by chief of Teton Sioux to lead parade." Imagine the horse that wore this, the white beads glinting in the July sun.

It's a wonderful piece of artistry in its geometric design and lazy-stitch technique, but what's unique about it is that it appears to have been made with the intention of later being recycled into many different objects. The beaded section, which would be placed over the face of the horse, could be remade into a pair of women's beaded leggings, and the area over the face of the horse could be made into a pipe bag. The upper neck section of the cover would have been made into a pair of tipi bags, also known as a "possible bag," because anything possible was stored inside. The lower neck section could be made into a pair of moccasins.

The resourceful woman who created this horse mask obviously had future plans for it—plans that were, fortunately for us, never carried out. A fusion of gifts never given, it is a reminder of Lakota traditions pieced together, a silent testament to what lies hidden within all those Fourths of July.

Image: Oglala Lakota beaded horse mask (ca. 1904)[6]

This mask was created at the Pine Ridge Reservation, South Dakota, most likely by a local woman artist. Today, the mask resides in the art collection of the Smithsonian Institution.

---

6   Oglala Lakota beaded horse mask, Smithsonian's National Museum of the American Indian.

DOCUMENT 33:

Wyoming rancher argues against no-kill policies for wild horses living on public lands: "Wild Horse Extremists Obscure Real-World Solutions," *High Country News* (2017)[7]

The *High Country News* magazine was founded in 1969 by a Wyomingite rancher interested in conservation and environmental issues. Since then it has become a well-known non-profit source for western environmental news. Here, Sharon O'Toole, a Wyoming rancher and writer, wades into the decades-long debate over the nature and impact of wild horses living on federal lands. O'Toole discusses the dilemma of the **no-kill** philosophy, the carrying capacity of the western environment to support horses, and the limited "social carrying capacity," as Jim Sterba has termed it, for the mustangs among many rural westerners who wish to see wild horse numbers reduced.[8]

no-kill: A practice whereby wild horses are captured and kept in holding facilities or, ideally, adopted out to farms and ranches instead of being sent to slaughter or otherwise euthanized.

e

Imagine a proposal to introduce an exotic species to the sagebrush steppe of the American West. This species could successfully reproduce and expand into forested areas, uplands and wetlands. It would be a large charismatic creature that attracted a passionate following—people who loved it so much that the management of its expanding population would be restricted by law. Some of them would be so passionate that armed guards would be necessary at academic meetings about the species.

The downside of this beautiful animal would be that it outcompeted native wildlife, plants and insects, degraded water sources and turned grasslands into deserts of cheat grass or dust. As its numbers increased, native species would be devastated.

The cost to the public of supporting these creatures would increase each year until it was projected to exceed $1 billion in 20 years or so. And ultimately, when the natural resources were exhausted, many would starve or die of thirst.

Clearly, this is a difficult scenario to support. It was not envisioned by Congress when legislators passed the 1971 Wild and Free-Roaming Horses and Burros Act. The act directed the Bureau of Land Management to manage

---

7   Sharon O'Toole, "Wild Horse Extremists Obscure Real-World Solutions," *High Country News*, 23 October 2017, accessed 30 January 2018, https://www.hcn.org/articles/opinion-wild-horse-extremists-obscure-real-world-solutions.

8   Jim Sterba, *Nature Wars: The Incredible Story of How Wildlife Comebacks Turned Backyards into Battlegrounds* (New York: Broadway Books, 2012), 75.

free-roaming horses to "maintain a thriving natural ecological balance and multiple use relationship."

The law has been amended several times to address the health of the land and management of the horses. It allows for the humane "removal or destruction" of "excess" animals "so as to restore a thriving natural ecological balance to the range, and protect the range from the deterioration associated with overpopulation."

The act further details practices like the removal of old and sick animals as well as the removal of horses from private land—private landowners are forbidden from shooing them off. It also covers proper adoption procedures. But in reality, due to lobbying efforts by horse advocates, actions by Congress and the lack of adequate horse management funding for the BLM, the wild horse population has exploded beyond the tipping point, both ecologically and economically.

I recently attended the **National Wild Horse and Burro Summit** in Salt Lake City—the meeting I mentioned earlier that required armed guards. Most of the attendees were academics, presenting research papers detailing the effects of overpopulation of horses and burros on rangeland ecosystems. Outside were demonstrators who dubbed the meeting the "Slaughter Summit."

Go to the websites of wild horse advocates, and you'll be told that wild horses, unlike their domestic counterparts, cannot overgraze or harm other wildlife species, and that they are native to North America, despite arriving on Spanish ships alongside pigs, cattle and sheep.

These supporters further argue that if only greedy ranchers would stop raising cattle and sheep, an infinite grass resource would exist for an exponentially expanding wild horse herd. Never mind that those ranchers produce food, manage the resource and support their local economies and communities.

The arguments of these advocates are countered by facts on the BLM's website.[9]

Forty-six years ago, an estimated 17,300 feral horses and 8,045 burros were on the range. In March 2017, about 73,000 horses were counted on the range. Another 46,000 were held in corrals, 29 percent of the total, and "eco-sanctuaries" held 1 percent.

These feral horses cost the BLM about $50 million per year, or 63 percent of the agency's total annual budget of $80.4 million for the program. Adoption, which is difficult and costs about $4,500 per horse, has declined by 70 percent over the past 10 years to 2,912 in 2016.

National Wild Horse and Burro Summit: A 2017 meeting of government, NGO, Indigenous, educational, environmental, and animal advocacy groups to discuss wild horses and sustainability in the West and ways of controlling and protecting wild horses.

9   United States Bureau of Land Management, https://www.blm.gov/.

PZP: Porcine zona Pellucida, an injectable form of contraception for horses and other wild animals.

gathers: A term employed by the Bureau of Land Management to describe occasions in which wild horses or burros are rounded up for administering birth control or for removal from a particular parcel of public land.

Fertility control has helped some, but the drug **PZP** must be administered every year to each mare. This is physically impossible in large, rugged horse management areas, and it requires horse "**gathers**," which some advocates consider unnatural and overly stressful. Spaying is not safe, because the mares are pregnant virtually all the time. Left unchecked, each herd increases by 20 per cent every year and doubles in four or five years. These numbers do not include the estimated 100,000 animals within Native American reservations.

Beyond the numbers is the heart-breaking reality—because everyone, really, is a horse-lover at heart. In our area, many of the horse advocates work hard for the horses and do not want to "love them to death." Some even adopt animals.

Fringe "advocates" have been effective at lobbying against the slaughter of old, unadoptable—or really any—horses. Only 10 states have horse management areas, and most of their congressional representatives want to find a better solution.

It is easy for people in the other 40 states to be swayed by the extremists. Their efforts are responsible for the current situation, in which taxpayers support at least 80,000 excess horses, leaving us with no end in sight, not in numbers, not in funding, not in ecological damage. What is a real-world solution?

DOCUMENT 34:

Image: Mustangs at Wild Horse Sanctuary, near Shingletown, California (2012)[10]

Animal "sanctuaries" are private, non-profit or not-for-profit organizations that provide permanent homes for unwanted animals who might otherwise be euthanized. For wild horses, such sanctuaries are a respite from the auction, slaughterhouse, or BLM facilities where horses are held indefinitely. Since mustangs learned generations ago how to prosper on Western lands and multiplied, a new problem arose once BLM contractors collected them from public or private lands. There were always too few people willing to adopt captured mustangs as rural pets for their hobby farms and ranches. With that in mind, what are the politics of this image by American photographer Carol Highsmith? And of a charity "sanctuary" for wild horses?

---

10   "Some of the hundreds of wild horses at the Wild Horse Sanctuary south of the little town of Shingletown, east of Redding, California," 2012. Carol Highsmith photographer, Library of Congress.

DISCUSSION QUESTIONS/WRITING PROMPTS

1. What regions, people, animals, and time periods are addressed by the primary sources here?

2. Thinking back to earlier periods addressed in this book, what new kinds of primary sources do historians have for the twentieth century? What are the advantages and disadvantages of the new sources in understanding the past?

3. What do we learn from these primary sources about how cowboying and ranch work had changed over the course of the twentieth century?

4. How and why did Westerners disagree about horses in the West, especially wild horses? How do these primary sources expose the complex politics that emerged in the twentieth century over whether horses were cultural, environmental, or economic resources?

PART 6

Range and Cattle Controversies

DOCUMENT 35:

Environmental scientist Dana L. Yensen discusses "The 1900 Invasion of Alien Plants into Southern Idaho": *Great Basin Naturalist* (1981)[1]

Dana Yensen, a researcher working at the Department of Biological Sciences at the University of Idaho, reports here on the history of **cheatgrass** after the Beef Bonanza era in Idaho and the work of determining what the West looked like historically. Environmental scientists used a variety of historical primary sources to piece together what plants appeared in the region, when, and how, and thus how the local ecology was changed. Yensen's article was just one of hundreds of studies, papers, conference, and community hall presentations produced by people interested in sustainability and the history of the land. Such research might also be reprinted or discussed in ranching and cattle trade journals, as well as Western newspapers and magazines. Yensen's piece shows us how scientists used political language at times to indicate how they believed people should identify problems in range ecology and their causes, and (like the mustangs discussed in Part 5) which plants rightfully belonged in the West. In some ways, this article is a secondary and a primary source at the same time. To view this document with its original illustrations and bibliography, visit the Internet Archive.[2]

❦

Several European annual plants invaded southern Idaho during the few years preceding and following the turn of the century. The spread of these alien plants, especially cheatgrass, was so rapid that it often escaped recording (Leopold 1941). Four important plants—*Salsola iberica* **Sennen and Pau,** *Sisymbrium altissimum* **L.,** *Descurainia sophia* **(L.) Webb.,** and *Bromus tectorum* **L.**—changed the ecology and the very appearance of southern Idaho. This paper presents some new information on documenting the

cheatgrass: Also known as *Bromus tectorum*, this is an annual grass originating in Europe. It is dangerous to rangelands in North America because it takes over land from diverse plant ecosystems, replacing them with a cheatgrass monoculture that is nutritionally insufficient for cattle, horses, and wild ungulates like deer.

***Salsola iberica* Sennen and Pau:** Also known as Russian thistle plant, native to Europe.

***Sisymbrium altissimum* L.:** Also known as tumble mustard plant, native to southern Europe and North Africa.

***Descurainia sophia* (L.) Webb.:** Also known as flixweed, native to Europe and Central Asia.

***Bromus tectorum* L.:** Also known as cheatgrass or downy brome, native to Europe, North Africa, and southwest Asia; an "invasive" species, it has spread around the globe in the last century, altering ecologies and habitats so endangering local animal and plant species in many regions.

---

1   Dana L. Yensen, "The 1900 Invasion of Alien Plants into Southern Idaho," *Great Basin Naturalist* 41, no. 2 (June 1981): 176–83.

2   https://archive.org/details/biostor-238834/mode/2up.

invasion of these plants into southern Idaho, and the means by which they came to dominate millions of acres of desert rangeland.

Presettlement Vegetation

The presettlement vegetation of southern Idaho consisted largely of open-canopied communities of low-growing shrubs, especially big sagebrush (*Artemisia tridentata*), as well as winterfat (*Ceratoides lanata*), bitterbrush (*Purshia tridentata*), rabbit brushes (*Chrysothamnus* sp.), and shadscale (*Atriplex confertifolia*) and other salt-desert shrubs. Most of the Snake River Plain was dominated by communities of big sagebrush with a rich understory of perennial bunch grasses (*Stipa, Elymus, Agropyron, Oryzopsis, Poa*, and *Festuca*) and herbs (*Balsamorhiza, Hydrophylhan, Tragopogon*, and *Agoseris*), or by winterfat or other salt-desert communities (Townsend 1839, Fremont 1845, Irving 1907, Elliot 1913, Ferrin 1935, Keith 1938, Stover 1940, Vahlberry 1940, Platt and Jackman 1946, Blaisdell 1953, Root 1955, Shirk 1956, Fulton 1965, Ellison 1960, Vale 1975, Gibbs 1976, Hironaka and Fosberg 1979, Meacham 1979, Young et al. 1979). The perennial grasses and several of the shrubs, notably winterfat, saltbushes, and bitterbrush, are highly palatable and nutritious to grazing animals (Kennedy 1903, Hodgeson 1948, Hutchings and Stewart 1953, Ellison 1960).

Originally, if sagebrush grasslands were burned, trampled, or otherwise severely disturbed and left wholly or partially bare of vegetation, snakeweed (*Gutierrezia sarothrae*) would appear on the disturbed areas within a year or two (Stewart and Hull 1949). Establishment of snakeweed was followed by the appearance of the short-lived perennial grasses bottlebrush squirreltail (*Sitanion hystrix*) and Sandberg's bluegrass (*Poa sandbergii*), along with big sagebrush seedlings. Finally, the large-culmed perennial grasses and the perennial broadleaved herbs would appear (Ellison 1960, Young et al. 1972). Revegetation occupied about a decade, and only occurred if the area was not significantly disturbed. In southern Idaho at the turn of the century, however, continual disturbance by fire, abusive grazing, agricultural practices, and construction (railroads, roads, towns, canals) created an environment in which presettlement patterns of secondary succession could not persist unchanged (Kennedy 1903, Piemeisel 1938, 1951). The stage was set for the invasion of alien plants (Young et al. 1979).

Conditions Leading to the Invasion of Exotic Plants

By 1900, native plant communities had been severely damaged by overgrazing (Hodgeson 1948, Piemeisel 1938). Pickford (1932) wrote that in the 30 years after 1880, burning and abusive grazing had resulted in an 85 percent reduction in native perennial grasses and a 40 to 50 percent reduction in the carrying capacity of the range. By this time, stands of native perennial grasses had been virtually eliminated from southern Idaho desert lands (Hodgeson 1948). Burning also caused serious and widespread damage to the vegetation. Many stockmen, erroneously believing that burning the shrublands produced good stands of grasses even when grazing pressure following burning was not reduced, deliberately set range fires (Griffiths 1902, Pechanec and Hull 1945, Vale 1975). Griffiths (1902), who traveled southwestern Oregon ranges in 1901, reported that such range fires were very common, and that many of the fires were set by sheepmen. The fact that sheepmen used to set many range fires is common southern Idaho lore (Hicks pers. comm., C.L. Stewart pers. comm.).

From 1900 until the end of World War I, large numbers of prospective farmers settled in southern Idaho (Rinehart 1932, Gibbs 1976). In the words of Hultz (1934), the country was "wheat mad." Railroads offered cheap one-way home seeker fares, and many settlers took advantage of them (Stewart and Hull 1949, Gibbs 1976). Large acreages of sagebrush lands were settled and cleared for planting row crops and orchards. However, during the 1920s, an agricultural depression began in Idaho. Many farmers went bankrupt and abandoned their homestead claims (Stewart and Hull 1949, Gibbs 1976). Thousands of acres of plowed farmland, many acres of which had been **dry-farm wheatfields**, were left unattended (Warg 1938, Piemeisel 1938, Stewart and Hull 1949, Young et al. 1979).

dry-farm wheatfields: Plantations on historically arid land by way of techniques that preserve limited soil moisture.

Several decades of burning, trampling, overstocking, and abusive grazing not only severely damaged the perennial grass and herb understory of the big sagebrush lands, but also greatly reduced the acreage dominated by the most valuable forage shrub, winterfat. By 1900 many hundreds of thousands of acres of big sagebrush remained, virtually bare of understory (Sweetser 1935, Chapline 1936, Stewart 1936, Taylor 1940, Hodgeson 1948, Reidl et al. 1964, Young et al. 1979). Erosion of the soil became a critical problem, both on the open range and on abandoned cropland (Clapp 1936, USDI-BLM 1974). And, with no easing of grazing pressure, rehabilitation of the weakened native plant communities was not possible (Young et al. 1979).

History and Ecology of Invasion

...

Cheatgrass.—The most important exotic annual to invade Idaho was the Mediterranean winter annual grass *Bromas tectorum* L., which in the West has been called cheatgrass, cheatgrass brome, downy brome, downy chess, Junegrass, bronco grass, and Mormon oats. Cheatgrass now occurs in every state except Alabama, Georgia, South Carolina, and Florida. In the eastern states it is a roadside weed, but in the West it has invaded millions of acres of rangeland and cropland (Hull and Peehanec 1947, Stewart and Hull 1949, Klemmedson and Smith 1964).

Cheatgrass germinates during fall rains and maintains small, dormant leaves during the winter. In spring, it grows rapidly and begins to form seed heads in April. In May, the seeds mature, and the plants turn purplish as they dry in the early summer heat. In June and July the seeds mature and fall to the ground, and the plants die. The dry plants, by then straw colored, persist upright in place for months (Stewart and Hull 1949, Klemmedson and Smith 1964).

Stewart and Young (1949) noted that cheatgrass was collected in Pennsylvania in 1861, in Washington in 1893, in Utah in 1894, in Colorado in 1895, in Wyoming in 1900, and was present in nearly all of its current range by 1900, though it was not as abundant as it was later to become. Stewart and Young implied that the spread of cheatgrass was from east to west. However, there is a strong possibility that the first cheatgrass to arrive in Idaho came from **awns** carried in the coats of sheep trailed from California through Nevada to southern Idaho.

awns: The bristle-like seed pod surrounded by barbed fibers that hook into fur and wool common to many species of grasses.

Cheatgrass awns catch in the coats of livestock and may be carried for miles before dropping out (Piemeisel 1938). The first instances of cheatgrass invasion in Nevada were in areas where California sheep had grazed (Kennedy 1903). Since bands of California sheep were trailed through Nevada and into Idaho (Wentworth 1948, Hanley and Lucia 1973), it seems reasonable to assume that cheatgrass awns could have been carried into Idaho by these sheep. Piemeisel (1938) notes that, as with other exotic annuals, cheatgrass seeds were often present in alfalfa seeds, and cheatgrass was also distributed in that way. An Idaho Historical Society photograph (IHS 503-F), taken at the mouth of Kuna Cave in southern Ada County in 1898, shows a dense stand of cheatgrass growing under a sparse cover of big sagebrush. This is the earliest photographic evidence of cheatgrass occurrence in Idaho, and even at the time of the photograph it appears to have been well established. Klemmedson and Smith (1964) note that cheatgrass is included in Piper and Beattie's 1907 *Flora of the Palouse*, Howell's 1903 *Flora of Northwest America*, and Piper's 1906 *Flora of Washington*. Cheatgrass, however, is not mentioned in Weaver's (1917) *Flora of Southeastern*

Washington and Adjacent Idaho. O.R. Hicks (pers. comm.) remembered that, just prior to 1906, cheatgrass occurred in south central Idaho between the towns of Glenns Ferry and King Hill in what was called a "railroad line"—a line of cheatgrass invasion originating on the railroad right-of-way and extending about 300 yards into the native vegetation on either side of the railroad tracks. Hicks believed that cheatgrass was fed to the sheep in the stock cars and that seed heads fell from the cars to ground along the tracks.

In the first few years after 1900, cheatgrass gained a foothold on disturbed areas such as railroad rights-of-way, road shoulders, orchards, fallow fields, and especially in dryland alfalfa fields which were grazed after having been harvested (Stewart and Hull 1949). In photographs, cheatgrass is not distinctive in appearance at a distance and can be positively identified only in uncommon instances. It is undoubtably present in many photographs where reliable identification is not possible. (Cheatgrass is a relatively small, fine-textured plant, and its delicate heads are stirred by a slight breeze, often blurring the photographic image.) Idaho Historical Society photographs in which cheatgrass can be positively identified show cheatgrass to have been present in southern Idaho by 1910 in areas along railroad rights-of-way, on roadsides, and in vacant, disturbed areas within towns. Severely damaged rangeland was also invaded about this time (Stewart and Hull 1949).

Cheatgrass has been called an aggressive invader of big sagebrush lands (Platt and Jackman 1946), but Piemeisel (1938), who did classic **successional studies** in southern Idaho beginning in the 1920s, concluded that invasions of big sagebrush lands by cheatgrass were largely limited to voids in native vegetation. Warg (1938) concluded that cheatgrass could not invade pristine native vegetation and that invasion by cheatgrass was an indication of disturbed range. Young et al. (1979) also felt that exotic annuals, including cheatgrass, did not invade stands of healthy native vegetation.

Many stockmen were enthusiastic about the appearance of the abundant new grass, and erroneously believed it to be superior to the native perennials it had replaced (Stablein 1940, Platt and Jackman 1946). Even though cheatgrass was a poor substitute for the native grasses, at the time of its rapid establishment and spread it was a blessing for the range because it did afford quantities of forage for livestock held on depleted ranges, and afforded some protection from soil erosion when much of the range was overgrazed and denuded of soil cover (Platt and Jackman 1946).

Cheatgrass burns. Because cheatgrass is the most inflammable of the range forage plants, range fires in southern Idaho became more frequent. Cheatgrass range is 500 times more likely to burn than any other rangeland type (Platt and Jackman 1946, Stewart and Hull 1949). Leopold (1941) wrote that it is in fact impossible to protect cheatgrass ranges from fire. Burning is very damaging to big sagebrush-grass communities (Pechanec et al. 1954, Vale 1974). The

successional studies: Scientific studies of ecological succession; namely, the process by which a group of inter-reliant species is established in a given habitat, how that network of species grows in complexity or otherwise changes over time, and the causes of those changes.

presence of cheatgrass in these communities can carry fires into areas that would normally not burn (Stewart and Hull 1949, Hull 1965, Pechanec et al. 1954).

Many early stockmen believed that fire did not damage cheatgrass stands (Stablein 1940, Pechanec and Hull 1945), since, once established on an area, cheatgrass will be present the year after it has been burned because cheatgrass seeds are not usually all destroyed by fire (Warg 1938, Leopold 1941). Many southern Idaho stockmen regularly set range fires, because the following year the burned areas were not camouflaged by shrubs or by the previous year's dried growth and so appeared greener (Hicks pers. comm.). Cheatgrass on the range increased very rapidly when fire was combined with overgrazing, which was often the case (Stewart and Young 1939, Leopold 1941, Ellison 1960, Ilironaka and Fosberg 1979). Cheatgrass replaced much vegetation on burned areas and came to dominate millions of acres, aided by its own flammability (Stewart and Hull 1949, Klemmedson and Smith 1964, Ilironaka and Fosberg 1979).

After cheatgrass became well established in southern Idaho, the pattern of secondary succession was changed. No longer was an initial disturbance necessarily followed by the eventual appearance of native shrubs and grasses. After the invasion of the exotic annuals, the secondary succession pattern became Russian thistle invasion initially, followed by mustard invasion, and finally by cheatgrass establishment. Russian thistle dominated for a year or two, mustards for two or three years, and then cheatgrass became the dominant species (Piemeisel 1951, Hironaka and Tisdale 1963). If undisturbed, cheatgrass stands were in turn invaded by bottlebrush squirreltail and subsequently by other native plants (Hironaka and Tisdale 1963). However, if cheatgrass were burned or grazed, it was able to maintain itself indefinitely (Piemeisel 1938, 1951). Overgrazing combined with burning helped to insure a continuous stand of cheatgrass and to prevent reestablishment of native plants (Piemeisel 1938, 1951, Leopold 1941, Stewart and Hull 1949).

In the years immediately following World War I, cheatgrass made its most rapid advances, colonizing millions of acres of abandoned farmland and disturbed range (Piemeisel 1938, Wentworth 1948, Stewart and Hull 1949). By the late 1920s cheatgrass was abundant in southern Idaho. An *Idaho Statesman* article dated 1 May 1928 reported that the desert bunchgrass had been replaced by grass that "grows in a day, ripens in a day, and blows away in a day." By 1932, the most important plant on Idaho desert ranges was cheatgrass (Rinehart 1932). By 1949, about 4,000,000 acres in Idaho were dominated by cheatgrass, and cheatgrass was an important component of the vegetation on 10,000,000 to 15,000,000 additional Idaho acres (Stewart and Hull 1949). This plant is now the most important forage plant in Idaho (Klemmedson and Smith 1964). The impact of cheatgrass is difficult to comprehend, for it has literally changed the appearance of southern Idaho (Young et al. 1979).

DOCUMENT 36:

Bureau of Land Management, Federal Public Land Surface and Subsurface Map (ca. 2005)[3]

The scale of federally controlled, public land ownership in the West has been controversial for decades, although it no doubt prevented many tragedy of the commons events. Advocates for local state or private ownership have argued since the early twentieth century that the federal government is too inefficient and distant from local concerns to manage public lands in local interest. They accuse Bureau of Land Management (BLM), National Park Service, or National Forest Service managers of allowing land to be exploited or, conversely, of being too restrictive when private interests ask for leases and other access to public areas. At the same time, many governors and state officials have known for years that their state budgets could not possibly afford to take on management of those lands, even if they know local constituents would support a transfer from federal to state control. Others have asked for public lands to simply be sold off altogether so that private citizens and companies can make their own use of them with less oversight.

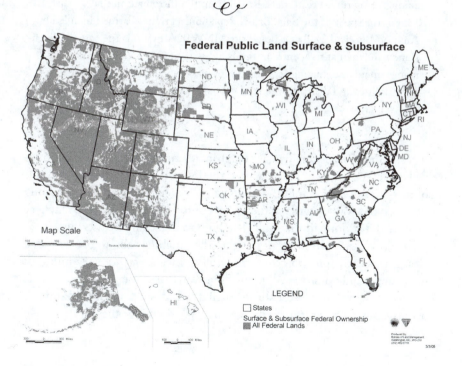

Federal Public Land Surface & Subsurface

---

3   https://en.wikipedia.org/wiki/Federal_lands#/media/File:Map_of_all_U.S._Federal_Land.jpg.

DOCUMENT 37:

Denzel and Nancy Ferguson criticize cattle grazing contracts: *Sacred Cows at the Public Trough* (1983)[4]

Nancy and Denzel Ferguson were among environmentalists who called for a reduction or elimination of extensive ranching on public lands. In the mid-1970s, the couple began work as managers of the Malheur Field Station, an educational and research facility within the Malheur National Wildlife Refuge (MNWR) in southeastern Oregon. The Oregon government describes the Malheur refuge as "a diverse setting of marshlands, desert basins, **alkali playas**, upland desert scrub steppe, volcanic and glacial landforms and **fault block mountains**, providing a rich outdoor classroom for the biologist, geologist, archaeologist, artist, astronomer or environmental science student."[5] The Fergusons charged that, despite the refuge's ecological fragility and importance, local cattle operations had leases to bring cows and calves onto refuge lands where the cattle did considerable damage to the land, plant life, and waterways, exposing the outsized political power of the minority of Westerners engaged in cattle production. The Fergusons' 1983 book, *Sacred Cows at the Public Trough*, contributed to public debates over federal land use among many rural Westerners. Recall from the Introduction that, in early 2016 in the spirit of the Sage Brush Rebellion, a group of armed men led by Ammon Bundy illegally occupied the MNWR. Ammon is the son of Cliven Bundy, the man at the centre of the Bundy Standoff protesting federal land management and grazing fees. The event was emblematic of continued far-right politics and distrust of federal power among some ranchers.

alkali playas: Evaporated lake beds covered in dried salts.

fault block mountains: Large block-shaped rock formations caused by shifts in the Earth's crust

℮

The *Wall Street Journal* (22 January 1982), in describing the routine operations of a large cattle ranch in Nevada, used the following lead: "Bleeding at four points on its body, a big bull calf bucks to its feet and plunges headlong into a nervous wall of cattle at the far end of the corral. What [the rancher's name] had just done to that bull is enough to make any man **cringe**."

The article goes on to point out that the ranch has about 7,000 deeded acres, grazes cattle on 700,000 acres (a block measuring 30 by 82 miles) of public range, and doesn't need to buy or grow hay because the cattle are able to graze all winter on desert shrubs such as white sage, shadscale, and salt bush. The ranch owner is quoted as saying, "We do things the old style"—in

cringe: Here the journalist probably refers to the moment a young male calf is first dehorned, castrated, and marked with a cut to one or both ears.

---

4 Bend, OR: Maverick Publications, 1983, 47–58.

5 Oregon Secretary of State, "Malheur Field Station," *Oregon Blue Book*.

other words, the same way things have been done in Nevada valleys for the past hundred years.

And the results are very much in evidence, for Nevada, which has more than 25 percent of all BLM[6] land in the West, provides an outstanding example of the low state of productivity of public rangelands. The BLM administers 49.1 million acres in that state—69 percent of the total land area—and when properly stocked, these lands have a carrying capacity of 1,836,912 AUM's.[7] Nevada's beef production in 1979 ranked 37th in the nation—on par with that of Vermont. In other words, an average of 26.7 acres of BLM land in Nevada is required to feed one cow for a month! The national average, which includes all public land, is about 5 acres (95 percent of all BLM land gets less than 15 inches of rainfall a year). In contrast, an Alabama cattleman can graze one cow for an entire year on 3.5 acres—that's slightly less than 0.3 acre per AUM, 91 times the productivity of BLM land in Nevada. (Note—Alabama pastures are also taxed for support of schools and local government). Exceptionally productive ranges, as in Puerto Rico, can support a cow year-round on only 2 acres.

In sticking to the old ways, the Nevada rancher is not unique. Most western ranchers continue to use traditional practices dating back to the original Spanish cattlemen. Of course some changes have occurred—winter feeding is standard in many areas, more of the public range is fenced into smaller grazing units, and the livestock industry is highly mechanized, with pickup trucks, fancy horse trailers, and fixed-wing aircraft taking on much of the original burden borne by the horse and cowboy. Other innovations involve breeding lines and veterinary practices. But the annual cycle of events, range practices, and operating philosophy of ranchers using the public lands have changed very little.

In parts of the West, where public grazing is limited to a portion of the year, typically April through October, the date of **spring turn-out** on the public rangelands varies depending upon locality and agency. Ideally, the date of spring turn-out should be sufficiently late in the season to insure melting of the winter snowpack, dry soils (to minimize effects of trampling), and a good head start in the growth of range vegetation. Grazing too early in the season can devastate good range.

Where distance permits, cattle are usually driven from home ranches to allotments on public land, at which time roads and highways, including major interstate routes, are temporarily clogged with milling herds of cattle. For motorists, large cattle drives can be exasperating and frightening—a

spring turn-out: The moment when ranch operators transfer cattle from a small range where they are supplemented over the winter with hay and other feed to a large range where cattle will forage for grasses and other plants on their own.

---

6   Bureau of Land Management.

7   Animal Unit Month, "the amount of forage required to feed a cow and her calf, a horse, or five sheep or goats for a month." Ferguson and Ferguson, *Sacred Cows*, 36.

moving sea of tightly bunched cattle, towering above the average compact car and obliterating everything but patches of sky. Although some cowboys will make an effort to clear a path through the bawling brutes, many delight in standing aside and regaling in the plight of helpless motorists.

In Baker, Oregon (population about 9,400), herds of several hundred cattle are driven down main street, which is also U.S. Highway 30, forcing pedestrians to flee for cover and bringing traffic to a standstill. Bellowing cattle **preempt** sidewalks, block entrances to stores, fill the streets, and splatter the route with excrement. Similar scenes are repeated in towns and cities throughout the West.

Because many home ranches are far from public grazing allotments, cattle are trucked to and fro. Large cattle trucks, loaded or not, can be a nuisance as they roar along highways spewing urine and feces to the wind.

In the past, typical allotments for public grazing, especially those on BLM land, involved enormous acreages of unfenced, remote rangeland. On such allotments, herds belonging to several different owners share the range, intermingled, and wandered great distances from original points of release. Because the cattle were unsupervised, large numbers concentrated in favorable sites and severely overgrazed the forage, while more remote or less favorable sites were lightly grazed or untouched.

On these large units, it was nearly impossible for agency personnel to detect **permit violations**. Knowing this, ranchers often extended the length of the authorized grazing season or put extra cattle on the allotment with little fear of being caught. Furthermore, stockmen who weren't even entitled to graze an allotment were able to trespass with relative impunity. Although some of these large units continue to exist, agencies have recently built thousands of miles of fences in a concerted effort to create smaller, more manageable units that can be assigned to individual ranchers or small groups. The extent of such fence building is well-illustrated in Oregon's Malheur National Forest, where a 28-mile segment of road crosses 22 fences at 13 single and 9 double-wide **cattle guards**, which cost $1,500 to $25,000 each, depending upon size and type. In recent years, smaller grazing units have gained added favor as the Forest Service and BLM have adopted various rotational grazing schemes involving periodic rest or deferred grazing allotments.

Management agencies are empowered to impound trespassing livestock and to assess charges against the owners for costs of capturing and caring for the offending animals and may even sell stock unclaimed by the owner in a specified time. But the legal procedures for dealing with cases of trespass are arduous, slow, and bound up in paper work. Consequently, the option of legal prosecution is often circumvented in favor of settlements based on gentlemen's agreement. Although conflict is avoided, violators usually get off

preempt: Appropriate or take over.

permit violations: When a rancher or ranching company gains a permit to graze cattle on a particular area of public land, the permit includes specific limits on how many cattle may graze, and when and where they may do so during the year. The limits are designed to prevent overgrazing of fragile areas and promote sustainability of the range indefinitely.

cattle guard: Sometimes known as a "Western gate" in eastern sections of the continent; a heavy metal grate installed across a road at an opening in fencing with a pit below the grate. The guard permits vehicles to drive over the grate, but prevents cattle or horses from crossing since their hooves slip off the round bars in the grate and will fall into the pit below. Horses and cattle learn when young to avoid cattle guards.

scot-free. Ranchers choosing to trespass on public lands are fully aware that the risks and costs are minor compared to the potential gains for undetected violations. Grazing permits may be cancelled after repeated violations, but such drastic action is rare. In fact, because of widespread feelings of open resentment of federal agencies in the rural West, successful violators are often admired in the community—sort of grass-stealing Robin Hoods. Many stockmen who trespass on public lands are among the most successful citizens and may attain high office, as in the case of Robert Burford, Director of the BLM in the Reagan Administration.

In 1977, eighty ranchers in Nevada were cited for 20,500 head of trespassing cattle, sheep, and horses on BLM lands, but were fined only $26,400—considerably less than the cost of grazing the same animals legally for a month. Furthermore, BLM officials in Nevada believe that prosecuted cases are only the tip of the iceberg. Most trespassing goes undetected with as few as two or three BLM employees overseeing as much as 4 million acres of rangeland. Nevada has more cases of trespass than any other state and accounts for about a fourth of all reported cases on BLM rangelands.

John J. Casey, a multimillionaire rancher and hotel owner who is known as the king of trespassing cattle and holds a 20-year record of illegal grazing in Nevada, California, and Montana. In just one area, near Susanville, California, in an 11-year period he was cited for 89 cases of trespassing in 140 incidents on BLM land. And largely to no avail, the federal government has spent more than $1 million prosecuting Casey for numerous trespass violations. When a judge asked him if he felt he had a trespass problem, Casey replied, "I feel I have been and am being picked on." Like Casey, many ranchers are aware of the impotency of the federal government in prosecuting cases of livestock trespass and are perfectly willing to risk the consequences, if any.

At spring turn-out, cattle are put on the allotment and left to fend for themselves—the rancher goes home. In mountainous terrain, the cattle are released at low elevations and follow melting snowlines and the new growth of vegetation up the mountain, often reaching subalpine or alpine meadows and range in late summer or early fall. With the arrival of fall storms at high elevations or with the drying and depletion of forage supplies on desert ranges, cattle often head toward the home ranch of their own volition. In any event, when the authorized grazing period ends, ranchers round up their cattle and drive or haul them to the home ranch. In some areas, other federal lands may be available for winter use. In southeastern Oregon, for example, many ranchers remove cattle from Forest Service or BLM allotments and move them to Malheur National Wildlife Refuge for the winter. Because modern ranches employ few hired hands, except for summer haying, neighboring ranchers often assist each other with the fall round up and brandings—such events being highlights of the social season, with ample food and drink.

From time to time, especially in the spring before turn-out and in the fall after roundup, new calves are branded. Using hot irons, cowboys burn the appropriate symbol into the living skin, usually on the upper thigh. The healed scar remains for the lifetime of the animal as proof of ownership. In addition to the brand, other symbols of identification are used. These include notches cut in one or both ears and the **dewlap wattle**, which is formed by cutting a six-inch flap of skin loose on the neck so that the bloody flap dangles free from the top of the incision as a pendant. Similar flaps of skin may be cut on the lower cheek. Some ranches use all of these disfigurements to mark their cattle. In addition, bull calves suffer the additional ordeal of castration at the time of branding and marking. Much of this gore is accomplished with a pocketknife, which the restrained animal bellows and writhes in pain. Sometimes, dehorning is added to the list of misfortunes. The entire procedure, which originated with Spanish cattlemen, has deviated but little in centuries. While this bloody mayhem remains standard throughout western rangelands, organizations devoted to the humane treatment of animals struggle to stop such atrocities as jumping frog contests, porcupine races, and greased pig contests! ...

Today, most ranchers using public lands have cow-calf operations, in which the basic resource is a herd of brood cows. The principal income is derived from sale of **yearling heifers and steers (feeder cattle)** to feedlots for fattening before slaughter. In the past, steers were often kept on the range for several years before being sent to market.

In assessing grazing fees, agencies do not charge for calves less than 6 months old. Because calving time can be set, depending upon when bulls are put with the cows, it is possible to have a fall calving season, however, most calves have traditionally been born in the spring. Spring calves are not charged for grazing. They spend their first summer loafing, following the cow, taking milk, and eating little forage. In contrast, fall calves eat forage the first summer on the range and make rapid weight gains, but of course require extra care the first winter after birth and count in assessments of grazing fees.

For winter feed, hay is cut from wild hay meadows or alfalfa fields, normally located on deeded property, although some agencies, such as certain national wildlife refuges, sell hay on a permit system. Cattle are usually fed on home ranches in feedlots likely to remain accessible and convenient throughout the winter. Most often, the hay is simply thrown on the ground for the cattle to gather. Although large crews were formerly required to harvest hay, the task has become highly mechanized, and today a single worker can harvest huge quantities of hay. The principal environmental

dewlap wattle: The flap of skin and tissue hanging below the neck.

yearling heifers and steers (feeder cattle): Year-old female and male cattle who have not bred and have grown enough to be transferred to a feedlot in preparation for slaughter.

impacts of winter feeding are conversions of valuable wildlife habitats to hay lands, intensive use of surface and ground waters for irrigation, wildlife losses associated with the use of haying machinery, such as mowers, and water pollution derived from feedlots.

In areas where year-round grazing is permitted on public lands, which includes about 21 percent of all Forest Service and BLM holdings, ranges tend to suffer extreme overgrazing. Because of severe overgrazing, cattle competition with wildlife becomes especially acute when forage is depleted in drought years or during unfavourable seasons. Also, because cattle are on the range when soils are wet, much damage results to the sparse plant life and fragile soils. In some areas, as much as 100 acres (or even more) are required to provide a month's forage for a cow—obviously, such lands should not be grazed at all.

In order to appreciate the cow as an instrument of range destruction, we need to examine its basic features and behaviour in greater detail.

Range cattle are out there—24 hours a day, 7 days a week, and for months or even years at a time. A standing cow exerts about 24 pounds per square inch upon the soil, and of course the pressure increases through the remaining feet if one is lifted or if the cow is in motion. Modern range cattle weigh 1,000 pounds or more, compared with the Texas Longhorn's average weight of 650 pounds. To obtain the amount of forage desired, a cow is willing to graze about 8 hours a day. When not actually gathering food, an equivalent amount of time is devoted to ruminating—regurgitating material from the first "stomach" and chewing it—or "chewing the cud," as the saying goes. About 25 pounds of native grass must be eaten to produce a pound of beef. When an 800 pound steer is butchered and the head, feet, hide, guts, etc. removed, the dressed weight is about 500 pounds. However, with the removal of fat and trimmings, the finished cuts, which include a considerable weight in bone, weigh only 340 pounds (42.5 percent of the original weight). In 1982, Americans consumed an average of about 77 pounds (retail weight) of beef per person.

Cattle are usually described as being grazers, meaning that they feed primarily on grasses and other herbage near ground level, as contrasted with browsers, such as deer, which feed principally upon shrubs. If given a choice in the matter, cattle prefer to graze, usually taking the tender tops and exhibiting little selectivity. As the forage supply is depleted, grazing becomes more selective, and coarser material, such as grasses and stems, are rejected. But as the available forage continues to diminish, stems are taken and the animals begin to **use larger quantities of browse**. Finally, when given no choice in the matter, cattle will feed almost exclusively on shrubs and other coarse material and gain weight in the process, as was the case for over-wintering cattle on the ranch described in the *Wall Street Journal*

use larger quantities of browse: If land is being overgrazed by supporting too many animals, in time those animals will consume all the new, high-energy forage, then resort to eating stems and remainders offering less energy and nutrition, which in turn damages those plants such that they cannot regenerate.

articles. So in the final analysis, the cow is a living vacuum cleaner, willing and able to move over the rangeland sucking up every bit of vegetable matter—right down to the bare soil if need be. This plasticity of the diet of cattle has made it possible for ranchers to "mine" overgrazed rangeland, while stubbornly insisting that the range is in good condition. No wonder cattlemen would rather have critics look at the cow instead of the range.

In humid climates, cattle consume about 50 pounds of forage a day, but in arid regions, such as much of the West, daily consumption is probably closer to half this amount (700–800 pounds a month). When slaughtered, a 1,000 pound feedlot steer will have consumed 12,000 pounds of forage and 2,850 pounds of grain and soy concentrates. When cattle can eat their fill every day, 70 percent of the digestible nutrients in the forage is required to maintain normal body functions, and only 30 percent goes to growth and reproduction (net gain). On the average, a range cow drinks between 35 and 70 pounds (5 to 9 gallons) of water a day. Producing a pound of beef, including the water required to grow the forage and the amount drunk by the animal, takes 25 times more water than producing a pound of bread. A hamburger for lunch and an eight-ounce steak for dinner require an investment of 3,910 gallons of water. The daily production of excrement by a cow is 52 pounds of manure and 20 pounds of urine, yet grazing does not significantly enrich range soils because large amounts of plant nutrients stored in cattle carcasses are eventually removed from the land and consumed elsewhere. According to one authority, the contribution of livestock to the nation's water pollution is 10 times that of humans and 3 times that of industry.

The carrying capacity of grazing allotments is set by agencies according to the amount of available forage. This procedure assumes that cattle will make uniform use of an allotment, regardless of terrain, slope, distance from water, and other variables. In practice, such is not the case. Cattle are basically lazy, and when they find ample food, water and shade, they stay right there until forced to move to another site. Consequently, lush bottomlands and riparian zones (the rich streamside habitat) are severely overgrazed, while forage on steep slopes, uplands, and remote parts of an allotment may go completely unused. Cattle prefer to graze 0–10 percent slopes, and use decreases markedly on slopes of 30 percent or more. Good range management practices dictate that cattle be moved from an allotment when half the current year's production of forage has been consumed in the riparian zone—even if not a blade of grass has been removed from steep slopes and other sites avoided by cows. Because agency permits entitle ranchers to a predetermined number of AUM's and length of grazing season, this precaution is universally ignored and accounts for a major portion of the grazing abuse on public rangelands. Given current practices, the only solution seems to be the use of riders to force cattle to disperse out from streamside and other points of concentration....

On arid rangelands, particularly during the summer, cattle congregate at water holes where they lounge about during the hot part of the day and move out to feed, primarily during cooler periods in the morning and afternoon. Because the immediate vicinity of these water holes is severely trampled, littered with excrement, and devoid of forage, such places are virtually destroyed and are commonly called "sacrifice areas." Forage use decreases with distance from water, and on relatively level terrain, use drops off sharply beyond a mile from water. The low mobility of modern cattle has intensified overgrazing—in contrast, Texas Longhorns were able to graze a radius of 100 miles from water and thrive....

The cow is a biological eating machine, and as such, is unbelievably destructive when turned loose to fend for itself on the fragile lands that make up the semiarid ranges of the West.

Rancher Linda Hasselstrom explains her environmental ethics: *Between Grass and Sky: Where I Work and Live* (2005)[8]

> The North Dakota rancher and writer Linda Hasselstrom lived through the conflicts of the 1990s between beef producers and environmentalists and wrote about how she understood herself and other ranchers to be stewards of the land. She is not uncritical of the commercial meat system in which she participates, which links food conglomerates, government agencies, and small businesspeople like herself to consumers. Still, her defense of her lifestyle and work shows she believes that outsiders misunderstand the dilemmas and trials with which rural people contended in producing food for the continent.

I'm a rancher, so when I want beef, I pick out a likely heifer from the hillside and encourage her to stroll calmly into a small corral containing feed. I kill her without scaring her, with one bullet in the center of her forehead, and cut her throat. I hang her body by the ankles from a tractor loader to skin and gut her, hauling her head and innards to a hillside where the coyotes will feast for several nights. I cut and wrap the meat for my own freezer and serve it to my guests as organic beef. I know—because I was present every day of that cow's life—that all she ever consumed was grass, hay raised without herbicides or chemicals, pure water, and salt.

Most urban Americans buy beef wrapped in plastic from a well-lighted supermarket. Relish that steak while you consider the life of the animal who furnished it. The calf may have been born on a ranch like mine, where someone helped the cow if necessary, and watched the calf for signs of sickness until it was six months old. Quietly, we herded the cows into the corral and separated them from their calves. Within an hour, we'd loaded the calves into a truck—we don't allow our truckers to use prod poles, electric tools that administer a shock. Unloaded at the sale right, the calf hardly had time to miss its mother before it entered the ring with fifty other calves and was sold to the highest bidder.

Then a trucker crowded as many calves as possible into his truck and sped east several hundred miles to a feedlot in Iowa or Nebraska. There the calf was dumped into a lot where it may not even have had the space to lie down. Shoulder to shoulder, hundreds of calves struggled to a feed bunk to eat corn protected by the latest agricultural herbicides, guaranteed, according to their advertising, "to kill everything." The biggest calves, like schoolyard

---

8   Reno: U of Nevada P, 2005, 162–64, 166–71.

bullies, always ate the most. Some of the weakest may have been injured, or died. When it wasn't eating, the calf stood idle, often knee-deep in mud for six months or more, until it was killed for your dinner....

If you eat supermarket beef, you might want to research Department of Agriculture inspection regulations; within the last few years the agency has reclassified a frightening collection of animal diseases as being "defects that rarely or never present a direct public health risk," and allowed "unaffected carcass portions" to be passed on to consumers. In other words, meat workers are supposed to simply cut out cancer, lymphomas and tumors, sores, and intestinal worms, among other things, and send the carcass down the line to be wrapped and sold to you. Some feedlots are experimenting with feeding the waste, including the diseased parts, to other cattle, though fear of foot-and-mouth disease may stop that nasty trend.

Feedlots where range-bred cattle fatten are often owned by the same companies that hold the farms where the **corn** is produced, the meatpacking plants where animals are slaughtered, and the grocery chain stores where the price is affixed. None of the steps by which the beef on your plate is produced compares to the risks and labor the family rancher puts into his herd.

On my ranch, calves range over miles of pastures, free to romp, grazing on native grass. Their wastes are deposited on the ground and scattered by bugs and birds. Rains wash a little manure into stock dams, but none of our cattle waste reaches water used for human consumption. Feedlot operators are regularly granted "permits to pollute" rivers and streams by county or state governments, who hope to bring jobs to impoverished rural residents. The average feedlot dumps tons of cattle waste into rivers in the nation's heart every week, corrupting more water than I've ever seen....

Every week someone somewhere mentions creating a "new paradigm for western environmental policy," probably in a meeting where experts declare the need to remove cattle from public lands. Environmental leaders hint darkly that cows exist only because "powerful ranching interests control Congress."

People who advise rural folks on economic strategies seldom live in the West or have the foggiest notion of how and why ranchers survive here. Public figures offering counsel on the West's problems appear not to grasp the reality every ranch kid knows at ten years old: resources—especially the soil and water imperative for life—are scarce. If shortsighted people govern the West in ignorance, ranchers in worn boots will jostle each other on every city street corner while public lands become dusty zoos full of starving elk.

Only grass keeps most of the West's thin soil from blowing east in swirling clouds to fall into the Atlantic Ocean. Evolved over millions of years, grasses utilize unique combinations of nutrients and water in specific ways unique to each prairie region. Grass is the main product of Western

corn: Beginning in the 1950s, government scientists and animal science researchers at many universities began recommending corn as an inexpensive cattle feed. Large industrial agriculture companies made this standard for feedlots, where cattle would gain great weight very quickly, although many were made sick by the feed. In response, feedlot operators treated cattle with an array of antibiotics and other drugs to suppress the digestive and other physiological problems caused by corn-based feeds, such as liver damage and internal-organ-constricting "bloat," from the painful production of excess intestinal gasses, including environmentally devastating methane. Although in the nineteenth century people sold older animals to the feedlots, by the mid-twentieth century most young cattle were being weaned and shipped to the feedlot by 6 months of age, then slaughtered by 14 months.

rangelands. Disturbing the surface of the earth—plowing and bulldozing space for houses, highways, and parking lots—destroys grass and encourages weeds. Even ardent vegetarians don't eat "creeping jenny" (field bindweed). Every farming method tried on arid prairies has been less successful than Nature's. Few crops could thrive under these tough conditions as well as grass does.

The most sensible way to sell grass—or "realize its market potential" if you think in economic language—is inside a grazing animal. If, as **Aldo Leopold** commands, we make the land's needs basic to planning in the West, we must consider two resources—water and grass—first. By Leopold's gauge, sustainable ranching may be the most logical and practical profession on the plains. If a ranch has been in business for a hundred years, its owners or managers are working to maintain its water, grass, and even wildlife.

Of course, my rancher father didn't teach me how to "sustain a naturally functioning ecosystem." He said, "This land will take care of us if we take care of it." I learned by watching his actions that he considered antelope, deer, badgers, and coyotes important to our ranch. He didn't call it an ecosystem, but it is. Much of our land lies on either side of a long, normally dry draw that drops out of the Black Hills on the west and stretches to the Badlands on the east. The antelope and deer graze among the willows, helping keep them in check; badgers and coyotes helped us keep the prairie dogs and moles under control.

Folks who live in town rarely consider predation relevant to their lifestyle unless they meet a mugger. Visiting Yellowstone Park, they expect to gawk at elk and geysers, but be protected from grizzlies and forest fires. Managing the park for those isolated elements has nearly eliminated everything else in the park—the animals and vegetation that create the variations of a healthy environment. As a rancher, I battle predatory blizzards, bankers, and environmentalists, but I try to remember that Nature thrives on conflict, and that I may survive through skill rather than power.

Undoubtedly, the West was settled by a rugged tribe chasing profits in cattle and grass. Gradually, though, they deduced why too many cows or too many people destroyed their livelihood. Ranchers who came west in the 1800s knew nothing of ecosystems, but if their descendants are still here, they know that any sustainable economy proposed for western prairies must start with consideration for grass and water....

Cooperation between ranchers and their critics is the way to find an answer to the challenge of land use in the West. Antagonism arises because neither faction knows enough about the other's position. Ranch publications make environmentalists' issues sound like an invading horde, while folks in favor of preservation portray ranchers as barbarians. Simple minds and one-dimensional thought processes are an advantage to an army, but

Aldo Leopold: Leopold (1887–1948) was an environmental ethicist and ecologist who advocated for conservationist policies allowing use of federal lands but in sustainable ways that would keep them productive and biodiverse. Conservationism is distinct from preservationist philosophy and practice, made famous by John Muir and others a generation earlier, which sought to reduce or eliminate human activities on particular areas of US Federal Lands, such as national parks. The tension between the two impulses, conservation versus preservation, has characterized political debates over land use in the US for well over a century.

residents of the West ought to know better. As an environmentalist born and raised on a ranch, I don't like to visit national parks or cities. Both resemble zoos too much for my taste—noisy, crowded, artificial environments that drive their inhabitants insane—in strong contrast with the well-managed ecosystem where I live....

Do you hear fiddle music as the last rancher rides off into the sunset? Many people think ranching is doomed, if not already dead and buried. I'm not ready to concede defeat, but if ranchers want to avoid extinction, they need to make some tough choices.

Already, the traditional rusty pickup with a dog drooling over the tailgate is being displaced by shiny double-cab jobs with dual tires lugging clipped dogs in cages. And no one wants to talk about water, the silent partner in any speculation about the future. The value of agricultural land is debatable, altered each time ranches are diced into subdivisions.

I remember the first rancher in the neighborhood who sold his ranch for double what the tax assessor said it was worth. He related the news with the self-satisfied air of someone who's just sold the Golden Gate Bridge. Loitering in the aisles of our local grocery store while the owner tallied the cost of our purchases in her old gray head, shoppers muttered to one another. "Did ya see that house them new people are building?"

"Hard to miss. If it don't **blow off the top of that hill** in the first blizzard, it's gonna be bigger than the town hall."

One chuckled wisely while the other repeated the old saying that we'd all make more money if we sold the land, put the money in the bank, and lived off the interest.

Gossip turned to bellyaching once we realized how much our neighbor's windfall was going to raise our taxes. Livestock raisers said they didn't know how they could hang on if the taxes went much higher and cattle prices didn't keep up. Each time another ranch sold, the selling price rose, making all the surrounding ranches "worth more"—but only if they were for sale. We congratulated all those canny former ranchers as they packed for the move to Arizona. No one mentioned that making money without working went against everything we believed.

Meanwhile, rumors flew: the newest buyer owns an island, and is going to use this place for hunting. Is he putting in gold plumbing? We groused at speeding construction vehicles on the dirt road, and a few of us lamented the number of deer, rabbits, badgers, and coyotes run over, happy none of our kids got in their way. Shrugging, we repeated clichés: "Got to get bigger to get better. It's progress; what can you do?"

Nowadays we don't stand around chatting. We toss remarks at one another as we fill our go-cups in the new combination gas station/bar/café out by the highway. Those newcomers from California occupy every hilltop in

blow off the top of that hill: Traditionally, ranchers and homesteaders built their houses at the base of hills or in small gullies to protect them from the freezing and harsh winds of winter, for which the northern Great Plains and Rocky Mountain regions are notorious. By contrast, those who build homes in the West as retirees and tourists conspicuously build houses on the tops of hills or the sides of mountains where they enjoy a beautiful view but are exposed to the region's harsh weather. As a result, the location of a house on the landscape reveals to people driving by whether the house is owned by local working people or people of leisure.

sight—apparently don't know the winter wind tugs at the roof and piles snowdrifts in front of garage doors. Maybe they don't care because they won't be here in the winter. Property taxes are so high our grandfathers are spinning in their graves, but the new highway makes trips to town easy, a good thing since most of us have jobs there. Instead of stocking up on groceries once a month, we pick up something for dinner at the deli on the way home. We don't buy anything but our daily coffee fix at the station on the highway, but it's sure nice to have those tourist dollars in the little town's treasury now that we need more deputies and a town marshal to catch the speeders, and isn't that regular trash pickup handy? Shame old Anna died before she had a chance to enjoy her retirement after she closed the grocery store. Gotta run!

Some cynics suggest that once all the recalcitrant old ranchers are replaced by politically correct tofu eaters, the West will be knee-deep in garbage shipped from the East Coast. Now that tourism has moved ahead of agriculture as the primary business in many states, some folks might welcome garbage. We could pave it, providing jobs, and creating ever-growing parking lots for convenience stores and tourist destinations like Mount Rushmore.

open range: A proposed rewilding project not yet enacted in which lands would be pulled back from ranching or other development, some semblance of nineteenth-century grasslands reinstated, and a bison ecology cultivated there. The Yellowstone to Yukon Conservation Initiative is a similar effort still active. https://y2y.net/.

A few activists predict an **open range** will stretch from the Canadian border to the southern tip of Texas, unfenced and untenanted except by wild bison, wolves, and other native animals. One group even wants to bring back the woolly mammoth but would settle for elephants....

By contrast, in my ideal future, ranching would remain the backbone of the arid shortgrass plains for simple economic reasons that affect both meat-eaters and those who prefer tofu. Millions of years of evolution have developed plants best suited to the western landscape. The best way to harvest their bounty is—so far—inside a grazing animal.

Image: Eat Beef: Plumas Sierra Cattlewomen sign, California (2012)[9]

The photographer Carol Highsmith captured this visual representation of the culture of ranchers, who encourage people to eat beef because cattle production makes their businesses and way of life possible in the rural West. This sign was erected by a local stock-raisers association Plumas-Sierra Cattlewomen, which was formed in 1966 in the Sierra Nevada mountains in Northern California.

---

9   "Eat Beef: Plumas Sierra Cattlewomen" sign, California, 2012, Carol Highsmith photographer, Library of Congress.

Table: Oxford University and thinktank Agroscope on "New Estimates of the Environmental Cost of Food" (2018)[10]

In 2018 researchers at Oxford University and Agroscope (an agricultural policy thinktank in Switzerland) compiled data from 40,000 farms, food processors, food-packaging firms, and retailers to explain the environmental costs of various types of food. In this graphic, they chart the environmental impact of animal and plant protein production. This table shows the "environmental impacts for 9 animal and 6 vegetable products from a sample of ~9,000 farms around the world." It was part of a larger study of 30,000 farms to understand the environmental impact, including water consumption, required to produce 25 food products.

The environmental impacts of protein-rich products are highly variable.

However, this variation fails to translate into animal products with lower impacts than vegetable equivalents. Today, diet change delivers greater benefits than purchasing sustainable meat or dairy.

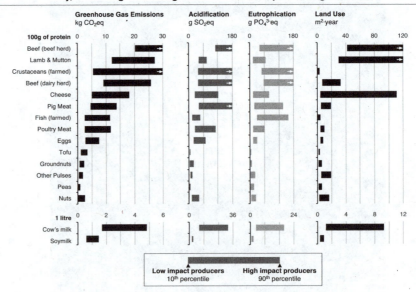

---

10   "New Estimates of the Environmental Cost of Food," 1 June 2018, accessed 14 February 2019, www.ox.ac.uk/news/2018-06-01-new-estimates-environmental-cost-food.

DOCUMENT 41:

Facebook status update, Northern Colorado Animal Save (2018)[11]

The Save Movement consists of hundreds of local animal advocate groups, members of which bear witness to the experiences of livestock by engaging through openings in the sides of stock trailers with cattle, pigs, turkeys, and chickens waiting to enter slaughter facilities. Beginning in 2010 with Toronto Pig Save, the now-global movement mobilized through social media. Its members have sought to expose—and give moral standing to—the suffering of animals in the food system, which is an element of food production that industry and government routinely obscure from public scrutiny. Certainly, cattle in stock trailers are not an element in the cowboy myth or stories celebrating the Old West, nor is the fact that today much beef is produced from the bodies of exhausted dairy cows—but why so? Here, a member of the group contextualizes a posted video of a vigil outside the JBS Greeley Beef Plant slaughterhouse in Greeley, Colorado. The JBS plant is one of approximately 150 owned by Brazilian meat processing company JBS, which is the largest such company in the world with facilities in dozens of countries. The JBS Greeley Beef plant is also one of many in the US that experienced severe COVID-19 outbreaks among workers and their families during 2020.

એ

What a powerful and intense vigil on Saturday, May 12 at JBS. I have not seen them this busy in a long time. Thousands of cows and bulls were packed inside these death trucks terrified out of their minds. The trucks were shaking and the cows were bellowing moans of pain and distress. We even found a horn on the ground outside of the truck that was ripped off of an **individual**. [From the processing plant] the smell of burning blood caused me to heave and gag. We witnessed the internal organs of many individuals being carted away in plastic bags and we witnessed dead individuals being hauled away in a truck to be made for pet food—and no one blinks an eye at this violence as it is entrenched in the culture of Greeley. A trucker got so angry at our presence, that he intentionally ran over my backpack, megaphone and sign. The Greeley police department were called and they handled the situation in the most professional manner. The trucker was cited with a criminal mischief ticket as well as a careless driving ticket. He will be forced to pay me restitution for my damaged property. I just wanted to thank the Greeley police department for delivering justice. We demand

individual: To acknowledge the sentience and moral value of livestock, animal activists refer to them as "individuals."

---

11 Northern Colorado Animal Save Facebook page, accessed 15 May 2018, www.facebook.com/northerncoloradoanimalsave/videos/2148769875137863.

that we are able to stand at JBS and bear witness peacefully and the police officers helped us secure our position.... I was able to connect with one of the officers and he shared with me his love for horses and said he donated to help rescue horses. He has a vegan heart! He asked me how I found myself at this location and I was able to tell him about my awakening and my vegan journey. I know this video is long, but please take a moment and bear witness from your computer or phone. Join us for our next vigil which will be on Friday, May 25th from 6–8. Event page coming soon.

DOCUMENT 42:

American Cowboy magazine celebrates the family ranch: "Ranching Legacies: Profiles in Persistence" (2008)[12]

American Cowboy is a prominent Western lifestyle magazine and one among many in a genre dating back to the nineteenth century. Many readers of such magazines reside outside the West or visit only periodically for work or vacations. Thus, magazines like *American Cowboy* function partly to present rural westerners to themselves and partly to promote tourism or investment in the West. The magazine does so with picturesque photography and stories that romanticize rural Western living. Readers are often people who frequently vacation in the West or move there to purchase a hobby ranch for their retirement. The magazine is also ideological, explaining the patrilineal (white) family ranch as both virtuous steward of the land and keeper of the "spirit of the cowboy." To see the striking color photography included with this story, look up this issue of *American Cowboy* on Google Books.

∾

These two ranches could not at first glance be more unlike, and yet the values of the McClaran and the Williams families are identical. Equal parts integrity, effort, and respect, their legacies are genuine, certain, and true.

The Pitchfork Ranch of Guthrie, Texas, has operated since 1883 as an outfit of the old school. Now in its fourth generation of family ownership, it has known every triumph and trial that cattle operations encounter in this big-ranch country 80 miles east of Lubbock.

Unlike most ranches established during the great cattle boom of the 1880s, the Pitchfork is the only ranch in west-central Texas today with more fenced acres than in its earliest years. With 125 years of continuous operation under a single family's ownership, the Pitchfork sprawls across 180,000 acres in two states, its 4,200 black and **black-baldie** cows watched over by cowboys riding some of the best ranch horses in the country. The "Pitchfork Gray" (with black manes and tails) has evolved over the last 75 years, building on the bloodlines of Joe Bailey's King, the magnificent quarter horse stallion who came to the Pitchfork in 1946.

The Williams family, descendants of Eugene F. Williams, the shoe salesman who made trusted friends wherever he went, monitors the Pitchfork with a herdsman's affection for the old ways, with a management style that is both hands-on for the family and hands-free for the manager. Witness

black-baldie: Hereford cattle crossed with a black breed, such as Angus.

---

12 John Brown, "Ranching Legacies: Profiles in Persistence," *American Cowboy* (June–July 2008): 34–40.

this: across its life as a multi-million-dollar agricultural undertaking, the Pitchfork's general managers have averaged 40 years in the saddle. (This is not counting star-crossed cowboy Rudolph Swenson, who introduced the American quarter horse to the ranch before a tragic encounter with a train in nearby Benjamin, Texas, took his life only 18 months after becoming the ranch's manager.)

Ron Lane took the managerial reins last May after the departure of Bob Moorhouse, the legendary 35-year veteran who was the successor to Jim Humphreys of similar four-decade tenure in the pastures along the Witchita River. Lane grew up as a neighbor, having been the son of the manager of the nearby 6666 Ranch's North Division. Being a Texas Tech alum just like Moorhouse, Lane brings business and finance experience, as well as a degree in animal science and a working cowboy's skills. It's all in service of the Williams family's only request: "Please leave this ranch better than you found it."

Careful management, and some white-knuckle luck in the confrontation with the weather and the market, has kept the Pitchfork debt free across its history. "The number of investors outside our family has shrunk, to be about 10 percent of the shares," says Gene Williams III, president and CEO of the Pitchfork's holding company, "and we realized quickly that, going forward, if the ranch were to survive and prosper, the family members needed to be accessible to our manager, but not so as to interfere with the workings of the ranch. We have always relied on our managers. At no time in the ranch's history did the prospect of a sale ever come up."

The Nature of Friendship

Dan Gardner came to Dickens Country, Texas, in 1871. Well-educated, a surveyor and a cowboy who had taken cattle up into Kansas, he partnered in the founding of the Pitchfork and, when the chance came, he called a friend with an offer to buy into the Forks. A Dickens County, Texas, historian of 50 years ago wrote that "Gardner has become acquainted with Eugene F. Williams of St. Louis, who was in the State in the interest of the Hamilton-Brown Shoe Company. Their families had known each other in Alabama and a warm friendship developed between the two men. So firm was his belief in Gardner [on buying into the Pitchfork] that he refused to make the 200-mile drive from Henrietta, then a railhead for the Fort Worth and Denver City Railway, to inspect the land and cattle. 'I am buying Gardner,' he said, adding, 'I believe what he tells me.' The story of the ranch's founding is refreshing and reveals the faith that two men had in each other, and of a business connection and friendship that endured so long as each lived. It tells, too, how this faith in West Texas and the future of its lands and cattle was handed down to the present generation, who hold the same belief as did their forebears."

"Our family has been blessed," Gene III says. "We have always appreciated the difficulties of the cattle business, the need for proactive management amid changing market conditions. We've been so fortunate in finding these accomplished and committed managers, each of whom has come from the west Texas ranching community. Ron grew up on the **Sixes**, and he knew our ranch from the neighbor work done over the years. He and his wife fully understand this lifestyle."

Sixes: The well-known "four sixes" 6666 Ranch in King County, Texas.

Ag Econ

Ag Econ: Agricultural economics.

Now larger and more diversified than at any time in its history, debt free of course, the Pitchfork Ranch is agribusiness at its best. Consider these characteristics:

The cattle: bulls selected for traits both maternal and carcass-based, all calves verified by source and age, all **USDA** verified as Non-Hormonally Treated and All Natural. In Gene Williams II's days, the purebred Herefords would ship to Pitchfork grass in Wyoming, two-year-old steers full of their unruly selves, and then under Bob Moorhouse's tenure, the Pitchfork's cattle moved slowly out of the Hereford breed, and black hides came to dominate the herd.

USDA: United States Department of Agriculture, the federal agency regulating animal agriculture.

Hunting: 165,000 acres of fields, pastures, thickets, canyons, and cedar timber is home to hordes of whitetail deer, mule deer, quail, dove, turkey, geese, and varmints, not to mention wild hogs with strong genetic and attitudinal ties to the Russian boar.

Farming: the wheat is green and growing, for both winter grazing and grain production.

Petroleum energy: discovery of oil in the Tannehill Sands beneath the ranch in 1980 meant zip to the cowherd. "The ranch had operated for a hundred years without oil income," Gene Williams II says. "While we were certainly grateful for the discovery, we understood that we were in the cattle business."

The McClaran Ranch

In 1904, C.A. McClaran came to the town of Wallowa in the Wallowa Valley, in the extreme north-eastern corner of Oregon. He operated the Eastern Oregon mercantile there and, interested in livestock, kept horses and a few

Ypres and Verdun: Famous battles of World War I.

cows around, and in time bought some sheep. C.A. and his son Joe ran those sheep straight into profitability, most especially when America entered the Great War. With the battles at **Ypres and Verdun** waiting directly ahead, Joe McClaran, at 18 years of age, on his way to war, sought out a financial advisor.

No banks operated in extreme northeastern Oregon in those days, and so young Joe found Earl Sherod, a prosperous neighbor, who counselled him on two options: a relatively safe investment that might bring a three-percent return, or a more speculative venture with greater risk but greater potential reward. Young Joe chose the safer place for stashing his savings. On his return from the war, his grubstake had grown to $7000. The more aggressive investment—stock in a little start-up venture called Ford Motor Company—would have returned 10 times as much, but Sherod suggested that a good lesson had been learned in his fiscal conservatism.

Joe was right back to running sheep with his dad, on 160 acres of native grass and on the higher surrounding elevations—ground steep enough that lost footing on a frozen hill meant almost certain death for creatures both two and four-footed. Soon enough the McClarans bought out a neighbor down the creek, acquiring more good bunchgrass and another 75 cows. Married now to school teacher Lorene, Joe saw his operation reach up into the high Wallowa Mountains.

Food and mail were floated up the Snake River from Lewiston, as were cook stoves, moving machines, and window frames—all the stuff of life arriving aboard the Idaho, a surprisingly deep-drafted boat that served all the ranchers up and down the drainage. The boat came every Friday, and supplies were packed the rest of the way home on mules.

By now, the Great Depression was finding its way into even the wilderness, its effects probably fatal on the ranchers there. Except, once more, for L.C. Johnson. Joe's son Jack remembers: "My dad had borrowed money from him, as had six or eight other ranchers in the area. Well, L.C. called his debtor ranchers together, and announced that he was suspending all regular debt payments until he and Dad and those other ranchers had ridden out the Depression together. There is no doubt in my mind that, without L.C. Johnson's enlightened self-interest, we would have lost the ranch."

charge across Europe: During World War II.

ovine: Sheep raising has been important in some regions of the West, with ranchers often switching from cattle to sheep depending upon market demand.

When young Jack went himself off to war, enlisting at 18 years of age to **charge across Europe** with Patton and the Fourth Armored Division, the ranch he left behind was largely a sheep operation. When he returned, the labor shortage of the war years had cut into the wool business, with its work-intensive lambing and shearing. The **ovine** phasing-out led to many a mutton-based meal in the K-rations of GIs everywhere, and the McClaran Ranch had switched to cows.

Growth came consistently through the decades, and the McClarans—Joe and Lorene, Jack and Marge—and their three children, Chris, Katy, and

Scott. Scott says that "my parents and grandparents couldn't rub two nickels together at year's end, but they were accumulating net worth in a rugged and beautiful place, living a life we all loved." Still, working on the ranch, Jack insists "only a certain kind of person can live up here. The challenges of making a living in a place like ours doesn't appeal to many people. But the country takes hold of you, and you find that you couldn't possibly live anywhere else."

Touching the Canyon

Scott and his wife, Vicki, became directly involved again in the ranch's operation in 1980, and their three daughters have grown up doing the work, both physical and cerebral, of a remote, high-country spread. An accredited teacher, Vicki homeschooled her girls, thereby saving a three-hour commute. Jill, the oldest, is pondering doctoral study. Beth and Maggie both attend Oregon State University, studying ranch-science.

After a three-day visit with Vicki for some electricity and some conversation, Scott McClaran rode back to winter camp today [March 11]. It's calving time at that higher elevation, where he reads by lantern-light waiting to help a heifer with her midnight calf. The McClarans revere the singularity of purpose in the responsibilities of a cow camp; they know first hand the rewards of simplicity. "Up there the rest of the world just disappears," Jack says. "It's not an easy life, but it's a great life." Scott serves the ranch's thousand head of mother cows as now four generations of his family have done ... with some necessary and convenient adaptations to these modern ways. An airplane, for example, sometimes flies in late-summer roundup, skimming the highest peaks, searching out stragglers before a couple of cowpeople and some exceptional border collies head out to bring them down.

The operation now includes seven different camps (four in winter country, three on summer ground); a house in town; a hay basin and a background lot; and two full-time employees with the cows and two more with the farming and the backgrounding.

"About the time we pay off a debt, the family will make a decision to add a **federal permit** or to buy a piece of private ground. We're not retaining ownership on some of our steers with a branded-beef program called Country Natural Beef. At our heart, though, we're a forage-based ranch operating year-round, without fences, in some big country.

Scott McClaran rides worry free these days: "I have three daughters who are as handy as anyone who wants to come along, I have a wife who is twice as valuable to this outfit as I am. With this kind of support, ranching is pretty easy." Maggie McClaran left home at four o'clock this morning [March 11],

federal permit: A contract to graze animals on land owned by the US federal government.

driving six hours back to Corvallis for an afternoon class. "Maggie needed to be horseback for a while," her grandfather says. "She needed to come home to, as we say in our family, 'touch the canyon'."

DISCUSSION QUESTIONS/WRITING PROMPTS

1. What regions, people, animals, and time periods are addressed by the primary sources here?

2. Many of the historical primary sources in this section are from the very recent past. How should we work with such sources? Is it possible to think and write historically with such primary sources so soon after their production?

3. According to the primary sources here, what constituted "rangelands" in the modern West? How and why did those lands change over the course of the twentieth century?

4. Since the mid-twentieth century, who has claimed authority over rangelands, and the animals and ecologies there? How did they characterize cattle and, by extension, the nature of those lands in order to justify their position and stake in the issue?

5. Considering all the various primary sources presented in this book, how should historians evaluate the histories of cowboying and ranching in light of contemporary knowledge about climate change, land-use sustainability, and animal ethics? Since the Beef Bonanza era, what has changed and what has stayed the same?

GLOSSARY OF KEY TERMS

Beef Bonanza: A period between the late 1870s and about 1886, the product of a number of years of maximum cattle production and record beef prices driven by external (mostly absentee British and east coast United States) investment and speculation in the industry, incomplete fencing that allowed big cattle holders to graze anywhere with few limits, and an unusually warm winter; the period was an economic bubble that collapsed with the Big Die-Up of 1886–87. In spite of its trials, many people romanticized this period as the heyday of the working cowboy and the era of unfenced "free grass."

Big Die-Up: 1886–87, a period of catastrophic losses for cattlemen and absentee ranch owners. A deadly combination of long-term drought and overgrazing of cattle produced depleted rangelands on the Great Plains; thereafter, starving and underweight cattle struggled to find forage, were trapped by new barbed-wire fences, and died by the millions in historically harsh winters of the period.

Bison ecology: A network of plant and animal species that remained relatively stable for several centuries with the American bison as critical keystone species; there were an estimated 30 million bison on the Great Plains around 1800. The bison ecology was destroyed by environmental changes up to the 1850s, including drought, habitat destruction, competition from exotic, introduced species like horses, and diseases like tuberculosis and brucellosis spread to bison herds by introduced species. With the proliferation of railways, intensive sport and market hunting, and to a lesser degree subsistence hunting, the population further collapsed to just a handful of individuals by the 1880s.

Carrying capacity: The maximum number of individuals of a particular species that can subsist sustainably on a given landscape or environment with respect to availability of water, edible plants or animals, and suitable habitat.

Cowboy/cowgirl: A person who engages in paid work with cattle, horses, or sheep for ranching or dude ranch businesses; may also be a ranch owner. Colloquially, the term also refers to rodeo competitors.

Cow-calf operation: A ranching business, either individually, family, or corporately owned, that keeps a herd of breeding cows and a small number of bulls. The herd produces calves that are raised to between one and three years old, then sold for slaughter or to a feedlot for fattening to market weight for slaughter.

Extensive ranching: A form of animal agriculture employing large areas of low-productivity land and limited inputs of human labor, capital, and supplementary feed to produce meat, wool, or further livestock on land unsuited to plant agriculture; generally extensive ranching involves livestock like cattle, sheep, bison-cattle hybrids, alpacas, or horses.

Invasive species: Non-native species introduced intentionally (e.g., horses, cattle) or unintentionally (e.g., brucellosis bacteria), who prosper and multiply; often they displace existing species or alter the environment such that native species and those who depend upon them struggle to survive.

Market steer: A castrated male calf raised to between one and three years of age for the purpose of slaughter.

Midwestern System (of cattle production): A practice developed in the later nineteenth century of raising crossbred cattle descended from heavy shorthorn beef breeds and Spanish cattle wherein ranchers kept smaller herds on smaller ranges and supplemented their forage with hay; market-weight steers were rounded up and sold to feedlots in the Midwest where they were fattened before rail transfer to a slaughterhouse.

Mustang: A wild or feral horse living on private or public lands in the West, descended from a diverse lineage of old Spanish breeds and, especially in the twentieth century, also Quarter Horses, Thoroughbreds, and heavy workhorse breeds like Clydesdales.

Pastoralism (patrilineal): A way of life in which male-led families raise livestock for subsistence and for market. With respect to ranching in the United States, generally family-owned ranches consist of one central ranch property and additionally graze cattle on leased federal land.

Sage Brush Rebellion: A rural political movement in the American West active in the 1970s and 1980s seeking through legislation or other means to transfer ownership and control of federal lands to individual states, which could thereafter lease or sell those lands to raise revenue and allow greater local influence over exploitation of public resources.

Vaquero: Spanish, later Mexican, Hispanic cowboys who adapted ranching and horsemanship traditions from Spain to the North American environment.

SELECT BIBLIOGRAPHY

Armitage, Susan, and Elizabeth Jameson, eds. *The Women's West*. Norman: U of Oklahoma P, 1987.

Cruise, David, and Alison Griffiths. *Wild Horse Annie and the Last of the Mustangs: The Life of Velma Johnston*. New York: Scribner, 2013.

Dant, Sara. *Losing Eden: An Environmental History of the American West*. Hoboken, NJ: Wiley & Sons, 2016.

Figueredo, Danilo H. *Revolvers and Pistolas, Vaqueros and Caballeros: Debunking the Old West*. New York: Praeger, 2014.

Flores, Dan. *American Serengeti: The Last Big Animals of the Great Plains*. Lawrence: UP of Kansas, 2016.

Glasrud, Bruce A., and Michael N. Searles, eds. *Black Cowboys in the American West: On the Range, on the Stage, Behind the Badge*. Norman: U of Oklahoma P, 2017.

Goetzmann, William H., and William N. Goetzmann. *The West of the Imagination*. Norman: U of Oklahoma P, 2009.

Hämäläinen, Pekka. "The Rise and Fall of Plains Indians Horse Cultures." *Journal of American History* 90, no. 3 (December 2003): 833–62.

Hixson, Walter L. *American Settler Colonialism*. New York: Palgrave Macmillan, 2013.

Iverson, Peter. *When Indians Became Cowboys: Native Peoples and Cattle Ranching in the American West*. Norman: U of Oklahoma P, 1994.

Lause, Mark A. *The Great Cowboy Strike: Bullets, Ballots, & Class Conflicts in the American West*. New York: Verso, 2018.

LeCompte, Mary Lou. *Cowgirls of the Rodeo: Pioneer Professional Athletes*. Champaign: U of Illinois P, 2000.

Marriott, Alice. *Hell on Horses and Women*. Norman: U of Oklahoma P, 1953.

Mellis, Allison Fuss. *Riding Buffaloes and Broncos: Rodeo and Native Traditions in the Northern Great Plains*. Norman: U of Oklahoma P, 2003.

Russell, Sharman Apt. *Kill the Cowboy: A Battle of Mythology in the New West*. 1993. Reprint Lincoln: U of Nebraska P/Bison Books, 2001.

Sherow, James E. *The Chisholm Trail: Joseph McCoy's Great Gamble*. Norman: U of Oklahoma P, 2018.

Slatta, Richard W. *Cowboys of the Americas*. New Haven and London: Yale UP, 1990.

Smalley, Andrea L. *Wild by Nature: North American Animals Confront Colonization*. Baltimore: Johns Hopkins UP, 2017.

Specht, Joshua. *Red Meat Republic: A Hoof-to-Table History of How Beef Changed America*. Princeton and Oxford: Princeton UP, 2019.

Starrs, Paul F. *Let the Cowboy Ride: Cattle Ranching in the American West*. Baltimore: Johns Hopkins UP, 1998.

Webb, Walter Prescott. *The Great Plains: A Study in Institutions and Environment*. 1931. Reprint Lincoln: U of Nebraska P, 1981.

White, Richard. "Animals and Enterprise." In *The Oxford History of the American West*, edited by Clyde A. Milner II, Carol A. O'Connor, and Martha A. Sandweiss, 237–73. New York: Oxford UP, 1994.

Wilkie, Rhoda M. *Livestock/Deadstock: Working with Farm Animals from Birth to Slaughter*. Philadelphia: Temple UP, 2010.

Young, James A., and B. Abbott Sparks. *Cattle in the Cold Desert*. Expanded edition, Reno and Las Vegas: U of Nevada P, 2002.

PERMISSIONS ACKNOWLEDGEMENTS

Abbott, Edward Charles, and Helena Huntington Smith. *We Pointed Them North: Recollections of a Cowpuncher*. University of Oklahoma Press, 1976, pp. 174–77. Republished with the permission of the University of Oklahoma Press, conveyed through Copyright Clearance Center, Inc.

Anonymous. "Adelina Ruelas Working at a Ranch in Box Canyon," c. 1920, Portraits-Ruelas, Feliz #79440. "Portrait of Felix Quiroz on horse," c. 1927, Portraits-Quiroz, Felix #62686. "Portrait of Luis Romero and Ramon Ahumada," c. 1890, Portraits-Ahumada, Ramon #66011. Arizona Historical Society, PC 1000, Tucson General Photo Collection. Reproduced with permission.

Anonymous. "Slaughter house, Crow Agency," c. 1890–1920?, Catalog # Lot 035 B11F12.11, Bud Lake and Randy Brewer Crow Indian Photograph Collection, Montana Historical Society Research Center Photograph Archives, Helena, MT. Reproduced with permission.

Belden, Charles. "Branding cattle," Accession Number 598, Box 10, Item 919. "People riding horses," Accession Number 598, Box 7, Item 493. "Sheep camp," Accession Number 598, Box 9, Item 736. University of Wyoming, American Heritage Center, Charles J. Belden Photographs. Reproduced with permission.

Blunt, Judy. *Breaking Clean*. New York: Vintage Books, 2003, pp. 210–11, 218–20. Copyright © 2002 Judy Blunt. Reproduced with the permission of Judy Blunt.

Brown, John. "Ranching Legacies: Profiles in Persistence," *American Cowboy* (June–July 2008): 34–40. Reproduced with the permission of Wright's Media, LLC as agent for Active Interest Media.

Bundy, Gus. "Men putting wild horse in trailer," 1946. Image ID: UNRS-P1985-08-32621.tif. "Roping a Wild Horse," 1946. Image ID: UNRS-P1985-08-32620.tif. "Wild horse roped to tires," 1946. Image ID: UNRS-P1985-08-32697a.tif. "Wild Horses," Gerlach, Washoe County, NV, 1951. Image ID: UNRS-P1985-08-32617.tif. Courtesy of the Special Collections and University Archives Department, University of Nevada, Reno. Reproduced with permission.

Doubleday, Ralph Russell. "Cowgirls," 1921. Photograph. Denver Public Library, Western History Collection, call #: Z-641. Reproduced with permission.

E.I. du Pont de Nemours & Company. "New! Self-Service Meats Make Shopping Quicker, Easier: DuPont Cellophane," 1949. Series 1, Box 43, Folder 27, dpads_1803-00325, E.I. du Pont de Nemours & Company Advertising Department records (Accession 1803), Manuscripts and Archives Department, Hagley Museum and Library, Wilmington, DE 19807. Reproduced with permission.

Emil Her Many Horses. "Remembering Lakota Ways," *A Song for the Horse Nation: Horses in Native American Nations*, ed. George P. Horse Capture and Emil Her Many Horses, pp. 11–13. Copyright © 2006 National Museum of the American Indian, Smithsonian Institution. Courtesy of the Smithsonian's National Museum of the American Indian. Reproduced with permission.

Ferguson, Denzel, and Nancy Ferguson. *Sacred Cows at the Public Trough*. Bend, OR: Maverick Distributors, 1983, pp. 47–58. Reproduced with the permission of Nancy Ferguson.

Fleischhauer, Carl, et al. "Buckaroos at Cabin," 1979. Photograph. Paradise Valley Folklife Project Collection, 1978–1982 (AFC 1991/021), American Folklife Center. Retrieved from the Library of Congress, www.loc.gov/item/ncr000462. Reproduced with permission.

Fleischhauer, Carl. "Cattle and Newly-Wattled Calves," 1978. Photograph. Paradise Valley Folklife Project Collection, 1978–1982 (AFC 1991/021), American Folklife Center. Retrieved from the Library of Congress, www.loc.gov/item/ncr001104. Reproduced with permission.

Hasselstrom, Linda M. *Between Grass and Sky: Where I Work and Live*. Reno, NV: University of Nevada Press, 2005, pp. 162–64, 166–71. Copyright © 2002 by Linda M. Hasselstrom. Republished with the permission of the University of Nevada Press, conveyed through Copyright Clearance Center, Inc.

H.H. Tammen Co. "Typical Cowboys Waiting Their Turn at Bucking Contest," c. 1900, colorized postcard. Photographic Study Collection, Dickinson Research Center, National Cowboy & Western Heritage Museum. Accession Number 2004.211.1. Reproduced with permission.

Levi's. "Fit for Action," *Rodeo Sports News*, May 15, 1957, p. 8.

Marcuerquiaga, Alfonso, et al. "At the Branding," 1978. Photograph. Paradise Valley Folklife Project Collection, 1978–1982 (AFC 1991/021), American Folklife Center. Retrieved from the Library of Congress, www.loc.gov/item/ncr001108. Reproduced with permission.

McErquiaga, Bruno, et al. "Branding, Grayson Ranch," 1978. Photograph. Paradise Valley Folklife Project Collection, 1978–1982 (AFC 1991/021), American Folklife Center. Retrieved from the Library of Congress, www.loc.gov/item/ncr001100. Reproduced with permission.

Miller, Fred E. "Blanket Bull and family," c. 1898–1910, catalog number N13658. "Children on horseback," c. 1898–1910, catalog number N13779. "Group on horseback," c. 1898–1910, catalog number N13772. Fred E. Miller photograph collection. Reproduced with the permission of the National Museum of the American Indian, Smithsonian Institution.

Monday, Jane Clements, and Betty Bailey Colley. *Voices from the Wild Horse Desert: The Vaquero Families of the King and Kenedy Ranches*. University of Texas Press, 1997, pp. 66–70, 102–07. Copyright © 1997. Reproduced with the permission of the University of Texas Press.

Northern Colorado Animal Save. Greeley Cow Save status update, 2018. *Facebook*. Accessed May 15, 2018. Reproduced with the permission of the Animal Save Movement. www.animalsavemovement.org.

Oglala Lakota (Oglala Sioux). "Horse mask," c. 1900. Hide, glass bead/beads, cotton cloth. National Museum of the American Indian, Smithsonian Institution (Catalogue # 1413). Photo by NMAI Photo Services. Reproduced with permission.

Oppenheimer, Harold L. *Cowboy Economics: Rural Land as an Investment*. Danville, IL: The Interstate Printers & Publishers, Inc., 1971. Copyright © Interstate Printers & Publishers, Inc. Jan. 20, 1966. Reproduced with the permission of Reed Oppenheimer.

O'Toole, Sharon. "Wild Horse Extremists Obscure Real-World Solutions," Opinion section, *High Country News*, Oct. 23, 2017. Reproduced with the permission of High Country News, Paonia, CO.

Poore, Joseph, and Thomas Nemecek. "Environmental impacts for 9 animal and 6 vegetable products." Graphs. "New Estimates of the Environmental Cost of Food," *News & Events*, University of Oxford, June 1, 2018. https://www.ox.ac.uk/news-and-events. Reproduced with the permission of Joseph Poore.

Russell, Charles M. "Waiting for a Chinook: Last of the 5000," c. 1903; 88.60. Courtesy of the Buffalo Bill Center of the West, Cody, Wyoming, USA; Whitney Western Art Museum. Reproduced with permission.

Smith, Erwin E. "African-American cowboys on their mounts ready to participate in horse race during Negro State Fair, Bonham, Texas," c. 1911–1915, nitrate negative, 5 x 7 in. Erwin E. Smith Collection of the Library of Congress on Deposit at the Amon Carter Museum of American Art, Fort Worth, Texas. LC.S611.016. Reproduced with permission.

Swift & Company Packers trade card, catalogue #529266, courtesy of the American Antiquarian Society. Reproduced with permission.

Tom Mix and Tony "The Wonder Horse" theatrical release film poster for *The Drifter*, 1929. Courtesy of Everett Collection, Inc./ Alamy Stock Photo. Reproduced with permission.

Ward, Fay E. Excerpts (pp. 101–05, 128); illustrations: Plate 27 "Wild Horse Trap & Corral Trapping Gate," (p. 103); Plate 33 "Bronc Busting," (p. 128). *The Cowboy at Work: All about His Job and How He Does It*, by Fay E. Ward. New York: Hastings House, 1958.

Yensen, Dana L. "The 1900 Invasion of Alien Plants into Southern Idaho," *Great Basin Naturalist* 41.2 (June 1981): 176–83. https://archive.org/details/biostor-238834/mode/2up. Used under license CC BY-NC 3.0.

This book is made of paper from well-managed FSC® - certified
forests, recycled materials, and other controlled sources.

 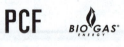